WOMEN AND CHRISTIANITY

Mary T. Malone

Women and Christianity

VOLUME ONE:
THE FIRST THOUSAND YEARS

NOVALIS

First published in 2000 by
NOVALIS
Saint Paul University
223 Main, Ottawa ON K1S 1C4
Canada
in association with The Columba Press, Dublin

Cover by Blaine Herrmann
Origination by The Columba Press
Printed in Ireland by Colour Books Ltd, Dublin

ISBN 2-89507-096-2

Canadian Library Catalogue No: 00-900270-7

Contents

Dedication

For the first time in my life, I write with the women of my family
close by, and so to them, in gratitude and admiration, I dedicate
this book. First of all, to my four sisters, Eileen, Marjorie, Olive
and Eithne, whose distinctly individual lives of grace and
courage have enriched mine so much, I dedicate this book in
memory of so much shared history. Then to my four nieces,
Carmel, Gillian, Helen and Carole, whose lives show, in abundance, the hopes of a blessed future, I dedicate the book, in hope.
And finally, to my aunt, Josephine, who has traversed, in her
own unique way, the extraordinary changes of the twentieth
century, I dedicate this first volume as a tribute to her ingenuity
in discovering the riches of life wherever she is.

Dateline

An event cannot be isolated by giving it a date, but it serves to anchor the attention and situate the persons involved in an appropriate context.

30 CE	Women disciples witness the death, burial and resurrection of Jesus, and make their report to the male disciples. Death of Stephen. Ongoing persecution by Paul of female and male disciples.
30-35	First missionary endeavours of Peter, James, Prisca and Aquila, and many other female and male disciples. Conversion of Paul Council of Jerusalem and the momentous decision to preach to the Gentiles. Execution of James the apostle. Though one of the Twelve, he is not replaced.
42-62	James, the brother of Jesus, is leader of the Jerusalem church.
49	Persecution of Christians in Rome. Prisca and Aquila are expelled and move to Corinth.
40s	Women and men form house-churches as well as being evangelists. We know the names of Prisca,and Aquila, Chloe, Nympha and Mary, the mother of John Mark, among others. Paul's first letter to the Thessalonians, first Christian writing addressed exclusively to men. Paul joins Prisca and Aquila in the Corinthian house-church. Throughout the next decade, Paul travels and writes to the Corinthians, Romans, Galatians, Philippians and Philemon.
50s	First official canonical and theological denunciation and silencing of women in 1 Corinthians. *(Approximately)* Mission of the disciples continues, including the apostle Junia and the deacon, Phoebe.
60	Execution of Paul at Rome.
64	Fire of Rome and Neronian persecution of female and male Christians.
66-70	Jewish war and destruction of the Temple. Scattering of Christians and Jews.
70s	Mark's Gospel, followed eventually by Matthew and Luke, and in the 90s, by John.
80s	*(Possibly)* Acts of the Apostles.

90s   Beginning of Deutero-Pauline literature and adoption of the
           Household Codes, which continue the theological and
           canonical exclusion of women from the core of Christianity.
107   Letters of Ignatius of Antioch: one of first references to the
           Eve/Mary dichotomy.
110   Correspondence of Pliny and Trajan, including the description
           of the torture of two Christian women slaves in order to
           extract information about the lives of Christians.
120ff   Gnostic literature.
           Martyrdom of Polycarp.
           Montanist movement: Prisca and Maximilla are the chief
           prophets of the movement.
           Blandina and companions martyred during the pogrom in
           Lyons.
178   Irenaeus becomes Bishop of Lyons: begins writing against
           heretics, including women.
180s   *(Approximately)* The beginning of the apocryphal literature,
           outlining the lives of Thecla, Mary Magdalen, and Mary, the
           Mother of Jesus, among others.
           Clement of Alexandria begins writing to encourage
           Christians to marry.
200ff   The writings of Tertullian against pagans, Gnostics, heretics
           and women.
202   Martyrdom of Perpetua and Felicitas.
225   Origen begins his voluminous writings.
           Martyrdom of Sabina and companions in Smyrna.
           (Approximately) Didascalia Apostolorum is written describing
           church order, including the Orders of Widow and Deaconess.
           Bishop Cornelius of Rome reports on 1500 Widows there,
           among other ministers.
250s   Decian persecution: Deaths of Origen, Cyprian of Carthage,
           Fabian of Rome.
270   Antony, the first hermit, begins his desert life.
303   The 'Great Persecution' is begun by Diocletian.
313   Constantine grants universal toleration to all religions of the
           Roman Empire.
325   Council of Nicaea: Among many highly significant edicts is
           one removing deaconesses from the orders of the clergy and
           returning them to the laity.
328-373   Athanasius, Bishop of Alexandria.

330s	Monasticism proliferates in the Egyptian desert.
	Bishop Athanasius visits Rome and stays as a guest in Marcella's house on the Aventine.
340ff	Marcella and other women begin the practices of women's urban monasticism in Rome.
347	Birth of John Chrysostom.
	Marcellina, sister of Ambrose, consecrated as a virgin in Rome.
354	Birth of Augustine.
	Martin of Tours becomes Bishop of Poitiers.
360	Hagia Sophia dedicated.
366-384	Damasus is Bishop of Rome.
370s	Birth of Hypatia, the philosopher.
	Ambrose consecrated as Bishop of Milan.
381	Council of Constantinople and the teachings of the Cappadocian Fathers, Basil of Caesarea, his brother, Gregory of Nyssa, and relative, Gregory of Nazianzen.
	Macrina, sister of Basil and Gregory, sets up her convent with her mother and whole household.
382	Jerome in Rome. Begins his translation of the Bible and begins his association with the communities of Marcella and Paula in Rome.
	(Possibly) Council of Nimes orders the ordination of women as deaconesses to cease.
	Death of Blesilla, daughter of Paula. Jerome expelled from Rome. Jerome and Paula set up their communities in Bethlehem.
386	Baptism of Augustine by Ambrose in Milan.
	Melania and Rufinus found their Bethlehem monasteries near those of Paula and Jerome.
	Augustine writes the Confessions.
397-404	John Chrysostom as Patriarch of Constantinople, supported by the deaconess, Olympias.
	Death of Paula in Bethlehem. Her daughter Eustochium and grand-daughter, Paula, take over the monastery.
410	Sack of Rome by Alaric. Some years later, Augustine begins writing The City of God.
415	Death of Hypatia at the hands of Christian monks.
	Augustine and Julian of Eclanum engage in the Pelagian controversy.
430	Death of Augustine after the Vandals had attacked Carthage the previous year.

431	Council of Ephesus: Mary declared Theotokos.
432	Bishop Patrick is sent to Ireland.
440	Leo I begins his episcopacy in Rome: beginning of papal authoritative activity.
451	Council of Chalcedon: end of one phase of christological controversy.
476	Death of last Western Roman Emperor.
481	Clotilde persuades Clovis to accept Christian baptism, leading to the conversion of the Franks and the Franco-Roman alliance.
	Birth of Benedict.
	Beginning of monasticism in Celtic Britain.
517	Council of Epaon: End of the Western Orders of Deaconess and Widow.
524	Birth of Radegund.
529	Founding of Monte Cassino by Benedict. His sister Scholastica, equally a monastic founder, is shunned by him. Marriage and subsequent flight of Radegund to found her monastery at Poitiers, in 550.
563	Columba arrives at Iona.
570s	Queen Bertha of Kent requests missionaries from Rome.
590-615	Missionary journeys of Columbanus.
	Augustine sent to Canterbury by Pope Gregory the Great, apparently in response to Bertha's request. King Ethelbert and ten thousand Englishmen are baptised on Christmas Day. Death of Columba at Iona.
619	Ethelburga and Bishop Paulinus travel to Northumbria for her marriage to Edwin.
627	Baptism of Edwin and his household on Easter Day. Among the group is Hilda.
632	Death of Muhammed.
	Hilda becomes Abbess of the double monastery at Whitby.
657	Aidan becomes the first Abbot of Lindisfarne.
664	Synod of Whitby and beginning of the dominance of Roman Christianity over the Celtic form.
680	Death of Hilda. Succeeded as Abbess by Queen Aelfled.
	Birth of Frideswide, monastic founder of Oxford.
700-716	Birth of Leoba, Anglo-Saxon missionary.
	Foundation of the royal Abbey at Wimborne.
	Birth of Walburga of Heidenheim, sister of the missionaries, Willibald and Wunnibald.
	Beginning of the mission of Boniface, Apostle of Germany.

718	Death of Erentrude, founder and first abbess of Nonnburg.
720s	Spread of Islam north of the Pyrenees.
732	Battle of Poitiers, stopping the Islamic advance into Europe.
735	Death of Bede, source of most of our information about Christianity in England
744	Foundation of the abbey at Fulda.
745	Boniface consecrated Archbishop of Mainz.
748	Thirty nuns, including Leoba, leave Wimborne at the request of Boniface. Leoba becomes abbess of Tauberbischofsheim.
751	The last Merovingian king is sent to a monastery. Last meeting of Boniface and Leoba.
754	Death of Boniface.
760	Tetta, abbess of Wimborne, dies.
778	Hugeberc, abbess of Hildesheim, begins to write the *Hodoeporicon*.
779	Death of Leoba.
782	Massacre of the Saxons by Charlemagne.
789	Charlemagne's *Admonitio Generalis*.
800	Crowning of Charlemagne as Emperor by Pope Leo III.
803	Nuns forbidden to teach young boys.
814	Benedict of Aniane begins the reform and standardisation of monastic life.
818	Birth of Joan, the Englishwoman who became Pope.
829	Council of Paris removes women from any contact with liturgical acts.
830	Birth of Irmengarde, saint of Bavaria.
842	Dhuoda's *Handbook* for her sons.
850s	Pseudo-Isidorian decretals.
856	Beginning of the two-year pontificate of Pope Joan.
857	Pope Nicholas I.
867	Destruction of the Abbey of Whitby by the Danes. Beginning of the Roman 'pornocracy.'
890	Theodora and Marozia in Rome.
910	Foundation of Cluny. Abbot Berno rules from 910-927.
932	Birth of Hroswitha of Gandersheim.
1002	Death of Hroswitha.

Introduction

When Freud said 'women are the enemies of civilisation', he was simply voicing the wisdom of the ages. Most of the so-called great moments of the human race were achieved at the apparently necessary expense of women. This is true both for religious and secular life. It is to give the lie to the Freudian version of human life that I have decided to write this book. In many ways, the book is an act of reminiscence, a cumulative memory of almost forty years as a teacher. I am mindful of the old adage that teachers often just have one year of teaching, repeated forty times over but, with the enormous change in the university student population over the past decades, this educational paralysis is no longer possible. Most of my teaching took place in Canadian schools, colleges and universities, and I owe a huge debt of gratitude to what, to my astonishment, I can name as generations of students. Above all, it was in Canada that I discovered myself as an educator, and it was also there that the intellectual challenges occurred that turned me into a feminist educator.

From childhood, probably egged on by brotherly teasing, I have been fascinated by the history of women, and more specifically by the women of the Christian tradition. The pale shadows of female living that were presented to me as Christian saints seemed profoundly unsatisfactory, and I set out on a journey, that still continues, to extricate from the tradition the reality of women's lives. This search led eventually to doctoral work on women in the first four centuries of the Christian story. It was simply fortuitous that my university studies coincided with the very early stage of the Second Wave of the Christian Feminist movement but, from the beginning, our shared agendas seemed destined to merge.

If I learned anything from my students, from all branches of Christianity, as well as Judaism, Islam and Hinduism, it was that the lives of Christian women from past centuries continued to have profound relevance for Christian life today. Undergraduates in their twenties wept over the horrific choice for martyrdom made by the twenty-two-year-old Perpetua, just as they raged at the almost complete absence of information about women of profound significance, such as Mary Magdalene. They were inspired by the courage of Leoba and exhilarated at the writings of Hildegarde and Hadjwich. And, more significantly, through all these stories they found the same challenges faced in their own lives: the cost of discipleship, the difficulties of finding one's voice as a woman, the intricacies of the mother-daughter relationship, and the ongoing dilemmas of the female-male relationship. Young men struggled also with their Christian heritage in an attempt to walk the fine line between frustration and empathy. My educational life was profoundly enriched by all these students as they challenged, reflected, argued vociferously and monitored their own lives of belief and unbelief in the light of this heritage. One thing was certain – they never found the history of their women ancestors to be boring.

Over the past four decades, this material has been discussed with hundreds of colleagues, friends and students in lecture-halls, church basements, condominium kitchens and pool-side patios. To all of these conversation partners I am intensely grateful. Their friendship and support, and more particularly their questions and challenges, have enriched my life and my scholarly work beyond calculation. In their presence, I first discovered myself as a feminist historian, and with their encouragement, I continue to do so. From so many, I choose to mention only two. Shirley Anne Majeau FCJ, one of my first Canadian friends and companion in many adventures, both orthodox and unorthodox, first pointed out to me the speciiic gifts that I had as an educator and communicator. Brid Murphy, my life-long friend and eagle-

eyed home-based editor and proof-reader, has given me incalcul-
able assistance in her own unobtrusive way. Each illustrates the
cumulative grace and richness of women's Christian lives. To
both of them, I state pubicly my profound gratitude and admiration. Finally, I wish to thank Seán O Boyle of The Columba Press
for his initial and continued interest in this project, nourished by
both the culinary and conversational dimensions of lengthy
lunches.

CHAPTER 1

Reading Women into History

In all of Jesus' teaching, as well as in his behaviour, one can find nothing which reflects the discrimination against women prevalent in his day. (John Paul II, Mulieris Dignitatem, 13, 1988)[1]

The church too, both consciously and unconsciously, has been guilty of prejudicial action, practices and policies against women. Many women relate how often they feel patronised, undervalued and trivialised by church leaders. (Bishop Howard Hubbard, Albany, 1990)[2]

When God is male, the male is God. (Mary Daly)

That is why we can never ignore the fact that Christ is a man. (Declaration on the Question of the Admission of Women to the Ministerial Priesthood, Paul VI, 1976)[3]

The history of Christianity shows great ambivalence towards women. On the one hand, women have been included, called, graced, inspired and canonised by Christianity throughout the centuries. On the other, as the quotation above from Bishop Hubbard's 1990 pastoral letter indicates, women have not always felt appreciated within the Christian tradition and indeed have often felt excluded and oppressed by church leaders. It is this ambivalence towards women that characterises the whole of Christian history.

The 'good news' for women rediscovered in the gospels forms the bedrock of the Christian tradition – some would say that this is one of its most radical innovations – and this 'good news' is rooted in the gospel portrait of the relationships between Jesus and women. From biblical times to the present, however, this gospel message for women has been variously

interpreted and, it must be admitted, during most of Christian
history, it was presented to women as a negative message of exclusion, trivialisation and often quite astonishing hostility on the
part of the clergy. This is what Bishop Hubbard alludes to, but it
is not at all difficult to find in the pages of Christian history
comments on women that make his allusions seem very tame by
comparison.

Here I will mention just two of these comments. The first is
from an eleventh century saint, Peter Damian, who was assist-
ing Pope Leo IX in the task of cleaning up the image and role of
the clergy. It is a shocking diatribe but it is not at all exceptional
in the writings of church leaders about women. The fact that he
is primarily addressing priests' wives as part of his celibacy programme does nothing to mitigate the utter nastiness of his comments:

> I speak to you, O charmers of the clergy, appetising flesh of
> the devil, that castaway from Paradise, poison of minds,
> death of souls, companions of the very stuff of sin, the cause
> of our ruin. You, I say, I exhort you women of the ancient
> enemy, you bitches, sows, screech-owls, night-owls, blood-
> suckers, she-wolves, ... come now, hear me harlots, prosti-
> tutes, with your lascivious kisses, you wallowing places for
> fat pigs, couches for unclean spirits ...[4]

And so it goes on for pages and pages. This form of discourse
represents a kind of Christian 'road-rage' against women, appearing at particular crisis points in the tradition, and in fact was
not as damaging in the long run as some more reflective comments. The second introductory comment sums up a tradition
which, in its very thoughtfulness and careful reference to scripture, has been much more influential in perpetuating negative
attitudes towards women. It is taken from a sermon of Pope Pius
XII to newly-weds, preached on 10 September 1941, right in the
midst of the Second World War.[5] The Pope speaks of the man
and woman entering marriage on a 'perfectly equal footing'
because of their equal creation by God, but then goes on to ac-
centuate the position of the husband as the head of this new

visible society called the family. The Pope stresses the need for such a male head as a result of the sin of Eve. The Pope then moves to the New Testament as follows:

> In holiness, by means of grace, both spouses are equally and immediately united to Christ. In fact, St Paul said that as many as have been baptised in Christ and who have put on Christ, are all sons *(sic)* of God; there is neither male nor female, because all are one in Christ Jesus. Not so, however, in the church and in the family, which are visible societies ...

Notice the ambivalence in the Pope's presentation. He announces the 'perfect' equality of women and men, both in their equal creation and in their equal baptism, and then seems to cancel out that equality by invoking the necessary arrangements of the visible societies of family and church. This sermon illustrates perfectly the 'give and take' quality of women's position in Christianity, but it also illustrates, as Peter Damian's outburst does not, the inescapability of the scriptural witness to women. This biblical testimony can be explained away, re-interpreted according to the needs of the author, or quite simply forgotten, but it cannot be removed from the record.

Re-reading the 'good news'

It is our first task, then, to look once again at this 'good news' for women as it appears in the whole biblical *corpus*, both canonical and apocryphal. A later and more extensive task will be to trace the historical development of this 'good news' throughout the Christian tradition. In both cases, our reading will be a gendered reading, that is we will explore and attempt to understand the multiple cultural and religious conclusions drawn from the biological fact of the division of the sexes into male and female. This will involve looking at the relationships between women and Jesus during the ministry period, and also the very diverse testimony to women in the earliest decades of Christianity and beyond. Since one of our operating definitions of history will be a 'fusion of horizons', this will also involve alternating our attention between biblical and historical times and the contemporary situation.

One of the major foci will be on the silencing of women and the ways in which the Christian tradition has succeeded in making women virtually invisible. We must also, then, ask questions about the blindness of women themselves in failing to see what was before our eyes in the biblical texts. Each century and each group of Christians have dialogued with the scriptures according to their own needs and faith experiences, so that when women today explore the scriptures from their own perspective, they are not doing anything novel. On the other hand, however, this contemporary search is a revolutionary act for women, or at least it was seen as such in the sixties and seventies of our century. For this was one of the very few times when women claimed the right to read and interpret the scriptures for themselves, and it is this initial re-reading that will be presented here, in order to share with contemporary readers the intense exhilaration of this first feminist re-reading. Since the sixties, there has been an explosion of biblical re-interpretation on every front, including very important feminist readings, and many of these will be explored as we follow the faith journeys of women through history. First, the decades of the sixties and seventies must briefly occupy our attention. What kind of time was it that gave birth to such a momentous turn of events for women believers?

The sixties and seventies
Nobody seems to be able to speak of the sixties without passion. Both chronologically and in a socio-religious sense, it was the century's turning point. Here, our focus will be on the Roman Catholic experience of the sixties, and from a fascinating canvas we will highlight four points of greatest relevance to our present purposes. These are, firstly, the new global perspective; secondly, the personalist emphasis in the psycho-social field; thirdly, the second wave of Christian feminism; and fourthly, the radically new Roman Catholic approach to the scriptures initiated by the Second Vatican Council.

For the Roman Catholic – and indeed the whole Christian – tradition, the Second Vatican Council (1962-1965) was a watershed. A whole generation of people still speak of 'before' and 'after' the council when situating themselves and their faith. The council crept up on the church quietly but as soon as the panoply of church-leaders assembled and began their discussions, the global significance of the event became clear. For the first time the news media became enraptured with the doings of the Roman Catholic Church. Perhaps what first became obvious was the new realisation of the global dimensions of the church. Bishops from all over the world with their diverse views and problems were featured daily in news reports. For many western Christians this was a revelation, their assumption having been that there was absolute similarity among Roman Catholics all over the world. There were inevitable coincidences with world politics. Many bishops represented countries seeking liberation, whether from colonial or racial exploitation, indigenous war-lords, or what was then called the western military-industrial complex. The bishops took stands for justice on behalf of their people and this raised many questions for Catholics of all stripes. The emphasis in Christianity seemed to move from private devotion to global justice almost overnight. Besides, the great world religions seemed to be grappling with exactly the same issues as Christianity, sometimes more effectively. Judaism, Buddhism, Hinduism and Islam came onto the agenda as dialogue partners for the first time for centuries.[6]

Needless to say, many did not like this one bit. The supposedly once uniform message of Christianity looked as if it were being stretched beyond endurance. And in another stretching experience, personalist psychology influenced the deliberations of the council in ways not perceptible before in Roman Catholic discourse. The Christian faith was portrayed as changing in emphasis depending on whether one was adult or child, first or third world, male or female, lay or ordained. There was a new quest for a relevant faith that responded to the needs and aspirations of contemporary believers. Sociologists pointed out that the old communities we all took for granted were losing their cohesion. Attention was turning to the internal dynamics of personal faith rather than the external hold of traditional religious life. Church leaders hastened to assure their 'flocks' that the faith had not changed, but believers were discovering that reading the gospel in a different context was, in a sense, reading a new gospel.

One of the key characteristics of the sixties for women was the birth of the second wave of the Christian feminist movement.[7] For the first time for centuries, the specific voices of women believers were heard in the churches. Indeed, since most women had been quite unaware of the first wave of feminism, this was an entirely new experience. Second wave Christian feminism, in the spirit of the times, focused particularly on the struggle of women for human rights in many spheres. Among the rights that were sought by Christian women was the right to be considered for the ministry, particularly the ordained ministry. This feminist quest coincided with a decline in male priestly vocations and the actual abandonment of the ministry by hundreds of ordained men. A similar movement was perceptible among the ranks of religious women. Seminaries, monasteries and convents were forced to consider their survival as membership fell dramatically. In a rather ironic turn of events, many of these institutions were saved from extinction by the arrival of hundreds of lay women and men thirsting to explore the theological and historical foundations of their faith. Within a very short time, these new theological consumers were experiencing at first hand the clash between traditional ministry and theology patterns and the needs of the contemporary churches. For women theology students, in particular, the ambivalence of Christianity about women became glaringly obvious, both in theory and practice. Women from the various Christian traditions turned to each other in an effort both to learn and to share these new experiences. Besides, the so-called 'sexual revolution' often stretched the relationships between women and their churches to breaking point and put the issues of women's personal sexual responsibility on the churches' agenda for decades, perhaps centuries to come.

Biblical renewal movement

One of the more dramatic changes in Christian life for many people was provided by the conciliar and post-conciliar deliberations on the scriptures, which created entirely new avenues of entry to biblical study. Among the last conciliar documents was the monumental *Dei Verbum* which opened the scriptures to Catholics with an urgency unheard of in previous centuries. Many Roman Catholics were not familiar with the Bible, seeing it as intrinsically related to the origins of Protestantism and the ongoing life of the so-called 'separated brethren.' It was assumed within the Catholic community, even if never actually taught in so many words, that the teaching and even the very existence of the Roman Catholic magisterium made scripture reading unnecessary for the Catholic faithful. This attitude rested partly on the assumption that scripture reading was too dangerous for the average lay person. Of course, it is quite true that the scriptures are revolutionary documents. As historians point out continually, every re-reading of the scriptures has led to a revolution in church life – and we shall have occasion to explore many of these revolutions.

What was the new conciliar teaching on scripture? In a word, it was invitational: Roman Catholics were invited to make the scriptures their own, to study them, reflect on them and share their insights with one another. Scholars were invited to study the scriptures and share their findings with the community. The result was, at least in some circles, an outburst of enthusiasm. This was especially so with many women. They gathered in ecumenical groups, feminist groups, study groups, prayer groups and charismatic groups and revelled in the newly-discovered biblical vision of inclusion, healing, compassion, call, and challenge. More particularly, the conciliar teaching directed Catholics away from a literal reading of the gospels and pointed them in the direction taken by many Protestant scripture scholars for decades. These scholars had come to the realisation that the Bible was like a library with many kinds of literature, many different authors (most of whom were unknown), and many different literary genres. This suggested to believers new questions to put to the scriptures and, above all, new ways of grounding their faith in a biblical spiritual vision.

In the mid-sixties, the Pontifical Biblical Commission pointed Catholics toward the realisation that the gospels were complex documents and much more diverse in their message and intention than a mere literal reading would indicate.[8] The commission pointed out that there were three stages to be taken into account in reading the gospels. In the intervening decades there has been a veritable mountain of research on these stages, and the volume of writing does not seem to be diminishing. Here, only an elementary account of the stages will be given.

The first stage refers to the gospel texts as we have received them, and as they are presented to us today. None of the gospels is an eye-witness account of the events it narrates and it appears that none of the named evangelists was an actual follower of the historical Jesus. Each writes from his own church context some forty to seventy years after the death of Jesus. Mark, for example, writes for a church enduring persecution in the early seventies of the Christian era, and so his main interest is writing an account of the sufferings of Jesus that will help his church to persevere. The vast majority of scholarly writing notes Mark's as the earliest gospel. Matthew and Luke follow some twenty years later, writing to their respective communities of convert Jews and Gentiles. These three are named 'synoptic' because of the obvious similarity of sources and narratives. John's gospel is dated another twenty years later and addresses a community whose needs are both more practical and more mystical. He also offers a corrective to some synoptic themes, and as an example of this, scholars point to his intentional placing of women at the core of the transmission of the good news. The Samaritan woman, Mary of Magdala and Martha take their place in this illustrious gallery.

The second stage in the composition of the gospels points to the period of oral transmission, when the stories and message of Jesus were passed on in the early communities, from the thirties to the sixties, in the context of liturgy and life. No actual written text remains from this period, though scholars are increasingly able to point out how the stories were selected and shaped. This is one of the most mysterious stages of the Christian story, when ministries and institutions were still fluid, and when women seem to have participated with full equality in the life of the young church. Much current research is focused on these earliest decades of Christianity, which seem at once so familiar and so strange to us. This was a time before dogma had been articulated and before the ministry had assumed the form we know today. It continues to be a time of utter fascination to women believers because, through the letters of Paul and the Acts of the Apostles, we meet women who are central to the mission and life of the young church. We know the names of many women who were co-workers and missionaries with Paul and who, in fact, preceded Paul in the church's mission. We shall meet many of these women teachers, prophets, house-church leaders and deacons in later chapters.

The final stage in the transmission of the gospels, that is the stage furthest from us, is the stage portraying the actual words and deeds of Jesus. A literal reading of the gospels has hardened our imagination about this period, as we have become accustomed to asking only questions of literal truth: did Jesus actually do this or say that? The recognition of the complex composition of the gospels, however, compels us to ask different questions. We wonder about the context of the preaching of Jesus and about the actual message of Jesus that lies behind several different versions of the same story. A good example of this is the story of the woman who anointed the head of Jesus (Mk 14:3-9). Each gospel treats the story differently for its own purposes, and so we are entitled to enquire about this purpose, and about the original intention of this woman's action and the response of Jesus, and even about whether or not the story has a historical base.

Enough had been said to show how the conciliar teaching on the scriptures opened up new avenues of study for believers

and, coming as it did, in synchronicity with the feminist movement, it opened doors for women to discover new resources and
challenges for their faith.

Good news for women
It is now time to ask what the women were finding as they read
the scriptures in a completely new historical situation and with
new literary tools. Many felt as if they had returned to the period
of the first Christians. They read in the gospels a message of inclusion and call that they had not heard before. They read that
they were a new creation, and in the reading, many actually experienced a newness in their relationship with God and with
Jesus. They discovered that the gospel values totally reversed
both contemporary secular values, and also the valuing of
women that had been presented as traditional church teaching.
They discovered that women and men had been equally called
to discipleship, and even to apostleship. And they met a glorious array of women, some of whose names had been familiar,
but who now seemed to take on personalities and to accompany
them in their faith life as closely as their best friends.

It is also clear that there never was a debate about the initial
inclusion of women in Christianity. Women have always been
admitted to baptism and are, therefore, included as *imago dei,* the
image and likeness of the creating God, as well as *imago Christi,*
the image of Christ, crucified, buried and raised. The pre-
Pauline understanding of baptism in Galatians goes on to de-
nounce all exclusions or oppressions on the basis of sex, race or
class (Gal 3:27-28). This baptismal faith is rooted in the teaching
of Jesus about the reign (or kin-dom) of God, which paints a vision
of a community rooted in truth, love, justice and peace. This vision
called all believers to a new ethic, a new way of life, where the
first were last and the last first, where the mighty are cast down
and the lowly raised up. This prophetic critique of a disordered
society has always been seen as central to the Christian vision.
The personal words and deeds of Jesus put flesh and colour on
this vision, and his life is seen as a model for all, especially in its
reversal of 'business as usual.'

Women silenced

Within this overall vision, women are held up again and again as exemplars of the life of discipleship through their faith and courage. Their fidelity is painted against the backdrop of male infidelity; their presence right to the end is deliberately written into the text in contrast with the cowardice and desertion of the male followers. Women began to read the scriptures with a new sense of their place within this 'good news'. But unfortunately, this is not the whole story. Despite the good news of the gospels, the actual fruits for women show a pitifully meagre harvest. Women are, in no sense, central to these texts, and often feel as if they are clutching at straws in texts that are thoroughly patriarchal. The earliest piece of Christian writing known to us – Paul's first letter to the Thessalonians – is written as though the Christian community were composed entirely of men. As the first century progresses, the prescriptions for the silencing and exclusion of women become more vociferous. The resulting invisibility of women has become part of our imaginative self-identity as women believers, and the silencing of women has been taken for granted in all subsequent teaching and theology. This does not mean that women were absent from Christianity, but that their voice, insight, experience, wisdom, and faith were considered unnecessary to the understanding of the tradition. This constitutes an unimaginable loss for believers, and when one adds the loss of women's contribution as leaders of Christian worship and proclaimers of the gospel, one can understand the demands for inclusion at every level that have rocked the churches in recent times.

In the final texts of the New Testament canon, patriarchal marriage, with all its strictures about the headship of the husband and the obedience and submission of the wife, is adopted as the normative Christian social relationship. This had practical consequences for the seclusion and relegation of women to a kind of second-class Christian membership. The espousal of Eve in the Pastoral Letters, as theological justification for the natural and necessary obedience of women, led very soon to the vilification of women as the source of all evil. In the case of women (though not only in their case), Christianity found itself to be practically incapable of incorporating the prophetic dimension of the message of Jesus.

All this has deprived women of a continuous story of public Christian activity. Women remain practically without models from the earliest periods, except for the women of the Apocryphal literature, who were very quickly assigned heretical status as a result of their struggles for full inclusion in the community. Another consequence of the exclusion has been the stereotyping of God-imagery and God-language. God has been overwhelmingly imaged in the light of his male spokespersons, and the language of theology, history, and liturgy continued for centuries to have a predominating masculine tone. Finally, today, as the voice of women is being heard as exegetes, preachers and teachers in some churches, a little light is beginning to be shed on solutions to some of these problems. At the close of the twentieth century, the presence of women does not have to be assumed, or tagged on as a footnote. Women are finding ways to voice their concerns and to begin to celebrate their journey towards full inclusion in the Christian community.

Making history

Chapters Two to Four deal with the biblical witness to women contained in both canonical and apocryphal literature. The remaining chapters pick up the historical thread to the end of the first millennium. Just as the scripture revealed new riches as feminist exegetes mined its depths, so too has history. For most of the Christian tradition – that is, until about the last twenty years – Christian history was written entirely from the perspective of male and clerical concerns. This version of the Christian story is so much part of our mindset that we hardly notice the virtually total absence of women. On the other hand, women are present everywhere as one of the major preoccupations of church leaders. Each generation presents us with volumes of advice to women on how to fulfill their allotted roles as repentant

daughters of Eve. But the voices and concerns of women themselves are rarely heard, especially at the institutional level. The
task, then, for historians is to include women in the story on an
equal footing. Some see this process as a kind of soup-making –
add a few women and stir – without altering the basic lines of
the traditional tale. Christian feminist historians see the task as
an act of re-visioning, of looking back with fresh eyes, and entering the old texts from a new direction and with new questions.
Many women Christians have come to see this re-visioning as an
essential task, rooted in the drive toward self-knowledge and
the search for our heritage as women.[9] So it is necessary, then, to
take a look at history-making, both old and new, in order to discover how the story of women Christians can be told without
seeming like an afterthought to 'real history'. We write history
for ourselves; so each writing will reveal as much about the
writer and her/his concerns as it will about the story of our fore-
bears.

Conventional history

Conventional church historians outline several stages in the
doing of history. First, the sources need to be identified and collected. These are the primary sources consisting of written texts,
monumental remains, inscriptions, and any other possible indications contemporary with the period under discussion. History
is only as good as its sources, but then these sources have to be
verified for their accuracy and authenticity. Besides, since ancient writers also had their own agenda, the purpose behind
their writing must be discerned, as far as possible. These sources
must then be interpreted according to the chosen stance of the
author and, finally, the whole must be presented in an accessible
fashion for the designated audience. The vast majority of historians
of Christianity were also believers, and their history was very
much concerned with demonstrating the necessary development of tradition and the need for ongoing fidelity to its man-
date. This methodology has left us with vast amounts of information about the chronological development, decisive turning

points, and important players in the Christian story – from a
male perspective.

The problems for women, however, are numerous. Here,
only two are identified. First of all, since history is written for a
purpose, this purpose can determine the content to an extraordinary degree. The purpose of most church history was to support
the orthodox teaching of Christianity, to justify the current
ecclesiastical arrangements in ministry and governance, and to
identify the one unbroken line of development seen as willed by
God. It is easy to see how, with this agenda, women disappeared
from the story as active participants. The second problem is that
this version was presented as the objectively true story of the
tradition. History was often defined as the 'record of things
found worthy of remembrance'. The content of such history,
then, depends on who is doing the remembering and this can
seriously damage any claims to objectivity. In recent times, this
form of history-making has often been termed 'his story' and
women's history has been designated 'her story'. This play on
words conveys pithily the point of a feminist re-writing of history.

Christian history
Two other introductory points are necessary before turning to
feminist history-making. First, I intend to focus here on
Christian history rather than church history. Church history entails a theological judgement about God's plan of salvation
working itself out in the concrete conditions of peoples' lives. It
presumes a shared faith between writer and reader and entails
theological choices about which events to include as 'worthy of
being remembered'. A history of Christianity does not make
such assumptions. It does not assume a shared faith, and so can
be more eclectic and descriptive in its approach. The church historian owes something to the self-understanding of the church,
and speaks to a defined audience. The historian of Christianity
speaks to a wider audience, and intentionally tries to present the
Christian story to believer and unbeliever alike. For both, however, history is an exacting science, and most contemporary hist-

orians declare their purpose very clearly. Not many historians today pretend to write about 'things as they really were', nor do they aim to present the one definitive version of the past.

The second point deals with what historians call periodisation. For the purposes of interpreting and presenting the past in a coherent fashion, historians divide their story into manageable periods. Christianity, for example, is often divided into early, medieval, pre-modern and contemporary periods. This imposes a frame on the writing in an effort to offer some understanding of such a diverse story. Periodisation, however, while dividing the story into manageable chunks, also distorts the story dramatically. Feminists were amongst the first to point this out when Joan Kelly-Gadol asked the seemingly simple question: 'Did women have a Renaissance?' She answered in the negative, and went on to illustrate that the great turning points of history were such for a very small number of people. Almost without exception, such turning points were at the expense of women. The conditions of some men's lives may have taken on a new dimension, but most men and all women were usually excluded from these developments. This applies to the Golden Age of Greece in the fourth century before Christianity as much as it does to the Golden Age of Christianity in the fourth century of our era. When we ask how these 'golden ages' affected women, we shall discover that it was mostly in terms of more restricted lives. Much of the content of the book illustrates this point.[10]

Christian feminist history

Most contemporary history-making, or historiography, seeks to access the story of all peoples, not just those at the top, or those of a particular sex or race. It seeks to raise to consciousness – to re-vision – suppressed aspects of the story, to write of a past which is critically related to the present. Feminist historians often describe their task as restoring women to history and restoring history to women. One of the recurring metaphors of feminist history is the recovery of voice. The New Testament silencing of women casts its shadow over the whole story.

Feminists, then, have tried to uncover women's voices in texts written by women, and to read between the lines of the abundance of texts written *by* men *about* women. The small number of texts written by women themselves presents its own problems to the historian. These are complex documents and have to be read within their own context. The women of the past were not feminist, in the contemporary sense of the term, but each text available to us is the result of a very specific choice to speak and write made by a woman in very specific circumstances, usually in situations of real peril to herself. Despite the discovery of some texts, we are faced with a real absence of concrete detail about how women really lived. The tangible reality of the lives of most women is now tragically lost to us.[11]

The task, then, of including women in the Christian story presents the historian with some real problems, not least because the accepted story was written in the firm belief that the voices of women were irrelevant and intrinsically false. Christians today have inherited the structures of dogma, theology, creed, liturgy and commandment, all built on a foundation which assumed the irrelevance of women's fidelity and wisdom. The intentional inclusion of women in the story means that much of Christianity will have to be re-thought. How are women to be included? Feminists have elaborated a six-stage strategy which attempts to provide steps toward an inclusive history-making.

Feminist methodology
The first stage is to notice the absence of women from the normative historical record. All the foundational documents of Christianity, most traditional teaching, and much contemporary writing of Christian history are based on the apparent premise that women are not needed for the understanding of the tradition. The language of history, theology, liturgy and dogma has excluded the voices of women almost completely. This fact, as yet, does not impinge on the consciousness of most people, but it is a necessary first step to righting the classical version of women's place in Christianity.

The second stage summons us to notice that when women *are* present in the story, it is often in an apologetic, trivialising, accidental or even hostile way. Women appear as afterthoughts, the exceptions that prove the rule. There never has been a time in the Christian story when women were not physically present – all popes, bishops, emperors and teachers have necessarily been involved with women, essentially as mother and life-giver, but also as wife, lover, mentor, teacher and, occasionally, as friend. The self-identity of every single male Christian leader was formed against the backdrop of the 'invisible' and silent women who made their public lives possible. As we shall see, hostility towards women always reached a higher crescendo whenever women themselves attempted to speak on their own behalf. So women need to be re-discovered as more than the 'underside' of history, and the objects of legislation and teaching. Misogyny and androcentrism form much of the historical backdrop to women's presence in the Christian story. On the other hand, it is from the long history of repetitive legislation against women that contemporary historians can begin to put together the threads of women's story. The very repetition of anti-woman legislation, century after century, illustrates that this teaching is prescriptive rather than descriptive. The fact of laws forbidding women to preach indicates that there were preaching women who needed to be silenced.

The third stage of the process is, perhaps, the one most familiar to readers today. It has been named the compensatory stage. By way of 'compensation', some women are being restored to history. Wherever possible, the gaps in the historical record are being filled in. A list of the names of 'great women' has now become familiar to many – Julian of Norwich and Hildegarde of Bingen, for example, now take their places beside Joan of Arc and Thérèse of Lisieux. The Roman Catholic Church has engaged in its own act of compensation by declaring Catherine of Siena and Teresa of Avila to be Doctors of the Church in the early seventies, and more recently, Bridget of Sweden and Catherine of Siena to be joint patrons of Europe with Benedict

and Boniface. So individual women have been restored to the
record. It is also the case that whole groups of women, whose
presence is crucial to the understanding of our past, have been
eliminated from the story and only recently restored to memory.
These would include the thousands of women who were burnt
as witches and heretics, and the thousands more who created
new forms of religious living, such as the Beguines.

This compensatory history has given contemporary women
a new list of fore-mothers. We can now speak, with much justification, of Mothers as well as Fathers of the Church. The basic
story-line, however, has not changed. These women are seen as
exceptional, known to us through the lens of their male biographers. They are remembered for particular ecclesiastical purposes. When we have access to the actual voices of women, we
are reminded again just how dangerous the act of speaking was
for a woman. Even women as great as Hildegarde of Bingen,
who would have been exceptional in any age, had to engage in
the 'rhetoric of diminishment' in order to deflect any hostile
reactions. Hildegarde belittled her own voice and wisdom and
attributed everything to her visions, in order not to give the
impression of authoritative teaching in a woman's voice.
Compensatory history has been immensely valuable but, at best,
it has provided a kind of parallel story of women, which is rarely
integrated into 'real history'. The old story, however, no longer
seems so stable. Events of huge significance, such as the witch-
craze, are now more likely to be given their proper place in the
story. The work of women religious, in their thorough research
on their own foundations, has added new chapters to the story
of the ingenuity of women in their fidelity to the voice of God,
often despite ecclesiastical intransigence. Despite all the positive
results, however, compensatory history raises as many questions as it answers.

The fourth stage of the process is an attempt to answer some
of these difficulties. The newly discovered 'great women' lived
and believed and their lives were recorded in patriarchal con-
texts. They are remembered, in part, because even though they

transcended the circumstances of their age, they suited patriarchal purposes quite well. And besides, the lives of these women gave few clues about the lives of millions of 'ordinary' women. Feminist historians set about the task of analysing the historical significance of these women, which meant that the actual *context* of their lives had to be examined. They revised their understanding of their task in the direction of attempting to write a total history, not just a history of great women. An attempt is made to look at families, social groupings, and, above all, sexual relationships. Perhaps the central theoretical point underlying this fourth stage is that the relationship between the sexes is socially constructed and not naturally – or divinely – appointed. The silence, submission and invisibility of women was not designed by God, but found to be socially useful to man. The underpinnings for such an arrangement were readily at hand in one reading of the biblical sources. As feminists re-read the Bible, they also sought to discern the consequences of biblical faith in the social and cultural arrangements of the Christian community.

With this insight, feminist historians turned to new sources, such as letters, diaries, and memoirs, documents not normally given much historical credence because of their supposed lack of objectivity. They studied the legal systems of church and state, examined property deeds, and explored the structures of social and ecclesial power. New interdisciplinary skills were needed for this task, and dialogue among formerly diverse areas of scholarship was begun. While compensatory history had focused on women's status, contextual history focused on her relationships, her power, her position in society. Contextual history examined the conventional turning points of history and critiqued them in terms of their liberation or oppression of women's potential. Women were seen as part of the civil and religious communities in the fullest possible sense.

Feminists questioned the ease with which the silencing of women was taken as a solution to the problems of the early church. As a consequence of this decision, the history of

Christian women has followed a different path from that taken by Christian men. These paths did not result from the divinely arranged natures of women and men, but from specific social, cultural and ecclesial choices. Contextual history also brought the realisation that the different experiences of women are class-related. Not all women had the same experiences, and all women did not experience oppression in the same way. But what all women did have in common was not being men. The sex/gender of women placed them in a particular situation in the patriarchal scheme of things.

The results of this process are, as yet, minimally included in most secular and church histories. They appear in journal articles and conference proceedings. It is not yet possible to write a complete history of women and Christianity. For this to happen, the whole discipline of history has to be challenged, and this constitutes the fifth stage. This challenge is being mounted, for the most part, in academic circles and almost exclusively by women historians. Whereas in most other areas of the new historiography, as for example in the history of workers, male and female historians share the task equally, the task of feminist historiography is left almost exclusively to women. Endless questions arise about the authenticity of such intentionally pro-woman history-making, but as feminists point out, all previous history was intentionally pro-men, without ever fully acknowledging this fact. In vignettes and tightly focused studies, a clearer picture is emerging for some women in some places at various times. All this exhaustive work prepares for the sixth stage, which is still far into the future.

What is finally needed is a new history of Christianity which will acknowledge the diversity of belief and membership among participants. Christianity has never been as monolithic as most Euro-centric history would like to believe. This new history will allow the stories of women and men to proceed hand in hand, as a development of the New Testament vision of co-discipleship. It will acknowledge that the visible, institutional history of the church is far from the whole story, and that, for example, a history of holiness might proceed with completely different emphases. It would not be a history that denied the past, but would attempt to portray the past in all its complexity and diversity. This implies that a full accounting of the implications of the omission of women would be undertaken, and that all the consequences of such omission in law, theology, liturgy, ministry and power would be faced. The utopian nature of such activity places it well into the future and well out of the reach of most contemporary believers.[12] Much of feminist Christian history is still only in its infancy, and almost entirely compensatory in nature. The present history is like a report from the trenches and will be valuable to the extent that it is recognised as such, and not as a final statement.

Goal of present work

The goal has not been to write a history of women, but to redirect our historical attention. There is no question of fabricating a history for women, for there has never been a single moment in the history of humanity when women have not been present. The problem with conventional history is that it has been presented as normative history, as if, having described the situation of the male, the whole has been attended to. History has, in theory and in fact, been the history of *everyman*. The impression has been given that we were being presented with the whole true and definitive story, and that there is little else of value to know. The story is told that the biographer of the great Anglo-Saxon missionary, Leoba of Bishofsheim, commented as he completed her story: 'Of what use this will be to history, I do not know.' This book is written, in part, to respond to his question. It makes no pretence of impartiality, but hopes to offer as much as possible of the truth about women in the first millennium of Christianity. It remains, nevertheless, an incomplete statement and has omitted as much and more than is included. None of it would have been possible without the passionate commitment of feminists to discover a continuous Christian heritage for women.

The Christian feminist movement

It is primarily feminist historians who are addressing these questions and attempting to restore history to women and women to history. It is time to focus attention, however briefly, on the nature of Christian feminism, and its development through the past four decades. The word 'feminist' seems to be a mid-nineteenth century coinage to describe the new challenges brought by women to existing social, political and religious structures. The immediate context was the initiative taken by some Protestant women in the movement to abolish slavery in the United States and Britain. As women fought for this cause, it gradually dawned on them that the political and religious philosophy which maintained slaves in their subjection, was not unlike the grounding for women's subjection. Eventually, with the realisation that male dominant positions were virtually unassailable, a new mind-set was born which was named feminist. Feminism, then, is an overtly political and interdisciplinary movement which now exists in any number of forms. All agree, however, on challenging the existence of any 'master-narrative' about the human race. All such versions of human reality are greeted by feminists with a 'hermeneutics of suspicion'.[13] This implies that all the historical, literary and religious texts, accepted as standard versions of reality, are esteemed by feminists to be flawed and partial statements.

What has been termed the 'second wave' of the Christian feminist movement is usually dated to the early sixties. It coincides with the Second Vatican Council, but in no way originated from this virtually all-male event. Nevertheless, the dynamism flowing from the council provided a fitting and beneficial context for the growth of feminism in Christian circles. Such feminists had a two-pronged agenda. One arose from the need to understand the facts of women's Christian presence and the underlying causes of women's silence and invisibility. As feminists came to realise the glaring contradictions between the scriptural vision of co-discipleship and the historical and current ecclesiastical arrangements, they diligently set about unmasking the causes of such incongruities. The theoretical notions of patriarchy, understood to refer to the male power monopoly in all areas of civil and religious life, and androcentrism, which referred to the normative value assigned to maleness, came to be accepted as key explanatory ideas for the understanding of women's position in the churches. These ideas were used in the exploration of the biblical, theological, liturgical and historical heritage of Christianity, and came to be recognised as a reality in the daily church experience of many women. Though the theoretical notion of patriarchy, especially, has been challenged on many fronts in the interim, no better word has presented itself to describe the full reality of women's ecclesial experience.

The second aspect of the Christian feminist agenda was in the exploration of the practical consequences of women's full church membership. Eventually, the feminist movement in the churches focused, sometimes practically, but always symbolically, on the reality of ordination. Many women in many church settings, with varying success, struggled to have their call to ordination recognised, affirmed and celebrated in their communities. Other women turned their attention to the issues underlying the exclusion of women from ordination. As the churches, especially the Orthodox, Anglican, and Roman Catholic traditions, were forced to elaborate their respective theological stances on this question, the issue of Christian anthropology came to the fore. To the astonishment of many, it was realised that basic human realities needed to be challenged. What does it mean to be human? To be female? To be male? Does the baptism of women imply something different from the baptism of men? Can women image God? Jesus? If not, why not? These questions and so many others still remain on the Christian agenda, even where the ordination of women has become a reality. As the questions become more basic, the real challenge of Christian feminism becomes apparent.

One of the hallmarks of feminist writing is the open acknowledgement of the stance from which one writes. This is necessary to counteract the temptation to make universal statements about realities beyond one's experience. It is time, then, to state my own stance. I write from a Roman Catholic background which, for the past thirty years has been informed by a clear feminist agenda. My earliest scholarly work in patristic literature was based on the need to find women – any women – with whom I could identify in the Christian story. My feminist convictions have carried me through historical research and critique, sixties-style activism in the area of the restoration of the diaconate for women, and decades of teaching feminist courses in theology, history, and spirituality. Over the decades my convictions about the flawed and partial realisation of the Christian vision have only deepened and given new impetus to the search which began over thirty years ago. My astonishment at the ingenuity of women grows with each new discovery. My despair that such faithful ingenuity will ever be fully recognised by the churches also continues to deepen. In general, the gift of astonishment and delight prevails, and I hope that this is what characterises this book.

I present myself, then, as a feminist historian, with no claim to neutrality or objectivity. I hope to write some of the truth about women's lives, by being attentive at all times to the gender constructions of history. Gender can be understood as the social, cultural and religious construction of sexual differentiation. Each age and each culture has inherited, and in turn created, differing expectations of women and men, supposedly rooted in the biological inevitabilities of sexual difference. We are all familiar with the 'common-sense' expectations that 'men do not weep', and that 'women are the power behind the throne'. Such gender constructions are in the process of being changed dramatically, often with a great deal of resistance, and an apparent need for compensation in one area for loss in another. The 'glass ceiling' phenomenon in politics and business is only one example. The dark-suited men still take up most of the pictorial and actual space.

As Joan W. Scott indicates, gender is primarily a metaphor of power. Throughout history, gender has played a crucial part in the organisation of equality and inequality.[14] The arrangements of systems of equality and inequality within Christianity are the particular focus of this book. Theoretically, Christianity is noted for its universality; it is open to all and welcomes all. The impression has always been created that, within Christianity, theological discussion and the working out of the spiritual life are far removed from gender. As feminists have pointed out, however, the more removed from gender religion claims to be, the more gendered it actually is. In political, historical, ecclesiastical, and theological realms, where women are most absent, there gender is most present.[15] The construction of gender, therefore, is coterminous with history.

The whole history of Christianity, then, can be seen as a continuous process of gender shuffling. Women may not be explicitly present in the traditional telling of the story. But this never means that they are not present. Generations of Christians have accepted the invisibility or forcible exclusion of women as an essential part of Christian reality, and have associated this with a particular organisation of gender: men lead, women follow, for example. More seriously for the Christian dispensation, this state of affairs has been interpreted as a necessary result of the position of women before God. Sometimes explicitly, always implicitly, the conclusion has been that there is something more divine about maleness than there is about femaleness.

The goal, then, of this book is to direct our gaze explicitly at the situation of women within Christianity. Of necessity, a large part will be compensatory, that is filling in the gaps in our knowledge of women's Christian history. We are quite simply not familiar with even a small number of the women available to us in the sources. This is intentionally a partial history, though an attempt is made throughout to situate women in their historical context, and to understand the working of gender in that context. This first volume traces the involvement of women in the development of western Christianity for the first millennium. Throughout, the struggle with inadequate sources, conventional omissions and misinterpretations, and the actual impenetrability

of the distant past, will be obvious. Even so, I have had to omit
enough material to make this present volume twice its size. My
hope is that readers will become as excited as I am at meeting
such an extraordinary gallery of fore-mothers, and that they will
share my joy of discovery and also my outrage at the depriv-
ation and tragic distortion of the Christian story.

CHAPTER 2

The Women Disciples

'There were also women ...' (Mk 15:40)

'Woman, great is your faith!' (Mt 15:28)

'Now it was Mary Magdalen, Joanna, Mary the mother of James, and the other women with them who told this to the apostles. But these words seemed to them an idle tale, and they did not believe them.' (Lk 24:10-11)

'And Jesus said to her, "Woman, what concern is that to you ...?"' (Jn 2:4)

One of the major discoveries of women in their contemporary re-reading of the Bible was the existence of two foundational texts which gave impetus to an almost total re-working of their lives of faith. These were the astonishing and revelatory texts of the first creation story in the first chapter of Genesis (Gen 1:26-27) and the inclusive baptismal formula in Paul's letter to the Galatians (Gal 3:27-28). In these texts, women found a charter of Christian equality which moved them deeply, and these texts have remained as a touchstone for testing all other statements about the life and role of women in the churches.

The first creation story served to restore to women a sense of graced presence before God that had been removed from them by centuries of misinterpretation of the Eve story. 'Then God said, "Let us make humankind in our image, according to our likeness" ... So God created humankind in his image, in the image of God he created them; male and female he created them.' This text threw a completely different light on the more familiar 'Adam first, Eve second' story, and removed at one stroke one of the foundational biblical reasons for the submission of women to men. While the story of Eve, the first sinner and cause of all human misfortune, had formed the substance of volumes of Christian preaching, the story of women and men, equally created in God's image, had rarely appeared as the stuff of sermons. For women, it cast the biblical testimony on women in a whole new light.

Likewise, the liberating and transformative teaching of the letter to the Galatians placed women in a new relationship to their church: 'As many of you as were baptised into Christ have clothed yourselves with Christ. There is no longer Jew or Greek, there is no longer slave or free, there is no longer male and female: for all of you are one in Christ Jesus.' The baptism of Christians, Paul seemed to say, included an inherent challenge to the community to remove all sexism, racism and exploitation from Christian life. Women felt called to a new responsibility to take their places beside their brother Christians as full and free members.

These two texts became a kind of biblical charter for a new community of female and male disciples and continue to act as inspiration to millions of women believers. It was, however, the women of the gospels and of the young church who put flesh on this vision and who sparked the imaginations of a new generation of women disciples to follow in their footsteps. There is a vast array of these women – one scripture scholar has counted 64 – but here we can choose only a handful from the gospels.

Women disciples: Mary

The image of woman that dominates Christianity is that of Mary, the mother of Jesus. Her portrayal has remained remarkably consistent throughout the centuries. How surprising, then, to find that the biblical images of Mary are quite varied and often differ remarkably from the traditional and conventional virgin-mother imagery.[1] In the synoptic gospels of Mark, Matthew and Luke, the testimony to Mary is often conflictual, especially in the scenes during the public ministry of Jesus. One such scene from Mark sets the tone for other similar events:

Then his mother and his brothers came; and standing outside, they sent to him and called him. A crowd was sitting around him; and they said to him, 'Your mother and your brothers and sisters are outside, asking for you.' And he replied, 'Who are my mother and my brothers?' And looking at those who sat around him, he said, 'Here are my mother and my brothers! Whoever does the will of God is my brother and sister and mother.' (Mk 3:31-35)

Here, Jesus seems to be making a contrast between the members of his new family of women and men disciples and his former family, based on biological relationships. There is a play on the words 'inside' and 'outside' and the family of mother, sisters and brothers seems to be designated as 'outsiders'. Jesus places himself with the new 'insiders' who are seated around him, namely his new disciples. These are characterised by one thing only, 'doing the will of God'. On the face of it, the scene is quite remarkable. It seems that Jesus does not have the same reverence for his mother that generations of Christians have had. In the gospels, there is a lessening of emphasis on biological family structures, and a continual raising up of the discipleship relationship. Even Mary, the mother of Jesus, is challenged to change her relationship with Jesus into one of 'hearing the word of God and doing it'.

And Mary is shown doing precisely this in Luke's portrait of her visit to her cousin, Elizabeth. This is a story composed by Luke to illustrate a theological point. He wants to draw our attention, right at the beginning of his gospel, to the reason for the coming of Jesus. Jesus is one who 'has brought down the powerful from their thrones, and lifted up the lowly'. (Lk 1:52) Luke deliberately chooses to put these words into the mouth of Mary so that she becomes, for him, the premier spokesperson of the good news of salvation. Mary is not here the submissive and retiring stereotype that she had often become in later ages. On the contrary, to quote Pope Paul VI:

The modern woman will note with surprise that Mary of Nazareth, while completely devoted to the will of God, was far from being a timidly submissive woman or one whose

piety was repellent to others; on the contrary, she was a
woman who did not hesitate to proclaim that God vindicates
the humble and the oppressed, and removes the powerful
people of this world from their privileged positions.'
(*Marialis Cultus*, 37)[2]

And indeed, the modern women took this new Mary to their
hearts. Her song of liberation for the lowly and despised became
theirs, and her challenge to the 'powerful of this world' encouraged them to make similar challenges. As we shall see, this initial
Marian meditation on power and its misuse by the powerful to
oppress the lowly, became one of the central themes in the writing and life of every single Christian woman known to us. We
shall be returning to it again and again.

The Women from Galilee

It is now time to name some of the other women of the gospels
and to recognise that there were countless women whose names
have not come down to us. The quotation at the head of this
chapter comes from the story of the passion in Mark. Mark has
already told us about the desertion of the twelve and the betrayal
of Peter. He has described the momentous events surrounding
the death of Jesus – complete darkness over the earth and the
tearing in two of the Temple curtain. He has described the great
cosmic cry of Jesus to God about being forsaken, and then,
almost casually, Mark tells us 'there were also women looking
on from a distance'. When the world had turned to darkness and
all the others had abandoned Jesus – including even his Father –
the women were still standing there. What an extraordinary
scene! As successive groups of women have recently rediscovered this scene, they ask themselves how they could possibly
have missed noticing it before. Pope Paul's 'modern woman' is
forced to ask about the Christian memory. Who handed on these
stories of the suffering and dying of Jesus? It seems that Mark
gives us our answer: the women. Apart from the single exception, also recorded by Mark, of the Roman centurion, there was
nobody else there.

And who were these women? Mark obligingly tells us. These were Galilean women who had followed Jesus up to Jerusalem, and the word he uses for 'following' is the technical biblical word for discipleship.[3] So these women were disciples of Jesus. Mark goes on to name three of them, names that must have had some ongoing significance for his community. They are Mary Magdalene, Mary the mother of James and Joses, and finally, Salome. These were accompanied by many others, who had come up to Jerusalem. So we are hearing about a whole group of women who, in an unheard of manner, had left their homes and country and had followed Jesus to the end. They had braved both the danger and opprobium that were part and parcel of being the friends of a condemned criminal, and they had stayed to the end.

Luke confirms Mark's story of women disciples accompanying Jesus. (Lk 8:1-3) Luke's scene is from the ministry of Jesus, where he is shown travelling through the cities and villages proclaiming the good news. Luke tells us that the 'twelve' accompanied him, as well as some women and, as usual, Mary Magdalene heads the list of women. This is a different list and includes Joanna, Susanna and the usual 'many others'. Luke's community – perhaps a generation later than Mark's – does not seem to be able to cope as well with stories of women in significant leadership roles. Luke characterises the women followers of Jesus as either grateful clients, who had been healed by Jesus, or wealthy women who 'provided for him out of their resources'. The singularity and courage of Mark's Galilean women has been removed, and instead we have a story of women who fit more stereotypical roles. It is rather amusing, also, to read how centuries of male exegetes have tried to argue away, even further, the significance of these women disciples. Luke's point about 'providing' for Jesus has been variously explained as cooking for him and the male disciples, taking care of their personal wants, even washing their clothes! How hard it is to break through centuries of conditioning about the proper role of women, even when the evidence is before our eyes in the text,

that Jesus made no distinction between his female and male disciples.

The Anointing Woman

One of the most moving stories, repeated in one form or other in
all four gospels, is the story of the woman who anointed Jesus.
Mark's version seems to be the earliest and contains remarkable
features that are subsequently toned down by the other evangelists.

While he was at Bethany in the house of Simon the leper, as
he sat at the table, a woman came with an alabaster jar of very
costly ointment of nard, and she broke open the jar and poured
the ointment on his head. But some were there who said to one
another in anger, 'Why was the ointment wasted in this way?
For this ointment could have been sold for more than three
hundred denarii, and the money given to the poor.' And they
scolded her. But Jesus said, 'Let her alone, why do you trouble
her? She has performed a good service for me. For you always
have the poor with you, and you can show kindness to them
whenever you wish; but you will not always have me. She has
done what she could; she has anointed my body beforehand for
its burial. Truly, I tell you, wherever the good news is proclaimed in the whole world, what she has done will be told in
remembrance of her.' (Mk 14:3-9)

This wonderful scene takes place in the darkening days before the arrest and execution of Jesus. The preceding chapter is
full of warnings to the disciples about fidelity, and right after
this scene, we are told of the betrayal of Judas. Mark deliberately
places the story of the woman's fidelity and loving care of Jesus
as a contrast with the expected infidelity of the male disciples.
Their anger at the woman shows that they are fully aware of the
implications of her actions.

Anointing on the head is an ancient biblical tradition for
portraying kingship, an act usually performed by a religious
functionary of high importance. 'The anointed one', the
'Christos', is a title so usually associated with Jesus that

Christians have come to use it almost as his second name. We do not know exactly when this usage started, but in Mark's story we are given the first visual representation of this anointing – and it is by a nameless woman. Jesus himself points out the significance of her action and defends her against the complaints of the others. Furthermore he directs that this story be told wherever the good news is preached. This, however, did not happen. We are not familiar with the story because it was dropped from the lectionary in favour of the more conventional versions of the story in the other three gospels. In order to go some way toward redressing this deliberate ignoring of the woman, Elisabeth Schüssler Fiorenza named her now classic book, *In Memory of Her*.[4]

Matthew's version of the story (Mt 26:6-13) differs from Mark's in one important way. Those who reproach the woman are specifically named as disciples of Jesus, thus pointing up the contrast between their understanding of discipleship and that of the woman. Luke's story changes the context and purpose of the woman's act quite remarkably. (Lk 7:36-50) She is now a sinner, presumably a prostitute. The men grumble at Jesus for allowing this 'kind of woman' to touch him. The woman weeps for her sins, bathes the feet of Jesus with her tears and dries them with her hair. It is a remarkable gesture of sorrow by a repentant woman and has been beloved by countless numbers of artists in the Christian tradition. This is the conventional image of the woman, daughter of Eve, who knows her place because of her sinful nature. In John's story (Jn 12:1-8), the foot-washing has become a loving act of hospitality performed by Mary of Bethany, the sister of Martha and Lazarus. In the long list of women remembered by Pope John Paul II in his Apostolic Letter, *On the Dignity and Vocation of Women*, it is the Lucan version which he quotes and makes no reference at all to the Marcan unnamed woman. It seems that, as far as the contemporary church is concerned, she will still remain unnamed and unremembered.[5]

The Healed Women

There are two stories in Luke's gospel which have become powerful instruments of healing and restoration for many contemporary women. One is the moving story of the woman who 'was bent over and was quite unable to stand up straight'. (Lk 13:10-17) The woman 'appeared' in the synagogue, was summoned by Jesus and healed 'when he laid his hands on her'. Her response is electric: 'immediately she stood up straight and began praising God'. There are so many situations today where this story is heard as a promise of release and liberation. Wherever women are 'bent' from poverty, abuse, battering, pornography, illness or just sheer exhausting work, this story is heard as a beacon of healing and freedom. It has motivated women not only to hope but also to act with the same kind of ingenuity and initiative which originally brought the 'bent' woman into the synagogue. And the story has also encouraged women to find their voice and move beyond the silence and invisibility of exclusion and oppression.

In the story of the bent woman, we are told that she had suffered for eighteen years; now we meet another woman, who has suffered from haemorrhages for twelve years. Jesus seems to display a special compassion for long-suffering women. This story in chapter eight of Luke (vv. 43-48) is set among several other stories of discipleship and healing. As we saw already, chapter eight begins with a list of women disciples. It then proceeds to relate the parable of the sower with its description of levels of fidelity in relation to hearing and doing the word of God. This woman, once again nameless, plots her approach to Jesus carefully. She has concluded that if she can just get close to him and touch the 'fringe of his clothes', she will be healed – and indeed, she was. Jesus, however, calls her from her invisibility and raises her up as a model of faith for all. She is an example of those who are 'good soil', where the seed of the word of God can take root and produce 'a hundredfold'. [6]

Martha and Mary

We have already met the members of the friendly household where Jesus seems to have gone often for some rest from his labours. It seems that Martha owned the house and lived there with her sister, Mary, and her brother, Lazarus. Both Luke and John tell us stories of these women and the two sisters have been used in hundreds of sermons about the roles of women. Luke's story (10:38-42) is familiar. Jesus and, apparently, his disciples came to Martha's home and while she busied herself about preparing a meal for her guests, Mary 'sat at the Lord's feet and listened to what he was saying'. Martha complains about being left alone to do all the work without her sister's help, and Jesus, apparently, takes Mary's side and says that she has 'chosen the better part'. This is one of those stories that, in its interpretation, illustrates perfectly the ambivalence of the church toward women. It has been seen to refer to the life of nuns as opposed to the life of the married woman. The quiet, meditative and silent woman is praised and the bustling, talkative and 'complaining' woman is blamed and seen to be rebuked by Jesus. On the other hand, Mary has been pointed out as the innovative one, breaking all the rules of her culture by acting the part of a student disciple, and taking on a role forbidden to her. Martha has also been praised as one who did not accept the conventional silencing of women, and did not stand in awe of male teachers, but challenged Jesus and his teaching. In another interpretation, both sisters in their respective choices are understood to point to the possible situation of the celebration of the eucharist in Luke's own Christian community, where women performed both the ministries of the word and the eucharist. There is no doubt that the scene has eucharistic overtones, and perhaps Luke is taking the side of those who are pushing for the removal of women from such ministries and restoring them to silence.[7]

Whatever the meaning of the story, this is one of those gospel passages that has endlessly fascinated women and also church leaders who feel called to write about women. Even contemporary feminist exegetes have not come to a consensus about the meaning of the passage. What can and must be pointed out is that this little tale has been used throughout Christian history to divide women from one another, by extolling one group of women at the expense of the other. Married women have not fared well in the Christian story – indeed, with very few exceptions, they have disappeared completely. Until fairly recently, married women were seen to have not chosen the better part. The vocation of marriage and motherhood was seen to be of less value than that of nuns. The life of consecrated virginity was praised at the expense of marriage, and every now and then, this attitude is heard still today. The story of Martha and Mary did not cause this situation, but was often used to illustrate the supposed mind of Jesus and will of God on the subject. When connected with the story mentioned above of Mary washing the feet of Jesus, it is easy to see how the tradition would have disliked the talkative and edgy Martha.

These two sisters appear again, this time with their dead and subsequently restored brother in John's gospel (11:1-44). It is a long passage, and we need not attend to the whole story here. In one sense, the personalities of the two sisters seem similar to the story in Luke, but there are several different elements in John's version. It is true that we have no word from Mary – but many tears of love and sorrow – and we have many words from Martha, still in a complaining mode. But it seems that, for John, Martha is the hero of this scene. It often seems that John's gospel presents something of a corrective to the synoptics. One example of this is that, whereas in the synoptics the twelve seem to predominate in leadership roles, these roles are, in John, often given to women. This is one such scene. Martha challenges Jesus about his delayed arrival and almost suggests that this delay caused the death of Lazarus. In response, John shows Jesus revealing to Martha the mystery of the resurrection of the dead, and goes on to portray Martha's firm act of faith in this revelation. In the other gospels, such revelations are made only to chosen members of the twelve. Martha here takes on an apostolic role and, as such, brings joy to the hearts of many women theology students, as she grapples with Jesus in a theological discussion of the resurrection. At the end, Martha proclaims: 'Yes, Lord, I believe that you are the Messiah, the Son of God, the one coming into the world.'

The Samaritan Woman

These words of faith are central to the synoptic gospels, but there, they are put into the mouth of Peter (as, for example, in Mk 8:29). There are several other instances of this apostolic replacement in John, but we will just refer to two of them here: the Samaritan Woman and Mary Magdalene. John's story of the meeting of Jesus with the woman of Samaria needs to be read at several different levels. It contains very touching moments illustrating an exhausted Jesus resting beside a well and looking for a drink, and the Samaritan woman pointing out that he came without a bucket. It shows the return of the disciples and their shocked mutterings – again – about Jesus talking to such a woman. Throughout all this, however, a much deeper conversation is taking place about the relationship between Jews and Samaritans, the gift of new life in the image of gushing and everlasting water, and the nature of true worship. Then, like Martha, this woman of Samaria, this despised outcast, makes her act of faith and sets off to proclaim the Messiah to the local residents, and 'many Samaritans from that city believed in him because of the woman's testimony'. Another woman, one of the most unlikely apostles, is given the apostolic role of missionary. She stands as one of the faithful ones who 'heard the Word of God and did it' and then went to proclaim it.[8] Many commentators on all the gospels have pointed out that the women stories in the gospels are often used to contrast the faith and full discipleship of the women with the cowardice and mutterings of the male disciples. There are many examples of this, but this version of events did not make it into the traditional interpretation of the good news in sermon or official teaching. A recent and telling change from such traditional interpretation is to be found in the previously mentioned Apostolic Letter on women by Pope John Paul II. At the end of his discussion on the Samaritan woman, he says: 'This is an event without precedent: that a woman, and what is more a "sinful woman", becomes a "disciple" of Christ.'[9]

Mary Magdalene

We come now to the acknowledged leader of the group of women who followed Jesus – Mary Magdalene. The Christian tradition has remembered her as a prostitute, in fact a kind of lovable and artistically titillating prostitute who repented of her supposed sin and then spent the rest of her life doing penance in the midst of the most romantic scenery. In most such pictures, she is naked and covered only by her hair. In most stories, she is confused with Mary of Bethany, the sister of Martha. Such a picture, though so familiar, bears no resemblance whatever to the biblical image of Mary Magdalene. The scriptures say nothing of a life of prostitution, but only acknowledge a healing by Jesus, which is shown as the origin of her life of discipleship. Given the usual toning down of the position of women in the company of Jesus and in the early communities, it is quite significant that the role of Mary Magdalene as leader of the women disciples remains constant in the gospels.[10]

Perhaps her most important role, however, is that of proclaimer of the resurrection. We have already placed Mary Magdalene in proximity to the events of Calvary with the other women when the men 'deserted him and ran away'. (Mk 14:9) The women remained as close to the scene as possible – in a stark statement we are told that 'Mary Magdalene and Mary the mother of Joses saw where the body was laid'. (Mk 14:47) The women witnesses, then, were present throughout all the events of the death and burial of Jesus. It comes as no surprise, then, to discover them 'very early on the first day of the week', returning to anoint the body of Jesus. Even though each gospel, as we have said, is engaged in its own theological purpose, our intention here is to demonstrate the collective weight of the biblical witness to the presence and significance of Mary Magdalene and the women in the resurrection scenes. Each gospel makes Mary Magdalene and the women the first witnesses of the empty tomb.[11] Each gospel tells of the women testifying to the male disciples and apostles about the resurrection. Each gospel tells us of the appearance of the Risen Jesus first to the women – and all the time led by Mary Magdalene.[12] This means that all the earliest Christian communities remembered this tradition, at least until the time of the writing of the gospels. It means that if there are memories of these foundational events, it is to the women, led by Mary Magdalene, that we owe these memories. It is sobering to reflect that, without these women and their subsequent proclamation, we would be left with no eye-witness accounts. All the more regretful, then, that later generations seem to have been blind to these testimonies, and recounted the stories with the male disciples as the main characters.

After the betrayal and death of Judas, the gathered apostles set out the requirements for apostleship, as they prepared to vote on his replacement (Acts 1:21-22). These requirements included the following of Jesus during his public ministry, the witnessing of the resurrection, and the subsequent command to go and proclaim it. A substantial case could be made that only the women fulfilled these requirements because they bore the only unbroken witness right to the end of Jesus' life, and they were the primary resurrection witnesses. Matthew has an angel command Mary Magdalene and 'the other Mary' to 'go quickly and tell' that 'he is risen from the dead'. (Mt 28:7) As they ran to do the angel's bidding, they met Jesus himself. They embraced him and then were instructed by Jesus to 'go and tell'. Luke tells a similar story but adds that 'these words seemed to them an idle tale and they did not believe them'. (Lk 24:11) In John, Mary Magdalene is portrayed as being alone and weeping outside the empty tomb when Jesus himself appears and calls her by name. She is then sent to 'tell' and John writes in solemn language: 'Mary Magdalene went and announced to the disciples, "I have seen the Lord."'[13]

This placing of women at the most significant event of the Christian story and their commission to announce it to the others cannot have been but a deliberate and intentional part of the gospel story. Bernard of Clairvaux in the twelfth century, as well

as many other writers both before and since, have called Mary
Magdalene the 'apostle to the apostles'. It is strange, then, that
Paul, in his much earlier account of the resurrection appearances, fails to mention the women at all and puts Peter back
firmly in the place of leadership as the first witness to the resurrection (1 Cor 15:5-8). As most Christian women can testify,
these stories and their significance failed to have an imaginative
and spiritual resonance in our lives until very recently. We had
internalised the Christian story as a story with a cast of predom-
inantly male actors. The women who were faithful to Jesus up to
and beyond death, and who had been held up as exemplars of
fidelity in contrast to their brothers, were by and large unnoticed
and our debt to them went unacknowledged for centuries. It
may be well to add here that these women were also present at
Pentecost, when, it is believed, the Christian church received its
identity and its mission to the world. It might be interesting to
check back to the pictures of this event that we all drew in
preparation for our confirmation. It is highly likely that, apart
from Mary, the mother of Jesus, there is not a woman in sight.

Women re-reading the Scriptures
We have touched here on just a few of the women around Jesus.
They have always been present in the text; they have always
been part of the story, but the stories had been interpreted,
preached and officially taught only by men, and so the women
had retreated to play only minor and conventional roles. The
traditional telling of the women stories owed more to stereotypical cultural and religious expectations than to the original and
radically subversive good news. When women rediscovered
these stories, or rather had the scales taken from their eyes so
that they could really see what was there all the time, they were
exhilarated and transformed by what they read. The concept
and, more importantly, the experience of discipleship and apostleship was renewed in their lives. Perhaps the interpretation of
these texts by the early feminists was not always focused, but
the excitement of discovery carried the women on to the next

more critical phase. It remains true that the lives of contemporary women need to be touched again and again by the stories of these women, so that the news of the coming of Jesus may indeed be experienced as good. So much seemed to have been hidden – the active roles of the women disciples, their exemplary lives of fidelity, their courage in remaining, despite personal danger, through all the events of the passion, the significance of the women in key moments of the life of Jesus and his inclusion of them as key recipients of revelation. And finally the named and nameless ones who now became part of the life of women readers of the New Testament. The names and stories of these women were repeated lovingly in liturgy and song and poem. Personal stories of inspiration, rooted in the stories of these women, became part of the gatherings of women in church, classroom and tearoom.

Accompanying this was the realisation that there was so little biblical evidence for current ecclesiastical preoccupations about roles, status and power. Many contemporary women felt challenged to a new praxis of discipleship and were wholehearted in their attempts to engage in this. They set off for theological schools, engaged in ministries and tackled head-on the language and practice of exclusion. There was a new generation of women disciples.

The attempts to actualise this new vision brought women a whole series of shocks. For the most part, church leaders did not read the scriptures with the same understanding. Women were often not welcomed as ministers, and were often ridiculed and trivialised. The question immediately arose as to why the biblical message was not as clear to all. Women asked themselves why they had been so blind to the message until recently, and besides, it became immediately obvious that not all women were equally open to the insights about women in the gospels. During the seventies and eighties, feminist scripture scholars engaged in a much deeper study of the scriptures, as they sought to root their faith lives more solidly in the 'good news' for women. They engaged in dialogue and discussion with male

scripture scholars and church leaders and, in fact, began a journey, whose end is nowhere in sight. Following is a brief overview
of some approaches to the scriptures elaborated by feminist
scholars. Scripture scholarship by feminists is an ongoing and
awe-inspiring discipline. The volume of studies seems unending,
so what follows is a snapshot study and meant only to give a
small indication of what is available.[14]

Biblical interpretation is theological interpretation – it is concerned with the divine presence among the people of God, past
and present. Feminist biblical interpretation makes explicit that
such divine revelatory presence and truth is also found among
women, till now the 'invisible' part of the people of God. That is,
feminists make it explicit that the receivers and proclaimers of
saving truth are not only men but also women. They seek to interpret the theological silence of women throughout history and
the ecclesial invisibility of women both historical and contemporary. And they insist that both the silence and invisibility have to
cease for the fullness of God's truth to be made manifest.

They aim for a critical re-reading of the biblical texts in a feminist key and from a woman's perspective so that the patriarchal
underpinnings of the scriptures are unmasked, mistranslations
are corrected and lost traditions are restored. They point out that
centuries of androcentric scholarship, that is scholarship done
from the point of view of male dominance and exclusivity, have
laid bare only partial truth about God and God's message. They
aim to discover new dimensions of the conventional biblical
symbols and their theological meanings, that is, new dimensions
of discipleship, apostleship, call, sin, redemption, salvation and
revelation, just to mention a few. In and through this process,
feminists realise that they are creating a whole new mental
discipline.

So feminist exegesis (extracting the biblical meaning as it was
intended at the time of writing), and feminist hermeneutics
(extracting the biblical meaning for today through the process of
interpretation), is a whole new intellectual and religious enterprise. This scholarship has several dimensions. It is a scholar-

ship that is compensatory, that is a scholarship that fills in the gaps in our knowledge about women. It is also revolutionary in that it challenges the accepted meanings of texts and interpretations in a most radical way. Feminist scholarship rejects the view that women's experiences, religious participation and cultural contributions are less important than men's. What is common to all feminist theology, exegesis, and hermeneutics is that it introduces a radical shift into all previous forms of these disciplines. The central commitment and accountability of the feminist theologian is not to the traditional male dominant church, but to a new church, which will be more faithful to the totality of the biblical revelation. Most feminists would agree that this task involves, as an initial step, an intense focusing on women only and their concerns, biblical, historical and contemporary. Therefore feminist exegetes focus, not just on the tradition, but on a feminist transformation of the tradition; not just on the Bible, but on the liberating Word of God for all, but especially for women. This, after all, has been the single most neglected aspect of biblical scholarship.

The Bible has been the book of the few, the elite. It has been used to support slavery, racist oppression and the dis-empowerment of colonised peoples. It has been used to promote anti-semitism and apartheid. And it has been used for the silencing and exclusion of women. So, the question that feminists, among others, ask is: How can this Bible be a saving word for women Christians? But the Bible has also been a source of insight, transformation and support for women and men who reject slavery, exploitation, sexism and racism. That is, the Bible can be – and always has been – used both religiously and politically.

Women have been reading the scriptures from the beginning, despite the fact that the major influence of the church was brought to bear to prevent this. We have some access, as we shall see, to the biblical insights of the medieval women mystics. One of their major struggles was the demand to be allowed to preach the Word of God, as they felt God had commanded them to do. For the most part, however, what we hear from the official teaching is that women cannot be trusted with the Bible. The book is too dangerous to be allowed into such untrustworthy hands. So, it is not until the first wave of the feminist movement in the mid-nineteenth century that we begin to hear the voices of women as biblical exegetes. It comes as no surprise that these first efforts were mostly compensatory in their scholarly purpose. These first women exegetes sought to find themselves in the text. They searched out positive texts about women in order to counteract all the negative teaching in the texts about Eve and her sinful descendants. They raised up the names and stories of the 'mouthy' women, to counteract centuries of admonitions to womanly silence. They rejoiced in the discovery of women who took bold and ingenious initiatives in order to counteract endless exhortations to submission.

In particular, they searched for a hermeneutical principle that would provide a central root for all that they wanted to say about their new discoveries, and they found such a principle in the liberating and inclusive message of Jesus. They restored to visibility and consciousness the hidden, omitted, and forgotten women as role models – Eve herself, and Lilith, Deborah, Ruth, Naomi, Esther, Mary Magdalene, Martha, Mary of Bethany, Phoebe, Dorcas, Prisca and so many others. Eventually, they came to the realisation, by the end of the nineteenth century, that despite such voluminous work, the Bible itself was a major problem. The Bible itself had been written by men, preached by men, interpreted by men and translated by men. It was at this time, in 1890, that Elizabeth Cady Stanton undertook the enormous task of writing *The Women's Bible*.[15] This women's Bible scared many people with its radical claims, and as a result of this and the warring turbulence of the first half of the twentieth century, feminist exegesis disappeared for about fifty years. The work of these first exegetes was virtually forgotten.

Some Feminist Biblical Principles
'Does the Lord speak only to Moses?' This was the question, articulated first by Miriam, the sister of Moses, and re-articulated

by a new generation of feminist exegetes in the early sixties, that inaugurated the second wave of feminist study of the Bible. This was a period of enormous enthusiasm for biblical study by women. As the decade progressed, these second wave feminists also discovered the limits of a compensatory approach to scripture study. The re-discovery, yet again, of the biblical women, was not enough to open up the churches to full participation by women. It would be impossible and indeed unnecessary here to recount the full story of feminist exegesis and hermeneutics in the succeeding decades. The task continues and one would need to be a devoted specialist to keep track of the volumes of writing. Here, I will just list some realisations and principles that continue to guide this study:

The biblical presentation of humanity privileged the male. This was not so just for individual texts, but for the text of scripture as a whole. The Bible was rooted in a patriarchal context and was androcentric and sexist in its attitudes towards women. Women were a mere backdrop and had come to be regarded as auxiliary figures. Stated like this, the biblical tradition seemed scandalously unfair to women and raised the question over and over again: 'What is the good news for women?'

The language of scripture was seen as alienating and almost idolatrous in its overwhelmingly male imagery. Feminist scripture scholars asked; 'How could women be included? Were women, in fact, intended to be included? What could be done about the language of scripture, as a starting point?' The problem of inclusive language had arrived, and with it a renewed realisation of the intransigence of the tradition. Even minimal requests for linguistic inclusion of women were met with entrenched negative resistance.

As women searched for more inclusive ways of reading the Bible, they took the inclusive vision of Jesus as a starting point. Scholars explored the texts for indications of the historical situation at the time of Jesus. They studied the significance and meaning of words such as 'disciple' and 'apostle' and found ways to explore the actual composition of the audiences addressed by Jesus. They studied the historical and sociological background of the women we have already met at the foot of the Cross and in Luke's list of women disciples. Many women found unbearable the tension between the assured biblical inclusion of women by Jesus and the ongoing excluding arrangements of many churches.

The search for a new God language was part of this process, and women began to experience the interconnections between their scripture study and their experience of prayer and worship. The unutterable God of scriptural revelation was routinely uttered in male language that had become commonplace in the normal worship service. Many women felt so excluded by this experience that they felt obliged to abandon their churches.

The study of Jesus' message revealed that even this 'good news' was not without its problems. There is no doubt that the good news of Jesus shows no demeaning word whatever towards women. There is no doubt that the invitation to co-discipleship seemed to be always part of the intention of Jesus in his words and actions. It is also clear, however, that this inclusive message seemed never to have been strong enough to alter the organisation of the churches. The Christian church, as an institution, seemed to have been constructed on the principle of the exclusion of women from public roles and responsibilities, and no words of Jesus seemed to have been heard strongly enough to challenge this. In this context, the question of the maleness of Jesus arose. Into whom were women baptised? Did the baptism of women bestow the same graces of inclusion as the baptism of men? Were women equally saved with men?

This questioning led eventually to an examination of the revelatory nature of the Bible itself. In what ways does God reveal God? What is saving truth for women? How is the Bible the Word of God? For women? For men? These are such fundamental questions that almost the whole effort of biblical study, by both female and male exegetes, is directed toward their resolution today. The initial joy of women in discovering women like themselves in the pages of scripture has not diminished. This joy is now, however, qualified by the enormity of the task facing all believers today. It is a question of exploring, again, how the scriptural revelation impacts on our contemporary world. No believer can absolve herself or himself from this challenge.[16]

One of the main resources for an exploration of renewed models of inclusive Christian community is to be found in the earliest decades of Christianity. We have the resources of the letters of Paul, dated from the early fifties, and Luke's *Acts of the Apostles*, to be dated from much later in the first century. It is to these that we now turn our attention. We will be entering a new era of ambivalence about women and their roles in the Christian community. This period, however, is absolutely foundational in its elaboration of a theological argument for the exclusion of women from public roles in the church. It is also foundational in providing us with the revolutionary words of Paul's baptismal formula, 'As many of you as were baptised into Christ have clothed yourselves with Christ. There is no longer Jew or Greek, there is no longer slave or free, there is no longer male and female; for all of you are one in Christ Jesus.' (Gal 3:27-28)

CHAPTER 3

Early Christian Women

'I commend to you our sister Phoebe, a deacon of the church ...' (Rom 16:1)

'For it is shameful for a woman to speak in church.' (1 Cor 14:35)

The early traditions out of which Christianity constructs its history were formed in the cultural milieu of patriarchal Mediterranean society. Thus the literary legacy of the first generation of Christian intellectuals is distorted by the cultural assumption that male activity is normative.[1]

Therefore both Jewish and gentile women's status and role were drastically changed, since family and kinship did not determine the social structures of the Christian movement.[2]

The decades of Christianity from 30-100 CE are completely fascinating in their diversity and complexity.[3] This rich tapestry will be the main focus of our interest here since, for most Christians, the presumptions are that Christianity proceeded in a calm, peaceful and unbroken line of development from the moment of Pentecost. The usual version goes something like this: Jesus left his chosen (male) apostles with a fairly clear blueprint for his church, which included instructions for ritual, leadership and doctrine. These men, led by Peter and eventually by Paul, then enacted these instructions and, using the gift of the Pentecostal Spirit, they handed on to the next generation what had been given to them. All Christian traditions have some version of this state of events, with varying emphases for ministry, authority, ritual and teaching, but, perhaps, the Roman Catholic version is the most intricately developed. Feminist (and other) scripture scholars have been challenging this monolithic foundation story for decades, and the fruit of their labours is now evident in hundreds of volumes, though perhaps not yet in any perceptible institutional changes. As mentioned above, with regard to the gospels, contemporary believing readers of these texts are amazed at what they have not seen with regard to women's presence. As is the case with so much of women's history, what we have learned to see is mostly behind our eyes. We see what we have been taught to see.

Sisters and Brothers

The quotations at the head of this chapter give some indication of the challenge to the traditional versions of the early Christian story. The cultural milieu of early Christianity was a patriarchal and androcentric one – male activity and male humanity were assumed to be normative. Men belonged to the public sphere and were actively engaged in 'making history'. Women belonged to the private sphere where they worked out their 'natural' roles of submission and obedience to the normatively male project. One of the main institutions of this society was patriarchal marriage. This does not mean that all women were in the same boat. There was a huge difference, for example, between the wife of a well-to-do public figure and a female slave of the household. There was an even greater difference between the surviving widow of such a male public figure and most other women. The main theme here, however, will be the cultural, and eventually religious attitude to patriarchal marriage as one of the main building blocks of society. The well-run patriarchal household was an image of the well-run state and, eventually, the well-run church. All were in their proper place and this place was assumed to be the plan of the gods and, in Christianity, the 'order of creation'.

We have already seen that Jesus seems to have challenged the arrangements of the biological family, not only in remembered attitudes to his own family, but also in his dealings with the women who left everything and followed him. We have seen that the group of disciples, as described in the gospels, is a mixed group of female and male disciples. This apparent challenge to normative family arrangements continues into the young church, and can often be seen as the main cause of division in the communities described in our sources. The intense excitement of early believers, both male and female, at the message of Jesus and the extraordinary transformation of their lives, as a result of their faith, appears on every page of our sources. Intense religious commitment challenges other human allegiances. While it is fair to say that Christianity changed the lives of male believers, the challenge to female and slave believers was even more dramatic. The Christian invitation was to form one community of believers, with no distinction of Jew or Greek, slave or free, male or female. One could say that all the succeeding centuries of Christianity faced and sometimes attempted to actualise this challenge as one of the central Christian tasks.

We focus here on one of the key moments in this journey. Christianity offered new choices to those who heretofore had no choice about their state of life. Slaves, wives, the poor and other marginal people were inserted into a pattern of life that benefited others. This does not suggest that all such patriarchal arrangements were necessarily harsh, but from our historical sources, tales of harshness far outnumber tales of compassion and respect. One of the main choices offered by Christianity to women was the choice of not marrying. It is hard to imagine today how socially disruptive the acting out of such a choice could be. This is precisely what is happening in these early Christian decades. In the chapters of the Acts of the Apostles and the Pauline letters, women seem to be covering the length and breadth of the Mediterranean world in fidelity to the teaching of Jesus. They travel alone, in pairs and in groups. They mingle freely and publicly with men as they go about their evangelising tasks. This kind of free association of the sexes was practically unheard of in the ancient world and brought opprobium on the Christian community in many places. Both ancient and contemporary authors call this kind of life structure 'syneisactic'.[4] It refers to an entirely new kind of gendered arrangement. Instead of the normative dominant/submissive roles of marriage and society, the early Christians sought to live in an inclusive community of shared discipleship. They seemed to have genuinely regarded each other as sister and brother through the new life of baptism. They had entered a 'new creation', where the old dispensations no longer held. The often startlingly radical early chapters of the story are amply illustrated in our sources, and to these we now turn.

What do the sources say?

As Bernadette Brooten has reminded us, we need to explore the lives of women if we wish to write women's history.[5] She points this out in contrast to the usual methodology of exploring what men have said about women. This, then, will be our first task. The intention here, as with the gospels, is to give a sense of the multiplicity and diversity of women's lives at the beginning of the Christian story. Then we will turn to the Pauline literature specifically, to explore Paul's Christian convictions and his struggles to live by them. We will then turn to the later canonical literature, closing with an examination of the influential message of 1 Peter.

After the death of Jesus c. 30 CE, his followers gathered in Jerusalem, where women as well as men participated in the foundational Pentecostal event. As the author of the Acts of the Apostles reports, 'they were all filled with the Holy Spirit'. (Acts 2:1-4) It seems that the impulse to spread the good news impelled them to go and preach immediately to the inhabitants of Jerusalem. This period of the 30s and 40s is without any written source, so the events are conjectured from comments at a later period. We learn that women and men in considerable numbers came to be 'followers of the Way', and that they very soon drew attention to themselves. From the account in Acts, it seems clear that the first believers tried to replicate the life they led with Jesus. We hear of sermons preached about the Spirit being poured out on 'all flesh', and about sons and daughters prophesying – 'even upon my slaves, both men and women, in those days I will pour out my Spirit; and they shall prophesy.' (Acts 2:17-18) A discipleship of equals was attempted where 'all who believed were together and had all things in common; they would sell their possessions and goods and distribute the proceeds to all, as any had need.' (Acts 2:43ff) The same text described the daily gatherings for prayer in the Temple and 'breaking bread' at home. The Acts of the Apostles has several such idealistic summaries, and it follows the author's (Luke?) plan to paint a picture of a community growing together in peace and harmony.[6] As we shall see, shortly, that was not always the reality. The earliest community seemed to have been an extremely lively assemblage of persons from all walks of life, with a variety of memories about the life and message of Jesus of Nazareth, and its meaning in their particular situation.

The presence of women in the earliest community drew the attention and ridicule of many contemporaries, but it seems, from several comments, that this aspect of the Christian assembly was particularly galling to Saul, later Paul. Since Paul seems to have become a convert about five years after the death of Jesus, that is, around the year 35 CE, the reports of his persecution of the Christians must refer to the first year or two after the crucifixion. 'Saul then worked for the total destruction of the church; he went from house to house arresting both men and women and sending them to prison.' (Acts 8:3) This seems to have taken place in Jerusalem, but two further accounts mention Saul travelling much further afield to persecute the Christians. Each time, women are mentioned as being the butt of his zeal, in a way that is quite unusual in early literature.[7] So, it is clear that women were visibly present in the early Christian groups. Here, in order to give a flavour of their visible presence, we will focus on just a few of these women and their quite significant ministries. It must not be thought, however, that this is a total picture. All these texts, as the quotation at the head of this chapter indicates, are male-centred in their concerns, but it is important to name all these women together in order to counteract the received traditions of all churches, where women are totally omitted from the foundational accounts.

The Leadership of Women

One of the most ubiquitous women is Prisca, who is always partnered with Aquila. They are mentioned six times in the New Testament. They preceded Paul in the missionary work of the church and, after Paul's conversion, he joined them in their house-church in Corinth, perhaps in the year 50 CE. Paul made tents in their workshop, as they shared this same trade (Acts 18:1-3). Prisca and Aquila had but recently come from Rome, having been expelled with other followers of Jesus by the Emperor Claudius. They are the earliest names that have come down to us associated with the founding of the Roman church. Later, the two travel on with Paul to Syria and we hear of them in Ephesus. So here is a woman and man missionary couple, whose main ministry seems to have been the leadership of the churches wherever they were. In Rome, Corinth and Ephesus, they founded house-churches. The house-church was the earliest organisational unit we know of among the early Christians. It is usually associated with fairly affluent believers, who owned a house of sufficient size to host the gathered community. We never hear of Paul founding a house-church; his particular ministry was as travelling missionary and initial evangelist of gentile communities. It is not at all unusual for him to mention and greet those who hosted him on his travels, and women are named as hosts in many such greetings.

One such is Mary, the mother of John Mark, one of Paul's companions. In what must be a very early memory, Acts recalls that Peter went to her house immediately after his escape from prison. This must have been a Hellenist house-church in Jerusalem, because the focus of the authorities (King Herod) at this time was the persecution of the original Jewish Christian community in Jerusalem. The apostle James was killed by Herod in 42, and it is interesting to note that, as one of the twelve, he was not replaced. The symbolic function of 'The Twelve' was no longer needed. Other women leaders of house-churches include Chloe (1 Cor 1:11), Lydia, the first European convert (Acts 16:14-15, 40), and Nympha and 'the church in her house'. (Col 4:15) These women are named plainly and without equivocation as the leaders in their respective houses. Lydia is described as a business-woman in the purple dye trade, and so must have been a woman of some financial independence. Again, we are told of a woman apparently living as ruler of a household. She is called a 'god-fearer' (Acts 16:14f), which usually indicates that, as a Gentile woman, she had lived on the margins of the Jewish community and followed Jewish religious life as far as possible. After listening to Paul's preaching, she and 'her household' were baptised. She then invited Paul to make her home his centre while he was in Philippi and, as the text tells us, she 'would take no refusal'. This implies that these women began to exercise their authority immediately in their communities, cared for its needs, presided at its celebrations and hosted travelling missionaries from other communities. We have no idea whatever how each community was organised, or even whether there was a distinctive organisation. All we are left with is the names of these women and their very specific designations. Traditional exegesis, in its false assumption of an institutional episcopate and priesthood descending directly from Jesus, felt free to ignore these women, or see them in the traditional roles of housekeeper and cook. Each text, however, seems to imply so much more.

Other roles assigned to women in these earliest settings include prophet, teacher, co-worker, apostle, teacher and widow. One of the few scriptural portrayals of a woman teacher in action is that of Prisca (or Priscilla, as she is called in Acts), who is named as the teacher of Apollos. This same Apollos is described as an 'eloquent man, well versed in the scriptures'. (Acts 18:24) He had spoken 'with burning enthusiasm' in the assembly, but he had known only the baptism of John. This implies a baptism of repentance, but not one in the Spirit. Acts reports that Priscilla and Aquila 'explained the way of God to him more accurately'. This would suggest that Prisca and Aquila were highly respected and authentic teachers in the community of Ephesus. It is, perhaps, the only laudatory report of an official Christian woman teacher for almost twenty centuries.[8] In several places, Paul identifies women as his 'co-workers'. This implies that they travelled with him and shared in the preaching and teaching. When the same word *(synergos)* is used of men such as Timothy and Apollos, this is what is implied. A number of these women are identified by name in the closing chapter (16) of the letter to the Romans. Mary 'has worked very hard among you'. Tryphaena and Tryphosa are 'workers in the Lord'. The 'beloved' Persis has 'worked hard in the Lord'. In each case, the word for work is the technical term for missionary labours. Prisca and Aquila show up here again and are described as ones who 'risked their necks for my life'.

Women Apostles

Two of the women in this list raise many other questions about the significant leadership roles of women in the early communities. These are Junia and Phoebe. Paul writes: 'Greet Andronicus and Junia, my relatives who were in prison with me; they are prominent among the apostles, and they were in Christ before I was.' (v. 7) We have no means of knowing what kind of partnership this was, but it is noteworthy that Junia is not characterised by being wife or sister to Andronicus. She is presented as an independent person in her own right, a relative of Paul's, a Christian before him and, what caused later commentators much more difficulty, a prominent apostle. In fact, the apostleship of Junia so bothered many later male commentators that she was changed into a male apostle – Junias. Several recent feminist exegetes have pointed out that there is no such male name as Junias in the whole of ancient writing.[9] But it seemed that the general consensus among male exegetes for centuries was that an 'outstanding apostle' definitely had to be a man.

There is very little consensus on the meaning or origin of the title 'apostle'. For the greater part of Christian history, apostle signified a member of the twelve and also, the self-proclaimed apostleship of Paul. Luke generally intends this meaning, but the other New Testament writings indicate that there were many more apostles in the early communities, performing a variety of functions. Common to all, however, seems to be the notion of 'being sent'. As we saw, this applies to the women and men at Pentecost, as well as the women witnesses of the resurrection. In Junia, we find another apostle, who preceded Paul in the Christian life and ministry, and therefore did not depend on him for her authorisation. In fact, as he tells us, they met on equal terms in prison, both arrested for their missionary and preaching activities. As Brooten points out, Paul had had to defend vigorously his own calling to be an apostle, so he was not likely to use the term loosely for anyone else, unless he was convinced of its authenticity

We have no further information about the activities of Junia. Like so many other women of the tradition, we get a brief glimpse of her and then she disappears. But it is clear that she was a woman with authority in the early church and was significant enough to be arrested for her activities. Phoebe, likewise, known to us from one brief reference in the same Pauline letter, is a woman with authority. Phoebe is named by Paul as 'sister', 'deacon of the church at Cenchreae', and 'a prostatis of many and of myself as well'. (Rom 16:1-2) The paragraph of recommendation of Phoebe seems to imply that she is the bearer of Paul's letter to the Romans: 'welcome her in the Lord as is fitting for the saints, and help her in whatever she may require from you.' Again, commentators have attempted to reduce the significance of the titles 'deacon' and 'prostatis' to make Phoebe a kind of generalised helper or servant of Paul's. This illustrates the translator's problem of 'seeing from behind the eyes' to which we have already referred. It is assumed – and taught – that women could not have been deacons on the same level as men, and so Phoebe is called a deaconess or servant. Phoebe, however, is given by Paul the same authority as the male deacons he names, for example Timothy, though it has been very problematic for later generations to recognise this. The Christian church, generally, has not been familiar with such authoritative women.

The title 'prostatis' is similarly misrepresented when it is applied to Phoebe. The male form usually means 'leader', 'patron', or 'president', all terms signifying authority. When applied to a woman, however, a term is sought which deprives the word and the bearer of this authoritative sense. Castelli quotes one such famous and well respected commentator to this effect: 'The idea is that of personal care which Paul and others have received at the hand of the deaconess.'[10]

Paul does not quibble about the women's authority, at least in the words he uses here. Even though we do not know the precise implication of Phoebe's role as deacon of the church of Cenchreae, leader of many and Pauline ambassador to Rome, it is clear that she was treated as a woman with official authoritative roles. Like Junia, she is not linked in relationship to any male relative. Paul's use of the Christian term 'sister' also indicates that Phoebe lived her discipleship in an outstanding way. She had made the Christian community her new family and this was the source of her identity.

These are some of the women, mostly known through Paul's writings, of whom we get a brief glimpse as they exercise their ministries in the early church. The information about them is tantalisingly sparse, but it is sufficient to let us know something of the diversity of faith life and ministry experienced by the first Christian women. Their very presence also contradicts, at so many levels, the accepted potted versions of early Christian history. There was not one straight line of development. There was not just a male-only ministry. The presence of these women, marginal though it be in a textual sense, places them in authoritative positions at the centre of their communities. We have Paul's authoritative voice for this. This presence discounts so much later biblical and theological groundwork on the proper roles for women in the Christian dispensation.

Women in Paul's Letters
We turn now to the genuine letters of Paul to explore his very concrete comments about women and their roles in the communities he addresses. It is necessary to state from the outset that women form a minor theme in his writings, for the most part. As

we have pointed out above, the very earliest piece of Christian writing that we possess, the First Letter to the Thessalonians, proceeds as if both the writer and recipients lived and believed and worshipped in a male-only environment. This letter can probably be dated to the year 50 CE, just twenty years after the death of Jesus and the foundational events of Christianity. It seems to contradict completely the images of vivid, enthusiastic missionary work of both women and men that we have seen in other sources, even in Paul's other writings. As feminist exegetes remind us, we must always presume the presence of women in such cases, because there has not been a human or Christian community without the presence of women. So the question is not, 'Where are the women?' but rather, 'What ideological choices govern Paul's total exclusion of them from the text?' 'Paul's man-to-man communication with his Thessalonian sons and brothers leaves no trace of Christian women's presence, let alone their status and activity as free and equal members of a democratic discipleship.'[11]

For our purposes here, I have chosen to explore only 1 Corinthians and Galatians among Paul's genuine letters. Space considerations make a consideration of most of the epistolary material impossible, but Ephesians, the Pastorals and 1 Peter also call for attention. First, it will be helpful to take a brief look at Paul's Christian vision.

Paul is a Christian mystic. He did not seem to have known Jesus and he expresses little interest in the details of the life and work of Jesus familiar to us from the gospels. Since his writings begin in 50 CE, we might expect to find some details about the life of his Christian contemporaries, but we are disappointed. There is nothing about miracle or parable, no detail about surviving followers from the time of Jesus, and one brief reference – by way of aside – to Mary, the mother of Jesus (Gal 4:4). What Paul is interested in are the great foundational events of Christianity to which believers have access through baptism. Christians are baptised into the life, death and resurrection of Christ – they are, in fact, buried and raised with Christ. Each

Christian is, then, a new being, a new creation, having membership in a totally new community. The Christian believer is 'in
Christ' and has moved to an entirely new place. Paul and Jesus
are at one in this – a new community has come into being where
there is 'no longer Jew or Greek, there is no longer slave or free,
there is no longer male and female; for all of you are one in
Christ Jesus'. (Gal 3:28) This is a ritual baptismal formula that
pre-dated Paul and there is no doubt whatever that it summed
up the actual experience of many early believers. They tried to
live in communities of co-equal disciples. That such an act of
faith in the effects of baptism had personal and political consequences is obvious. It is these inevitable social and ecclesial consequences that form most of the substance of Paul's writings,
and of the greater part of all later Christian theology. How does
one form and organise such a community of equality? Much of
Paul's energy was directed to nullifying the distinctions between Jew and Greek, but the slave/free and male/female distinctions awakened in him feelings of great ambivalence. As we
have seen, some of this vision of equality of discipleship seems
to have prevailed in the concrete details of Christian life; when
faced with verbalising his responses to the inevitable social and
ecclesial difficulties, Paul's nerve seems to have failed him.

There is no doubt that the first believers, including Paul,
were actually transformed by this belief. Christians felt as
though they lived in a new age of grace. The Spirit of God was
the acknowledged community leader and all were subject to and
led by this Spirit. In both Paul's letters and Acts, one can sense
the bustle and excitement as male and female missionaries,
apostles, teachers, prophets seem to rush explosively through
the Mediterranean cities, and are hosted by the resident house-
churches. Behind the often idyllic picture of Acts, however,
there are tensions between Jew and Greek, male and female,
slave and free, and it is to one set of those tensions that we now
turn our attention in the Corinthian community.

The Corinthian community
Paul had arrived in Corinth, one of the crossroad cities of the an-

cient world, in the year 50 CE and, as we have seen, was greeted
and accommodated in the household of Prisca and Aquila. He
knew the community well though he definitely had not founded
it. There were tensions in this multi-racial community, and several years later, 'Chloe's people' wrote to Paul reporting many
community factions and asking for advice (1 Cor 1:11). Whatever
the actual situation – the letter describes the scene as a fairly
complex struggle for authority – the group that most seems to
attract Paul's ire are the women prophets. Chapters 5-14 deal
with a variety of issues relating to women – marriage and re-
marriage, virginity, dress, meal preparation, and hints of insub-
ordination and immorality. This is obviously, from Paul's point
of view, a community in trouble. At any rate, by the time the letter reaches Chapter 11, Paul advocates a triple subordination for
women, prophets included: 'But I want you to understand that
Christ is the head of every man, and the husband is the head of
his wife, and God is the head of Christ.' (1 Cor 11:3)[12]

Paul continues to castigate the women prophets specifically.
He uses words like 'shame' and 'disgrace' about the way women
are prophesying in Corinth, with uncovered heads. 'For this reason a woman ought to have a symbol of authority on her head.'
(1 Cor 11:10) Paul seems to be invoking the honour/shame system of the ancient world, which basically saw women as
'shamed' whenever they ventured outside of the boundaries of
patriarchal marriage. The male prophets of Corinth seem to have
experienced the prophesying of the women as more powerful
and a challenge to their own position. The whole section is
phrased in the language of unedifying competition. Whatever
the situation, it is the women's power that Paul wants to de-
stabilise, and just a few chapters later, Paul's patience runs out
and the women are commanded to be silent.

> As in all the churches of the saints, women should be silent in
> the churches. For they are not permitted to speak, but should
> be subordinate, as the law also says. If there is anything they
> desire to know, let them ask their husbands at home. For it is
> shameful for a woman to speak in church. (1 Cor 14:34-35)

These few sentences have had enormous historical consequences in Christianity. They represent the first official and explicit
modification of the Christian vision with regard to women.
Indeed, they are found to be so offensive that many scholars,
both male and female, see them as an interpolation in the text
here, and not from the hand of Paul at all. Antoinette Wire, however, shows convincingly that this final silencing of women is
the natural climax to the argument of the letter. The issue is the
proper subordination of a woman to her husband, including the
assumption that all women should be married or in some situation of submission. A second assumption is that women do not
have any right whatever to speak in the churches. This includes
the right to participate in worship, to prophesy or to preach.
Women are silenced and returned to the invisibility that the letter to the Thessalonians illustrates. A third assumption is that, in
fact, the women did have a 'need to know'. The women seemed
to have wished to study the Christian message and to share their
insights with the believing community. Paul will have none of
this, outside of the appropriate environs of patriarchal marriage.

We do not know what happened in Corinth. Paul's dicta may
or may not have been obeyed. Such a strong group of women,
able, apparently, to excite such resistance in Paul and the male
leaders, cannot have given in without a struggle. And what a
powerful group of women they must have been. What we do
know is that these words have been repeated down through the
years, fortified by Paul's invocation of the 'Law' as the basis for
his words, even though in almost every other instance, Paul decrees the 'Old Law' to have been surpassed by the 'New Law' of
the Spirit. The loss of the voice of women in officially interpreting and preaching the Christian message constitutes an enormous loss to the churches. There are only rare exceptions to this
silencing, as we shall see in later chapters, but from this time forward, the choice by a woman to speak was made at her peril.

Household Codes
Two other theological modifications of the original Christian
message appear in the Deutero-Pauline letters. One is the first

Christian elaboration of a 'household code' in Colossians (3:18-4:1) and the other is the Ephesian invocation of bridal imagery as another way of enforcing the triple subordination of women in the formula: God, Christ, man, woman. The letter to the Colossians is generally agreed today not to have come from Paul's hand, but from one of the Pauline communities.[13] While it is true to say that, in the genuine letters, Paul remains ambivalent about the roles of women, seeming to struggle between vision and practice, in the letters from the Pauline school, this ambivalence has been resolved in favour of the re-enforced submission and silencing of women. The use of the household code here is a deliberate tactic and is used to 'christianise' the patriarchally subordinate state of women, children and slaves. The household code was one of the normative articulations of civic duties in the ancient world. It posited the father as head of the household and outlined his power over its members and their obligations of submission and obedience to him. Supreme power resided in the Roman Emperor, the father of his dominions.

In Colossians, the household code is stated, in part, thus (Col 3:18-4:1): 'Wives, be subject to your husbands, as is fitting in the Lord. Husbands, love your wives and never treat them harshly. Children, obey your parents in everything ... Slaves, obey your earthly masters in everything ...' The Christian addition here is contained in the words 'in the Lord'. An attempt is made to find a compromise between the Christian vision of equality and the absolute demands of a patriarchal household. What we end up with is a semi-Christianised notion of male domination, which has been called 'love patriarchy'. The old structures are to remain in place, but Christians are called to recreate them 'in the Lord'. Much of Colossians deals with the relationships between slaves and their masters, and it is obvious that the propertied slave-owning classes have become Christian. The social implications of slave-owner and slave meeting on a footing of Christian equality seem just as incapable of solution as the Christian equality of husband and wife, father and children.

Bridal Imagery

The idea of marriage in the ancient world was governed by the Aristotelian notion of marriage as the union of a natural ruler and a natural subject. This arrangement was the basis for household and imperial rule. The model was taken from the notion of the priority of the soul over the body. This dualistic way of thinking makes its home in Christianity from this time forward. The world was seen as a system of graded dualities – soul/body, reason/emotion, divine/human, heaven/earth, spiritual/earthly, master/slave, culture/nature, male/female and husband/wife. Eventually the dualities of white/black and a host of other racist and classist dualisms were added.

   Another example of the adoption of the pagan household code as the basis for Christian behaviour occurs in the letter to the Ephesians. This particular version has, perhaps, been even more effective in silencing and marginalising women in the churches. Before examining Ephesians 5:22-6:9, it is worth remarking that Christian feminist exegetes have raised serious questions about the revelatory status of these texts. An important feminist principle, which is the basis for much of Rosemary Radford Ruether's work, is that anything that silences, oppresses and marginalises women, thus diminishing their humanity, cannot be regarded as saving truth, cannot be from God. It is certainly not good news for women.[14] The argument of Ephesians is placed in the context of a great cosmic battle between good and evil. This warfare between heaven and earth, reconciled by Jesus Christ, has been named the 'great mystery' and the sign of this restored cosmic unity is the unity of the church. Thus Christians are called to live in unity and resist the 'principalities' and 'powers' and stand against 'the spiritual hosts of wickedness in heavenly places'. (Eph 6:12) It does not seem at all accidental that the Ephesian articulation of the household code occurs just before this passage. It is now a familiar list: 'Wives, be subject to your husbands as you are to the Lord.' (Eph 5:22) 'Children, obey your parents in the Lord, for this is right.' (6:1) 'Slaves obey your earthly masters with fear and trembling, in singleness of heart, as you obey Christ'. (6:5)

As we have already seen, Christianity began as a household movement and, for at least two centuries, Christians relied on the 'house-church' as their meeting place.[15] It is not surprising, then, that when the writer of Ephesians, at the end of the first century, wants to speak of the church as a battle ground of warring cosmic forces, his attention turns to the household relationships as the bulwark against division. The path to unity was not rooted in the biblical vision of baptismal equality but rather in the pagan vision of the graded subordinations of the household codes. It is true that there is, at least initially, a constant attempt to 'christianise' these codes in demanding some mutuality between husband and wife, master and slave, but the obvious trend is toward the increased subjection of the weaker parties. In this way, the burden of unity is placed, as a challenge, on the shoulders of wives and slaves, not on the more powerful husbands and masters. This Christian change of plan is all the more striking since, in the house-church, women were able to act in a discipleship of equality. When a woman acted as leader of a house-church, the old lines between public roles for men and private roles for women were all but obliterated. In the first decades of Christianity, the leadership of women seems to have been celebrated, but by the end of the first century, it is consistently challenged and, in another few decades, the renewed patriarchalisation of Christianity is almost complete. This development is all the more insidious when the husband/master is compared to Christ and the wife/slave is compared to the necessarily obedient and submissive church. The subjection of the church to Christ 'in everything' (v. 24) strengthens the argument for the submission of wives and slaves to their masters in everything. There is no loophole, Christian or otherwise.

The bridal imagery in this section of Ephesians has been beloved of male Christian writers throughout the centuries. 'Husbands, love your wives, just as Christ loved the church and gave himself up for her, in order to make her holy by cleansing her with the washing of water by the word, so as to present the church to himself in splendour, without a spot or wrinkle or anything of the kind – yes, so that she may be holy and without blemish.' (Eph 5:25-27) The passage goes on to quote Genesis about the male and female 'becoming one flesh'. (Gen 2:24) No matter how gloriously this union is described, there is no doubt that this is not a union of equals. In *Mulieris Dignitatem*, Pope John Paul II writes at length about this passage in moving terms, constantly invoking the 'mysterious' quality of the relationship, but no amount of poetry can remove the necessity of submission on the wife's part.[16]

Silent Suffering

The writer of the letter to the Ephesians is, presumably, speaking to wives and husbands in a Christian household. One hopes that the writer of 1 Peter is not. The church context described here is a harsh one: wives and slaves are instructed to submit even to 'harsh' masters. The household code in 1 Peter 2:18-3:7 has an increasingly oppressive tone. This particular passage has been used to justify the suffering and abuse of slaves, wives, and all who are oppressed. It is all the more fearful because the model is Christ, the one who was innocent and suffered in silence. We shall return again to this 'suffering servant' theme, but it is important to note here the images of God as a harsh and punishing judge, Jesus as a silent and innocent sufferer, and the consequent justification of harshness in the dominant and silent suffering by the weakest in society. The demand for justice and mutuality on the part of husbands and rulers grows dimmer and the demand for unquestioning obedience gets louder. Slaves and wives are instructed to internalise the Christian message and be like Christ, but no such demand is made of rulers and husbands. Wives and slaves are to know that they are saved, that their hearts are free. In fact, by this silent suffering, they may even save their rulers. Wives are instructed to win over their husbands without a word by the purity and reverence of their lives. The husband will then 'pay honour to the woman as the weaker sex'. (1 Pet 3:7)

Both Ephesians and 1 Peter offer a vision of universal peace and a vision of a united church but, in these texts, this peace and unity is to be acquired somehow at the expense of the baptismal formula of equality. Jews and Gentiles are instructed to live in peace as equals, but the wife and slave are instructed to subordinate themselves for the sake of the community. There is freedom for slaves – in the eschatological future. There is freedom for wives in obedience and motherhood. The husband is frequently commanded to love his wife in imitation of Christ, but the imitation of Christ by the husband is understood hierarchically and patriarchally. The husband takes his place in the graded setting of God, Christ, man, woman. This, then, is yet another theological justification of patriarchy. Christ is used to cement the inferior position of the wife and the slave. Now, the submission of the 'lower orders' is a Christian as well as a civic duty. In this way, despite Christian affirmations to the contrary, the position of the wife has deteriorated with the institutionalisation of Christianity. This is particularly tragic in being stated in the context of a vision of universal peace. The unfortunate message is that Christian peace is won by the unjust suffering of the weak. No such challenge is made to the upper grades of the various hierarchies, who, in the working out of Christian history, are uniformly male.

The rethinking of ministry follows the same logic. During the second century, there is more and more emphasis on local leadership in the now patriarchal house church, and the roles of travelling missionaries are downplayed. The move has been made from the house church to the 'household of God', which is based on Aristotelian ethics, with an overtone of Christian love. The true freedom of all has been postponed to an indefinite future and the day to day running of the church has been re-ordered in line with contemporary hierarchical and patriarchal models. The prophet and apostle are merged with the office of bishop and the leadership of women is regarded, more and more, as one of the sure signs of heresy and a disordered community.[17]

The Pastoral Epistles
The final comments in this section will deal briefly with the

group of writings known as 'The Pastorals'. These consist of two letters to Timothy and one to Titus, all claiming to be from the hand of Paul. These letters are variously dated from the 60s of the first century to the 90s or much later. Most exegetes opt for the later dates. This set of writings is very important, because although they continue, and even intensify, a harangue against the leadership of women, they also illustrate that what is said about women in the letters we have studied so far was prescriptive rather than descriptive. This means that women had not necessarily followed the precepts laid down for them. The intensity of the discussion about women in the Pastorals shows that they are addressed to communities where women are well organised and highly vocal. Women have not gone away. They are not being noticeably submissive. They are still experiencing the freedom offered by the good news. But now the resistance of the male leaders increases in crescendo. Rather than repeat the phrases now familiar to the reader, we will simply make some general comments about the Pastorals. Feminist interpreters ask serious questions about the revelatory content of these letters – they are often patriarchal to the point of absurdity.[18]

There is no doubt that the author of these letters had a definite vision of how the church should be run, and that one of his major problems was the role of women. The letters initiate a form of writing that becomes common in Christianity – women are present as a constant pre-occupation of male leaders. While this fact is often depressing to the woman reader, it does illustrate the fact that women continued to make their presence felt. Because of this the prescriptions for women's silence, submission and passivity continue to resound through the centuries. The major problem of these texts is that, by this stage of Christian development, there is no room in the churches for strong, articulate, active women. This does not mean to imply that all such women are saintly characters, but it does mean to imply that the silencing of all women has done untold damage to Christianity, not to mention to the women themselves. Linda Maloney points out in her commentary that in the letters of Paul considered genuine, the voices of his opponents are often heard with fairness. He argues with them. The writer of the Pastorals has no such intention. He makes no effort to cater to the reality of opposing groups, but rather vilifies them with a standard polemic. His opponents become stereotypes. His aim is not to discuss but to ridicule and silence.

Sound doctrine is the key concern of the Pastorals, and this is maintained by a tightly structured church, where God is the head of his household, Christ is son and heir, the *episkopos* and elders are stewards and all the rest are to be obedient. Since the greatest demands for obedience are made on the women, this seems to be the quarter of most resistance. A new theological explanation for women's silencing appears in the first letter to Timothy, even though the letter also reveals that women are acting as deacons in the community. 'Let a woman learn in silence with full submission. I permit no woman to teach or to have authority over a man; she is to keep silent. For Adam was formed first, then Eve; and Adam was not deceived, but the woman was deceived and became a transgressor. Yet she will be saved through childbearing, provided they continue in faith and love and holiness, with modesty.' (1 Tim 2:11-15) This is the first deliberate theological linkage in Christianity between women and Eve. It was an explanation that dominated later writing about Christian women to the extent that one often wondered whether women were included among the redeemed. From now on, women bore the burden of Eve's sin. It is interesting that Paul himself (in 1 Cor 15) laid the burden of the first sin on Adam. Here, however, the author seems to be seeking a definite argument for the final silencing of the women teachers in the community. This, again, is prescriptive, not descriptive, teaching. He is not describing his actual community of authoritative women teachers and deacons but his desired community of silenced women. But it is probably this text, linked with 1 Cor 14:34-35, which, throughout later centuries, was used more than any others to deprive women of an authoritative voice in the Christian community.

This letter also introduces what became the ongoing Christian emphasis on marriage as a way of removing women from public life. Married women and, in fact, all women are to lead a hidden and passive life away from the public eye. The author saw clearly that it is patriarchal marriage that deprives women of a voice, and later generations of women, who felt called to a public role of teaching in the church, knew instinctively that their first task was to renounce marriage.

In the space of this chapter, then, women have come full circle. From leaders of house churches and co-workers with men as Christian missionaries, they are being directed by male Christian leaders to become prisoners in their own homes, for the sake of sound doctrine in the community. The only teaching role left is that prescribed to the older women and that is the passing on of household wisdom. In the Pastorals, we are told that, as far as the official handing on of Christianity is concerned, women are not needed.

CHAPTER 4

Women in Apocryphal
and Gnostic Literature

'In the name of Jesus Christ I baptise myself on the last day.' [1]
'Blessed are you for not wavering at seeing me.' (Jesus to Mary
Magdalene)[2]
*The threat of being perceived as a bad woman works very effectively to
keep us as women in our place, or at least looking like we are in our
place.*[3]
*The understanding of church that won out advocated accommodation
to the kyriarchal order of the Roman state. Consequently, the orthodox
'fathers' argued not only against women's ecclesial leadership but also
against their public speaking and writing of books.*[4]

The biblical period is necessarily the touchstone for everything
else in Christianity. It is the source of vision and also of self-crit-
ique. As we have seen, this has constituted a very mixed inheritance for women. Centuries of women have been consoled, inspired and challenged to lives of quiet belief or heroic faith by
the scriptures while, at the same time, centuries of religious
leaders have used the scriptures to silence women and render
them effectively invisible as people of significance in the story of
Christianity. In this chapter, we will be examining one of the last
struggles in the church to marginalise women and, as Elisabeth
Schüssler Fiorenza says, in the above quotation, to impose a
patriarchal and 'kyriarchal', that is a 'lord and subject' model,
on the Christian church.

Some of the scenes of this struggle are available in the semi-
canonical texts of the Apocryphal and Gnostic literature.
Christian scholars had always been aware of the existence of this

extraordinary body of writing, but it was only with the *Nag Hammadi* and other discoveries in the mid-forties of this century, that many of the actual texts have become available.[5] I call this literature 'semi-canonical' because in some churches, at some times, some of this literature was deemed to be part of the canon of the New Testament.

Pagan hostility

As the Christian community grew in numbers, it attracted to itself the attention of the Roman world. The Romans prided themselves on their openness to all religious traditions, as long as the worship of the ancient Roman gods continued, because this worship assured the continued power and prosperity of the Roman world. From the beginning, Christians challenged this attitude, announcing fearlessly that their God was the only true God. The Romans, then, blamed all national disasters on this new group with their new gods, who refused to do the very little required of them to uphold the Roman state. As we have seen, there had been some disturbances in Rome in the late 40s resulting in the removal of Prisca and Aquila to Corinth. There are various disturbances recalled in the Acts, resulting in the arrest and executions of James, the brother of John in 42, and of James the brother of Jesus around 62. A strong tradition names the year 64 as the execution date of both Peter and Paul in Rome, and it is at this time that the persecution of Nero struck terror into the hearts of Christians, and even disgusted many of the pagans by its cruelty. We will return to these persecutions in the next chapter. I mention them here to contextualise the choice of becoming a Christian from the middle of the first century onwards. It was a dangerous choice, requiring a deep commitment and a knowledge of the possible consequences, namely martyrdom. No one took this choice lightly but, in general, the courage of those who did make the choice seemed to make Christianity even more attractive to converts. So, at the beginning, hostility from without seemed to strengthen the church. As we have seen, the gospel of Mark was written against such a background of persecution:

'you will be hated by all because of my name. But the one who
endures to the end will be saved.' (Mk 13:13)

During periods of persecution, Christians were called on to
present a unified face to the world. All the more reason, then,
why inner disunity caused the church much more heartache
than external persecution. Indeed, disunity may be the wrong
word here. From the beginning, there were diverse understand-
ings of the Christian message. The very fact of four gospels,
Acts, and the Pauline and post-Pauline writings testify to this.
These documents have provided centuries of scholars with
material for reflection, and this does not seem to be at an end.
Nevertheless, the Pastoral letters to Timothy and Titus represent
a tightening up of Christian teaching and organisation and a
reaching toward one orthodox version of the Christian faith. The
official teaching of the *episkopos* is upheld and all other teaching,
especially that by women, is comparatively diminished. In the
case of women, as we have seen, it is silenced. If we were to
judge from the canonical biblical literature, we would be justi-
fied in drawing the conclusion that this newly adopted patriarchal authoritative structure prevailed without opposition.
Indeed, for the most part, the writings go to some pains to give
this impression. The renewed study, however, of Apocryphal
and Gnostic literature reveals quite a different scenario. It is time
to take a very brief look at this literature in general and to explore a few texts in a little more depth.[6]

Apocryphal and Gnostic literature

Nobody seems to be quite sure of the origins of Gnosticism – it
preceded Christianity, but then seems to have accompanied it
throughout its history. Until the *Nag Hammadi* and other recent
textual discoveries, what we knew of Gnosticism was learned
from its arch-enemies in Christianity, men like Irenaeus and
Tertullian. Gnosticism, as its name implies, is a system of religious belief wherein knowledge is the key to salvation. Such
knowledge is graded and only the most pure are deserving of
the most refined knowledge. This indicates immediately that

Gnosticism was dualistic in its strict division between matter and spirit, but quite egalitarian in allowing spirit-filled women and men to speak and teach. The lines between Gnosticism and Christianity were quite fluid. Gnosticism seemed to be more eclectic in its choice of religious ideas and, inevitably, clashes of authority took place. There is no doubt that many opted for Gnosticism rather than the Bible alone, but with so many competing traditions, the distinctions must not have been too clear for everyone. Perhaps the most familiar form of Gnostic thought is its understanding of the fall as the gradual descent of the soul from heavenly purity to worldly matter, and the understanding of redemption as the gradual return of the soul from matter and the body to its original pure spiritual state.

It is clear that many of these ideas overlap Christian ideas of creation and salvation, sin and evil. The Gnostic system was extremely popular and was eventually seen as the great rival of Christianity. It is the openness of Gnosticism to both masculine and feminine spirits, and a masculine and feminine aspect of divinity that, on the one hand, made it abhorrent to an increasingly orthodox Christianity and, on the other, made it more attractive to women, who were being silenced in the Christian communities. As we shall see later, the Gnostic dualistic attitudes to matter and spirit led to an emphasis on penitential asceticism, which was designed to help the believer live in the spirit, at the expense of the body. Eventually, this ascetic tendency kept returning to haunt Christianity as the monastic movement developed. Even today, many Christians associate a spiritual life with an anti-body otherworldly life, an attitude that is, in essence, more Gnostic than Christian.

The other body of literature to be explored here is Apocryphal literature. This refers to a body of literature which, like Gnosticism, interweaves with the canonical writings of the Christian testament. The Apocrypha are a series of gospels and acts, modelled on the traditional four gospels and the Acts of the Apostles. Some of these texts, like the gospel of Thomas, seem to contain genuine traditions not found in the synoptics and John.[7]

Other texts, like the proto-gospel of James were deemed canonical in some churches for a time. Many feminist scholars return to the Apocrypha with interest because here, just as in the Gnostic literature, the position of women seems to take on a different colouring from the canonical literature. The Apocrypha tend to fill out some of the missing details of the four traditional gospels. They give biographical details, for example, for the lives of Mary, Joseph and Jesus which have become so beloved of Christians that they seem unaware that these details are the stuff of legend. Those who name the parents of Mary and the names of the Maji are quoting the Apocrypha. Movies have been made and novels written about the lives of Joseph and Mary that are rooted in these stories. On the other hand, the Apocrypha record sayings of Jesus and conversations between the male and female disciples and between the disciples and Jesus which throw light on what might have happened in the earliest times after the death of Jesus.

So in both the Gnostic and Apocryphal literature there are traces of the lives of women not available to us from the canonical sources. Hence, feminist scholars speak of 'transgressing canonical boundaries' in their search for the story of women behind the patriarchally conceived canonical texts.[8]

The selection of the texts which would eventually form the New Testament was rooted in both religious and political ideologies. It is a large part of feminist supposition today that any text which acknowledged the leadership of women or portrayed a woman as an authoritative teacher was an immediate candidate for exclusion from the canon. From this time the naming of heretical tendencies became a central Christian pre-occupation. Women teachers, women church leaders and, above all, women who presided at ritual and worship constituted annoyingly frequent examples of 'bad' and 'heretical' women. The imposition of the household codes, particularly in relation to marriage, seem to have been the chosen church instrument to silence, disempower and eventually exclude women totally from public church life. One can only lament that more details of these astonishing debates are not available to us.

We turn now to just three of the Apocryphal texts in order to get just a glimpse of life in Christianity in the latter years of the first century. It is not necessary to insist on the historical truth of the events narrated in these texts. The very fact of their survival and even more of the extraordinary details of the lives and beliefs of the participants give us an insight into the preoccupations of early Christians not otherwise available to us.

The Acts of Thecla

Whenever a later Christian woman wanted to assert her right to speak and teach publicly in the Christian community, it was often the example of Thecla that she invoked. Christian women do not enjoy a consecutive narration of their involvement in the tradition. Women pop up in disparate fragments and scattered tales, but there is no real psycho-history for a woman to internalise. Hence, each generation of Christian women has had to start almost from scratch to create a spiritual and ecclesial identity. The abundance of prescriptive teaching about women and who they should be and how they should behave gives the illusion of continuity, but unfortunately, the story of women's Christian involvement will never be completed. One of the very few names available to women as exemplar was Thecla. Her story was all the more remarkable in that she was linked with Paul as his co-apostle, but in every version of the story, the real actor is Thecla. She pushes Paul and when he does not act, she acts for herself. Her performance of a self-baptism, as illustrated in the quotation at the head of this chapter, is only the most extraordinary example of this.

Thecla was a beautiful young woman who renounced the excellent marriage arranged for her by her parents, cut off her hair, dressed in men's clothes and ran off to join the Christian movement. Each detail of this initial part of her story is repeated over and over again throughout Christian history. In order to follow God's call, a woman must defy her parents and their marriage arrangements, disguise her socially required femininity and leave home – that is, the patriarchal home, where neither freedom of movement nor independent choice of believing nor the disposition of her own body is permitted.

The story tells of Thecla's absorbed attention to Paul's preaching in her home town of Iconium, so much so that her mother complains to the jilted fiancé: 'And my daughter too, like a spider at the window, bound by his words, is dominated by a new desire and a fearful passion; for the girl hangs upon the things he says, and is taken captive. But you go and speak to her, for she is engaged to you.' (Acts of Thecla 8-9) The extent of the mother's rage at Thecla's choice to follow the Christian teaching on virginity is obvious later in the story. Paul has been arrested and brought before the governor, where Thecla stands at his side. Thecla's mother addresses the governor: 'Burn the lawless one! Burn her that is no bride … so that all the women who have been taught by this man may be struck with terror!' (v. 20)

This the governor agrees to do because, in disobeying her mother and resisting her fiancé, Thecla is seen as disrupting the social order. The fire is quenched by a rain-cloud, Thecla escapes and embarks on a fabulous series of escapades in an effort to follow Paul. When Paul, too, resists her pleas, Thecla baptises herself, and eventually wins Paul's blessing for her teaching activities.[9] The story eventually brings Thecla back home where she is reconciled with her mother.

The story of Thecla remained enormously popular and she was revered as a saint on 23 October until the revision of the calendar of the saints after the Second Vatican Council. Before leaving this wonderful tale, several points need to be made. Whether or not there is an historical basis to the story, the very fact of the existence of this tale and its emphases indicates the presence of a lively body of opinion about Christian women. The pre-arranged marriage often set children and parents in opposition when the daughter felt called by God to a more intensive following of the gospel. There is no suggestion here that all women have to be unmarried, but the Christian option of virginity set women in direct opposition to parental and social expectations. This text is dated to the mid-second century, but the story itself must have been circulating prior to this. It records the ongoing expectation by women that, when called by God to teach, they have to endure all opposition in order to follow this call. One of the astonishing features of Thecla's story is the description of the supportive community of women who surround her at all the important events of her life. In the tale they act almost like a Greek chorus, invoking retribution on Thecla's judges. A few examples will suffice: 'But the women were panic-stricken, and cried out before the judgement-seat: An evil judgement! A godless judgement!' 'But the women with their children cried out from above, saying, O God, an impious judgement is come to pass in this city.' 'But all the women cried out with a loud voice, and as with one mouth gave praise to God, saying: One is God who has delivered Thecla! So that all the city was shaken by the sound.'

It is not to be wondered, then, that later women remembered Thecla and invoked her name to justify their own choices. It is also not accidental that nearly all these women were virgins, because from the end of the second century, it is only virgins who break through the universal Christian silence about women. 'Good' women are consigned to the silence and invisibility of marriage. Eventually 'good' virgins are consigned to the silence and invisibility of the cloistered convent. But the choice by a woman of virginity, in response to God's call and in fidelity to the option provided by the words and example of Jesus, has always been a double-edged sword for the church. On the one hand, there was the danger for the church of resisting the Spirit and, on the other, there was the danger of women like Thecla launching themselves on society in obedience to God's command. We shall see this dilemma played out over and over again.

A final word, for now, about virginity. It seems clear that both Jesus and Paul – though not the other male apostles – opted for the single life. Their words, also, offered all Christians the possibility of making a similar choice. Initially, there was no hint that this choice was made to belittle the choice of marriage, but eventually this strain of thinking became common in Christian teaching. We see here the interweaving of Gnostic and Christian thought and an example of a frequent historical occurrence. What Christianity condemns as heresy in Gnostic dualism returns to haunt it in the Christian adoption of dualistic asceticism. This has twin implications for women. First, virginity is seen as an excellent remedy for the sins of Eve and, secondly, the flesh of non-virginal women is considered to be even further removed from things of the Spirit and even more thoroughly sunk into matter. We shall see many more chapters of this drama.[10]

The proto-gospel of James

The proto-gospel of James, in its bias towards the continued physical virginity of Mary, the mother of Jesus, seems a natural follow-up to the story of Thecla. This proto-gospel has provided some of the most familiar details of the Christmas story, as well as the details of Mary's life, even though most believers have never heard of it. Much devotion to the Virgin Mary is to be rooted here rather than in the canonical gospels. This text reflects the struggles of Christians, of around the same period as the story of Thecla, to come to terms with the perceived gospel demands for chastity in their particular life circumstances. The story is usually called the 'gospel of James', that is, James the brother of Jesus, and so it claims family connections for knowledge of the intimate details of the story. The gospel provides the details of Mary's biography, her betrothal to Joseph, the confusion around her pregnancy, the birth of Jesus in the 'cave', the proving of Mary's physical virginity, the punishment of the doubting mid-wife, the stories of the Magi, the star of Bethlehem and the slaughter of the Innocents, and finally, the execution of John the Baptist's father, Zacharias. It closes with the identification of the author as James.[11]

The whole point of this tale is to proclaim the total virginity of Mary. Her birth is announced by an angel, in response to the prayers of her parents, Joakim and Anna. From the beginning, Mary's life is a marvel. She walks seven steps at the age of six months, after which her mother scoops her up and swears that Mary's feet will never touch the ground again. Mary is then taken to the Temple at the age of three, where she dances on the third step of the altar and is henceforth fed only on spiritual food. At the age of twelve, Mary is deemed to be at the stage of puberty and therefore capable of polluting the Temple. A council of priests is held and the widowers are assembled. The lot falls on Joseph, who protests mightily that he is too old for the task. After priestly threats, he relents, takes Mary home and then disappears from the story. When he returns, Mary is six months pregnant. The story follows Luke's gospel from here but, like most apocryphal gospels, it fills in some details for local colour. The whole focus of the story is on Mary, her pregnancy, and her continuing virginal state after the birth. The child Jesus had appeared in a great light. It is a miraculous birth but, even so, Mary immediately breastfeeds her child. This is the first Christian portrait of the 'Virgin Mother'.

One midwife has already testified to this 'new sight', but another, Salome, now appears and refuses to believe without putting Mary through a vaginal examination. Her hand is immediately withered as a punishment for her unbelief but, at the bidding of an angel, she touches the child and is restored to health. This very physical description of a conception without intercourse and a birth without a broken hymen pushes the story of Mary's virginity much further than the canonical texts. It defines Mary's virginity in the narrowest possible physical terms, and begins a Christian preoccupation with physical virginity that has been death-dealing to many women. The story now picks up the details from Matthew's gospel about the Maji and Herod, with the addition of a few more miracles.

This is a wonderful story, marvellously written, with several flights into poetic fancy. Despite its supposed Jewish Christian sources, however, it displays a real ignorance of Jewish tradition, and is therefore presumed to come from a Gentile hand around the year 150 CE. The story seems to have its origin in efforts to counteract accusations of the illegitimacy of Jesus, accusations first made, of course, by Joseph in Matthew's gospel. It is clear, from the infancy stories in both Matthew and Luke, that many theories about the birth of Jesus are possible. This 'proto-gospel' aims to give the real story from the family archives, so to speak. There was a well known story about the rape of Mary by a Roman soldier, Panthera, which is reported in an apologetic Christian document at this period. The proto-gospel of James corrects all previous thinking about the conception and birth of Jesus and gives the purported real story. Indeed, he was extraordinarily successful. This apocryphal tale has coloured centuries of interpretation of the canonical text. It illustrates the beginning of attention to Mary's body, a body never touched by a male and certainly never penetrated by one. We get no insight whatever into Mary's feelings – in the tale, she appears only as an untouched body, which will be an appropriate instrument for the birth of Jesus. She speaks no word, makes no decisions, is manipulated by parents, priests, Joseph and all she meets – all for the accomplishment of God's will. And it is not without interest that God is named as a 'despot' several times in the course of the narrative.

This story, then, in its intermingling of canonical and apocryphal interests, and especially in its absolute insistence on Mary's physical virginity before, during and after the birth of Jesus, sets the scene for some very unhealthy pre-occupations with women's bodies throughout Christian history. The tale has had amazing staying power. Some of the influences of the narrative will be taken up again in later comment on Mary, but here it is important to emphasise once again the Gnostic influences on these tales. These Gnostic themes found a home in canonical literature. The gospels never show Jesus actually praising the family – indeed, his stated goal was to set up a new family of disciples. Paul, in his dealing with the Corinthians, could be interpreted – indeed this consistently happened – as advocating that it is good 'not to touch a woman'. In the next chapter, we shall see that women's bodies were redeemed through martyrdom, but before that, we shall turn to one other sample of apocrypha, the gospel of Mary Magdalene.

The gospel of Mary Magdalene

Before the recent re-examination of Apocryphal and Gnostic literature, the story of women's public involvement in Christianity was generally assumed to have been part of a necessarily radical beginning to the Christian movement – a kind of dramatic opening event, to get things started. Recent official writing, including papal writing, has often pointed out that Jesus did not seem to have been engaged in anything resembling the liberation of women. Those women named in the gospels are assumed to be either affluent women who provided for the mission, or else grateful suppliants who had been healed and/or forgiven. These women were forced, by commentators, into conventional women's roles, and the impression was given that such conventions had not been challenged by Jesus. Once Christianity had settled down, it was implied, such unconventional womanly behaviour was at an end. In fact, as we have seen, there is much evidence for this in the way the community of Luke's gospel viewed the role of women. It became possible to tell the story of Christianity without ever mentioning women. There was, however, one major exception to this. One woman's story was rewritten to fit androcentric categories and concerns and she became the darling of multitudes of writers, preachers and artists. This woman is Mary Magdalene.

This woman is, of course, a creation of the male mind. The gospels do not speak of such a woman. The figure of Mary Magdalen there is of a woman who was healed by Jesus, perhaps from epilepsy, and thereafter became the chief woman disciple and, after the resurrection, its first witness and proclaimer. As we have seen, she fulfilled all the requirements of an apostle and, in a strange twist of logic, was so recognised for centuries in the Roman Catholic liturgy when, as befitted an apostle, the Creed was recited at Mass on her memorial day, July 22. What happened to this woman? Medieval legend has her arriving in Marseille in southern France, with her supposed sister Martha and brother Lazarus. Until quite recently, she continued to be confused with Mary of Bethany. The trio were pictured as evan-

gelising bishops, and are often pictured as such in medieval
art.[12] Later, her body was fortuitously discovered, and many
churches fought vigorously to have their relic declared the authentic one. These churches became centres of pilgrimage and
continue so to this day. This is the stuff of legend, and while one
may wonder where and why such legends are created, they tell
us nothing of the real Mary from Magdala – beyond the fact that
she was loved and remembered.[13] We have one group of texts,
however, which seems to provide us with more likely historical
information about the eventual fate of the real Mary Magdalene,
and these are the Apocrypha. We focus here on just one of these,
the gospel of Mary Magdalene.[14]

The gospel of Mary Magdalene takes its place among the
'heretical' texts excluded from the New Testament canon for the
political reason that it illustrates the leadership of women, in
this case, of Mary. The first section of the gospel is not of interest
to us here. It consists of a lengthy Christian Gnostic discussion of
sin, human nature and salvation between Jesus and the disciples. Finally, Jesus departs, leaving everyone in a state of de-
pression until Mary takes up the task of comforting them. It is
significant that, in our present text, she has not been mentioned
up to this. Now she steps forward to take the place of Jesus in
comforting, teaching and challenging the other disciples. She ex-
plains to them that Jesus has made us 'true human beings', who
have discovered their true spiritual nature within. Mary is asked
by Peter to teach them, implying that Mary may have had some
teaching from Jesus that the others have not heard.

Mary then launches into the authoritative teaching that she
has received straight from Jesus. There is no doubt that much of
the teaching, as related in the text, is Gnostic in origin, but this is
not unexpected, given the mid-second century dating of the text.
As soon as Mary stops speaking, she is challenged by Peter and
Andrew. She is accused of fabricating the whole story and of
giving the impression that Jesus loved her more than the others.
Levi defends Mary, calling Peter an arrogant hothead. An argument ensues about Mary's character and Levi insists that it is

Mary's spiritual qualities that have attracted the attention of Jesus. The text ends with a fairly divided group of disciples.

Several other texts from the same period share similar traditions about the significant place Mary Magdalene enjoyed among the disciples. She is always portrayed as having special understanding and as being specially loved by Jesus for this. Other texts show the disciples, especially Peter, demanding that she be expelled from their group because of her flighty nature. In this way, the real Mary Magdalene disappears from history.[15]

Feminists exegetes are in no doubt that these texts, scattered and incomplete though they be, give us a real insight into a final stage of women's efforts to be treated with dignity as equal partners in the preaching of the good news. Their credentials are as genuine as those of the male disciples. Their faith has remained steadfast. But the weight of ancient tradition seems too heavy to be lifted by the good news preached by Jesus. Women are returned to their 'rightful' places in the private realm and, in many ways, the gospel challenge to the social arrangements of the ancient world seems to have failed. But women did not disappear, though most subsequent histories act as if they had. The major Christian invitation to discipleship was not taken away from women, and the rest of our story illustrates the courage and ingenuity of women as they remained faithful. But from now on, we have only tiny slivers of the story of women. Tragically, from this period, there is no consecutive account of women's involvement in Christianity. Women appear in vignettes especially at moments when the normal social and Christian routines have broken down. There is only one continuous strand of Christian tradition where the presence of women may be detected in every age, and this is in the option for a life of virginity. Much – but not all – of the remaining story will focus on this.

Reviewing the issues
Before leaving this chapter, it might be well to itemise the issues that have continually come to the fore since the arrival of the Jesus movement. These same issues represent, in many ways,

the unfinished agenda of Christianity. They return to haunt us at every stage of the Christian story, and they appear in many a letter to the editor, even in our own day.

While Christianity has built an astonishing history and has travelled to every corner of the globe, it has survived thus far by steadfastly ignoring many basic questions about the presence of more than half of its membership. What we have inherited is only a small part of the possible story. We have received a Christianity that is built on the exclusion of the voice of women – as a necessary foundational building block. This state of affairs cannot be altered. History cannot be re-written. Most of the story of women Christians has been lost forever. But the buried issues have remained as a kind of Christian neurosis that has the power to strike fear into many a church leader. Women are often astonished at the intensity of emotion aroused by the demands of women for equal inclusion. Not ten years ago, an Anglican cleric, outraged at the demands for priestly ordination by Anglican women, is reported to have said: 'We burned them before: we can burn them again.' He is obviously aligning himself firmly with the late medieval inquisitors who were engaged in the burning of witches. He thinks of Christian women seeking equality as witches. He professes himself quite ready to engage in a new orgy of burning women. Whence this huge fear and rage? It comes from the buried issues that were forcibly removed from the agenda in the second century of Christianity.

What are these issues? At the core of Christian pre-occupation is the issue of *authority*. Who has it? How does one get it? Who is automatically excluded from its use? The issue of authority is always bound up with the issue of women, because they are the largest group excluded, until very recently, from its use. Of course, in the Roman Catholic tradition, this exclusion still prevails. And since women have constituted more than half of the active membership of the churches, the issue is always visibly present.

The issue of *ministry* is also close to the core. Who acts and speaks for God? Who acts and speaks for Jesus? Allied to this, in

recent times, is the issue of *God language*. Is God only and exclusively male in the language of worship and prayer? What kind
of Father is God? Always linked to the issues of authority and
ministry has been the issue of *sexuality*. Must one be celibate to
minister? Is abstinence from sex better than involvement in sex?
While heterosexuality seems to have been somewhat rehabilitated
in recent times, anxieties now focus on homosexuality. And
what of women's bodies? Many of the same arguments that
clothe discussions on abortion continue the attitudes that were
evident in second century discussions of women's sexuality in
any context. And finally, what of *a dualistic approach to all creation*?
Is the world still polarised into body/soul, female/male,
earth/heaven, the colonised/the usually white coloniser, the
slave/the free, the Semite/the Gentile, the old/the young and
the poor/the rich?

Many of these issues come straight from a second century
agenda, though updated many times over, and not from their
supposed rooting in biblical revelation. Christian history is a
wonderful illustration of the maxim that whatever is not faced
in one period of history, will return to haunt us in another.

CHAPTER 5

Women Martyrs

'I am a Christian and I follow the authority of my name.' (Perpetua)[1]

'You are the one who opened the door to the devil ...' (Tertullian)[2]

The misogyny to which Tertullian appealed so insistently was, in his opinion, based on unalterable facts of nature: women were seductive, and Christian baptism did nothing to change this fact.[3]

Since women are most often assigned the role of suffering servant in church and society, some believe it encourages martyrdom and the continued victimisation of women.[4]

From about the year 100, Christian leaders were engaged in the task of trying to create a normative and uniform basis for faith. The excitement and diversity of the early decades seemed now to be in danger of fragmenting the community and, as the second century developed, the challenges to Christianity from within and without seemed only to intensify. Gnosticism was no longer just stray ideas floating in the air: it was organised around recognised leaders who attracted enormous followings. On the other hand, Christianity of all kinds continued to grow rapidly in numbers, and could not fail to attract the attention of the Romans who were themselves trying to consolidate and unify their empire. For the first fifty years of the century, there are several vicious outbursts of Christian persecution but, in the second half of the century, this persecution is much more intentional and put on an empire-wide legal footing. Both the Gnostics and the persecutions will occupy our attention in this chapter. Our main focus will be on what we know of the women Christians of the period, but this exploration will have to be contextualised and set in its proper focus.

Christians and the Empire

At the beginning of the second century, the Roman Empire was confident in its identity and future and even professed that war was now but a memory.[5] More and more publicly, this confident Empire credited its prosperity and peace to its fidelity to the ancient gods, and with increasing assent by all, these gods were seen to be represented in the person of the Emperor. Undoubtedly, the Emperors relished the divinisation of their persons, and, as might be expected, began to demand that all recognise this and acknowledge it publicly. Here was a real sticking point for Christians. As strict monotheists, the acknowledgement of the divinity of an emperor was unthinkable. Already, in the year 112, we find evidence of this in the remote Roman province of Bithynia where the new governor, Pliny, had to deal for the first time with recalcitrant Christians. He wrote to his overlord, the Emperor Trajan, in order to gain an understanding of imperial policy and practice. The Christians are being persecuted, but Pliny is not sure why. He mentions, more or less casually, that he has tortured two slave women with important positions in the Christian community in order to find out more about the inner life of Christians. He reports to the Emperor that he finds nothing alarming – they rise early, they pray, they share goods, they lead moral lives – but, and this is the cause of his puzzlement, they are unaccountably stubborn. They are absolutely intransigent about recognising their God as the only God. Such stubbornness is, to Pliny and most of his contemporaries, completely un-Roman. We hear nothing more about the tortured and murdered women deacons who may have been slaves – they disappear into the vacuum of history. But it is from such situations of intransigence that Christians stood accused of 'hatred of the human race', and of being members of a 'third race'. When the Romans also noticed that the numbers of Christians were increasing visibly, on an empire-wide basis, alarm bells began to ring.

The early martyrs

Initially, for the most part, the persecution of Christians coincided with major festivals and major catastrophes. Christians were scapegoats. All calamities were blamed on their 'atheism', that is, their unwillingness to worship the old gods. While the two slave-girls from Bithynia may have disappeared without a trace, that is not the case with many later martyrs. One of the greatest and most loved was Polycarp, who had been Bishop of Smyrna for about sixty years, when he was executed in 165. It was generally believed that Polycarp had known the apostle John, and this link with the apostolic church was of enormous use later to one of Polycarp's friends, Irenaeus of Lyons. One can easily see the enormous propaganda value for Irenaeus, fighting against the Gnostics, in being able to say: 'I knew Polycarp, Polycarp knew John, John knew Jesus.'

The account of Polycarp's death is considered to be the earliest genuine martyrdom account and, as such, it set the model for the 'Acts of the Martyrs'.[6] The quiet courage of the old man cannot fail to impress, and his profession of faith set the example for many more. As was usual, the Roman Governor tried to persuade him to recant: 'Revile your Christ.' Polycarp replied: 'Eighty and six years have I served him and he has done me no wrong. How then can I blaspheme my King and my Saviour?' As the governor persisted – a recantation was of much more value than a martyrdom – Polycarp said: 'If you still think I am going to swear by Caesar's Luck, and still pretend not to know what I am, let me tell you plainly now that I am a Christian; and if you want to know the meaning of Christianity, you have only to name a day and give me a hearing.'

It was this kind of bold speech that astonished both pagan and Christian alike. And while one might have expected this kind of courage from a bishop, it was the bold and courageous speech of Christian women that seemed to raise the stakes for everyone. Inevitably, these tales are elaborated, and eventually can seem like a competition between towns about whose martyrs endured the most.

Blandina

There are two women, however, whose stories can be vouched for with some degree of certainty, Blandina and Perpetua. Around the year 177, the Christians of Lyons in what is now southern France were drawing the unwelcome attention of the authorities, and several were put to death. Among these, the acknowledged leader of the group was the slave-girl, Blandina, who apparently outranked in bravery even her mistress, her companion in suffering. She was 'like a noble mother encouraging her children'. But she was also the image of the crucified Christ. She had been hung from a post with her arms outstretched, so that her companions 'saw with their outward eyes in the person of their sister, the One who was crucified for them'. For the first time since the New Testament, women are raised up as exemplars for the community: 'Blandina, through whom Christ proved that the things that men think cheap, ugly, and contemptuous are deemed worthy of glory before God, by reason of her love for him ...' When Blandina died at last, she was reported to be oblivious to all pain because she was 'rapt in communion with Christ'.[7] For the Christians of Lyons, and all who heard of her, this was an image of human nature at its highest. The narrator of her story knows exactly why she deserves great honour. Blandina may have been 'tiny, weak and insignificant', but 'she had put on Christ, that mighty and invincible athlete'.[8] She represented the culmination of God's gradual work of raising the human race to 'bear the mighty weight of God'.[9] The extraordinary disruption of imprisonment and martyrdom created a new set of circumstances where the egalitarian conditions of the early church reasserted themselves. We are told that these prisoners addressed each other as 'brother' and 'sister', and, as we have seen, divisions of class, race and sex did not apply.

Perpetua and Felicitas

The same is true of the story of Perpetua and the slave-girl, Felicitas, two young women in their early twenties who, like Blandina, were executed for their faith. We have an account of their imprisonment from Perpetua's own hand, an extraordinary survival of a woman's voice in the Christian tradition. Vibia Perpetua and Felicitas are parents. Perpetua has a baby at the breast when she is arrested and Felicitas gives birth to her baby in prison, three days before her execution. We hear nothing of either father, which may indicate that the men remained outside the Christian community. In prison, the two young women and their male companions attained an equality of status, which was not possible for them elsewhere.

Perpetua and Felicitas lived in the north African city of Carthage and together with their teacher, Saturus, as well as three others, Revocatus, Saturninus and Secundulus, were engaged in the study of Christianity, with a view to baptism. This process of initiation was called the catechumenate, and was designed to assist Christian converts to pass over from the world and manners of paganism to the new world of Christianity. Despite the account in the *Passion of Perpetua and Felicitas,* it is extremely difficult to know the exact circumstances of their life. This document is the oldest piece of Christian literature available to us from a woman's hand. It is dated to the year 202 or 203 CE during the reign of the Emperor Septimius Severus. It is a highly stylised account and contains not only Perpetua's prison diary, but also an unknown editor's introduction, the dream of her companion, Saturus, and some concluding material about Felicitas and the other martyrs.

This is a story about women and their bodies and the violation of these bodies in the course of imprisonment and execution. As we have also seen in the account of Blandina's death, the bodies of women carry enormous significance for the Christian community. Almost every other woman whose life is available to us in Christian history is remembered because of her asceticism and her virginity, but Perpetua and Felicitas are mothers and presumably wives. As such, their bodies become part of the story. We hear of the pains of childbirth endured by Felicity, and the breasts of Perpetua aching from unused milk after her baby's removal from the prison. Scholars who have studied the *Passion* are convinced that here we have the women's own words. This is an extraordinary and unprecedented gift to us from almost eighteen hundred years ago. We are allowed to enter into Perpetua's preparation for her death, her love for her child, her problematic relationship with her father, her leadership of the other prisoners, her demands for better treatment from the prison authorities, and her account of the dreams which she interpreted as the voice of God helping her to deal with the horror that was to come.

By now, the early third century, there was a mystique of martyrdom in the Christian community. The stories of Polycarp, Blandina and others were related in letters, passed on from community to community. These accounts emphasised the presence of Christ to the martyrs as they identified with his suffering. It was believed that they experienced no pain and that, after death, the martyr achieved instant union with Christ in heaven. The trial and execution of the martyrs presented an opportunity to make public testimony of their faith, and many used this opportunity to remind the Roman rulers that the situation would soon be reversed. The Romans now seemed to win and the martyrs seemed to lose. But the reality was precisely the opposite. As the little group of five marched with 'gay and gracious looks' into the arena, 'when they came within sight of Hilarian, they began to signify to him by nods and gestures: "Thou art judging us, but God shall judge thee".' The execution of Perpetua and her companions took place in the 'Circus', that is, in the public arena, for the entertainment of Governor Hilarian and the city of Carthage. It was the Emperor's birthday and, on this special occasion, something special was offered to the city. According to the account, the extraordinary bravery of the young women martyrs, especially in the face of such mindless cruelty, shocked even the hardened Carthaginians and somewhat spoiled their enjoyment. We will focus here on Perpetua's struggle with her father, her dreams, her relationship with her companions and finally, her death.

'When I was still,' she says, 'with my companions, and my father in his affection for me was endeavouring to upset me by arguments and overthrow my resolution, "Father," I said, "Do you see this vessel for instance lying here, waterpot or whatever it may be?" "I see it," he said. And I said to him, "Can it be called by any other name than what it is?" And he answered, "No." "So also I cannot call myself anything else than what I am, a Christian".'[10]

This famous passage begins Perpetua's own account. There are three other sections of dialogue with her father, all confrontational and unutterably poignant. In a few words, Perpetua places herself at odds with the whole of the ancient world and its assumptions about the father/daughter relationship. The father has been brought in by the local governor to make Perpetua obey him and end her resistance. Perpetua, in her 'waterpot' illustration, tries to show her father that she has achieved a new identity. She is no longer his daughter. He has no power over her. She cannot and will not obey him. She has moved to a new place, beyond his and the governor's control. She is a Christian. What an extraordinary statement of power by a twenty-two year old woman! This type of parental defiance is repeated endlessly in the stories of Christian women and, as we have said previously, it is only such women who are remembered, even minimally, in the unfolding of the Christian story. The good and obedient women who did their fathers' bidding have disappeared without a trace.

The father is furious at her words and tries to 'pluck out my eyes'. He departs for the moment and Perpetua tells us that she is refreshed by his absence. It was during these few days of refreshment that she and the other catechumens were finally baptised in prison, knowing full well the consequences of this action. Her baby was brought to her in prison where she suckled him and 'my prison suddenly became a palace to me, and I would rather have been there than anywhere else'. A few days later, her father returned to beg her to have pity on him:

'Daughter, pity my white hairs! Pity your father, if I am worthy to be called father by you; if with these hands I have brought you up to this your prime of life, if I have preferred you to all your brothers! Give me not over to the reproach of men! Look upon your brothers, look upon your mother and your mother's sister, look upon your son who cannot live after you are gone! Lay aside your pride, do not ruin all of us, for none of us will ever speak freely again, if anything happens to you!' So spoke my father in his love for me, kissing my hands, and casting himself at my feet; and with tears called me by the name not of daughter but of lady. And I grieved for my father's sake, because he alone of all my kindred would not have joy in my suffering.

They wept and kissed, as she tried to comfort him, but 'full of sorrow he left me'. During the public trial, her father again tries to reason with her – 'Have pity on your baby' – but to no avail. He is beaten with rods in her presence and the baby is finally taken away from her. They do not seem to have met again.

This is a very vivid description of how the old Roman system of being in *patria potestate* – in the father's power – could, and did, break down for a daughter. As Perpetua had tried to explain to her father, the power of God had now taken over in her life and earthly systems of power were irrelevant. One cannot help but be struck with compassion for the father who, while he may not be able to call her 'Christian', is more than ready to address her, in an unprecedented way, as 'lady', *domina*. He acknowledges that she has been his favourite child, but Perpetua is now beyond recall.

What an extraordinary and tragic dilemma for a young woman. Perpetua tells us: 'I knew myself to have speech of the Lord, for whose sake I had gone through so much ...' It is possible to trace in the text how Perpetua's sense of her own authority increases after her baptism. She demands better conditions in prison, but her whole attention is now on her one goal – perseverance through the suffering of the body which lay ahead. She tells us that her 'brother' suggested that she should ask for visions to strengthen her, and this she does. She goes on to recount four dream/visions, which she describes as gradually preparing her and her companions for their ordeal. Perpetua, thus, becomes the voice of God for her companions. She dreams of ladders and dragons, heavenly gardens and good shepherds and cool refreshing waters. Through these dreams, she experiences the healing of all her relationships with her old family and the beginning of her total concentration on her new heavenly family. Her final dream well describes her new state. She dreams that she is going to her fate in the arena, but that when her clothes are removed, she discovers herself to be a man. In antiquity, the male body was considered the norm, and the strong woman was described as 'becoming male'. This phrase will also later be used about virginal women. The act of 'becoming male' indicated that all the carnality of the woman/Eve had been left behind, and a new creature was produced. This dream convinced Perpetua that she would prevail on the morrow, when she went to meet the wild beasts in the arena.

An editor gives us the account of Perpetua's 'passion' and death in the arena, and as we might expect, it was exemplary. She is gored and tossed by animals, but requests a pause in the proceedings so that she can re-arrange her clothes and her hair.

> Sitting down she drew back her torn tunic from her side to cover her thighs, more mindful of her modesty than her suffering. Then having asked for a pin she furthered fastened her disordered hair. For it was not seemly that a martyr should suffer with her hair dishevelled, lest she should seem to mourn in the hour of her glory.

She also wishes to encourage her companions to perseverance in their sufferings. Since the completion of her dreams, Perpetua shows herself to be in charge. She does not, in any sense, consider herself to be a victim. She died with total dignity and, at the age of twenty-two, confounded the total power of the Roman Empire, and of the traditional male *potestas* over women's lives. The power of the Spirit which was communicated to Perpetua through her baptism, continued to act in her life but through no mediation of clergy. Rather she felt herself to be in direct contact with her God. To the limited extent that was possible to a prisoner in the process of execution, Perpetua took control of her own life. It was, of course, a strange victory. All the cruel power of Roman imperialism was able to prevail against her in bringing about her death, but it was not able to conquer her spirit. In the end, she had to help the 'wavering hand' of the novice gladiator to find the right path for his sword because, as the editor remarks, 'so great a woman, who was feared by the unclean spirit, could not otherwise be slain except she willed'.

And what of Felicitas? Felicitas is introduced in the beginning of the story as a slave together with Revocatus. She was eight months pregnant when arrested and feared that her pregnancy would interfere with her martyrdom. 'It is against the law for women with child to be exposed for punishment.' Two days before the date for execution, all the prisoners joined together in prayer for Felicitas' safe delivery. Immediately, her birth pains started and she gave birth to a girl, 'whom one of the sisters brought up as her own daughter'. As she cried out in pain, the warders taunted her about the much greater pain which awaited her. Felicitas answered: 'Now I suffer what I suffer; but then Another will be in me who will suffer for me, because I too am to suffer for him.' As Perpetua, the 'darling of God', led them to the arena, Felicitas rejoiced about her safe delivery: she was going 'from blood to blood, from midwife to gladiator, to find in her second baptism her childbirth washing'. Even the pagan audience was horrified when 'a woman fresh from childbirth with milk dripping from her breasts' was brought forward for execution. She was gored by a heifer and eventually dispatched with a sword.

These women martyrs had a unique relationship with God which put all their other relationships, even the most intimate, in jeopardy. It is astonishing how much the women's concern for their bodies marks the telling of the story. We hear about their food, their clothing, their breast-milk, their birthing pains, their breast-feeding. There is hardly another account from the ancient world that concentrates with such detail on women's bodies as central to their identities. But this is not a stereotypically carnal concentration on the weakness and sinfulness of the

woman's body. Rather, the body is central to their Christian
identity. With their baptism, this little group of martyrs has entered a new set of relationships. A new egalitarian sister- and
brother-hood is evident among them. The normative ecclesial
arrangements do not apply to their liminal existence. God com-
municates to them directly, and directs them on each step of
their journey. All the classic conflicts of a woman's life appear in
their stories: the desire and duty to please and obey the father
against the absolute priority of following God; the sense of responsibility for and love of children against the harsh exigencies
of martyrdom; the real fear of bodily pain and humiliation
against the search for consolation and healing wherever it could
be found. At the end they went towards martyrdom with 'gay
and gracious looks, trembling, if at all, not with fear but with
joy'.

Much as the Christians loved the powerful imagery of martyrdom, the actual persecutions were disruptive events for the
church. Not all Christians acted with dignity. Some bribed their
way out of the dilemma; and some, in an excess of enthusiasm,
threw themselves on the Roman governors and begged to be executed. In the last half of the third century, persecutions were
more legally defined on an empire-wide basis. Many more were
martyred, but many defected, including some bishops. The
growing wealth of the church attracted some rulers and the un-
reliability of Christian soldiers in times of stress antagonised
others. As the century drew to a close, Christian leaders sought
for a recipe for stability. They were tired of enthusiastic outbursts, Gnostic speculations, and the last traces of women's claim
to leadership. The courage of the women martyrs was as much a
curse as a blessing in this sense. In Irenaeus' list of heresies, any
group that honoured the leadership of women had been roundly
condemned. It was to Irenaeus, then, that the church turned for
the lineaments of orthodox Christianity.

Irenaeus

It seems, from his writings, that Irenaeus had felt himself to have
been plagued by Gnostics in southern Gaul. He railed against

their 'fantastic speculations', and provided what was to become
the classic Christian denunciation of all things Gnostic. The
Gnostics were playing havoc with his communities and, as
Bishop of Lyons, he felt that he had no choice but to extirpate
this false Christianity from his territories. He denounced their
strange initiation ceremonies, their public confessions and
prophecies, and above all, their claim that all this was rooted in
the scriptures. Over and over again, he denounced especially the
'silly women' who 'prepare a marriage couch and go through a
mystical performance, pronouncing strange formulae over
those who are being initiated and declare that it is a spiritual
marriage after the manner of the heavenly unions.'[11] Irenaeus
also tells us of women who continue to preach and teach boldly,
and who even insist on celebrating a form of the eucharist. What
disturbs him even more is that these women are considered by
many to be holy – in his view, they are leading many astray. We
also hear of groups of women claiming the biblical figures of
Salome and Martha as their inspiration. Both Tertullian and
Irenaeus had been especially traumatised by the story of the
prophetesses Prisca and Maximilla, who had been so significant
in the Montanist movement from about 177 on. The hallmarks of
Montanism had been prophecy, asceticism and preparation for
martyrdom. Their reliance – and the reliance of all women
prophets – on the Holy Spirit, put the clergy in a quandary. They
could not appear to resist the Spirit, but they were also convinced, by this time, that the Holy Spirit had little to do with
women. These are but glimpses of the continued efforts of
women to gain full participation within Christianity. What we
hear of them, we hear from their sworn enemies, Irenaeus in
southern France and Tertullian in north Africa. We hear enough,
however, to be assured that many women, in many different
parts of Christianity, still sought access to teaching, preaching
and priestly roles.

There were, of course, more men martyrs than women, but
the courage of the women brought all to a standstill. Nevertheless, this did not alter the church's attitude to the proper roles

of women. The women martyrs were seen as an exception, though an exception of enormous propaganda value. Throughout the latter part of the second century, there was increased resistance to an egalitarian ethos within Christianity. Single women presented a real problem, especially those who were calling themselves Widows and Virgins. There is no doubt that Christianity had given women the option of living the single life in such roles, but the leaders of the community were unwilling to accept any kind of public ministerial role for them. The frequency and tone of the denunciations show that women were not only not accepting such restrictions, but that they were organising themselves to resist them. Since patriarchal marriage offered no opportunity whatever for egalitarian relationships, the life of asceticism and virginity presented itself as an ideal solution. As Christianity organised itself, it was obvious that the emancipation and co-equal inclusion of women were no part of the agenda. The option for ascetical virginity became a two-edged sword. While it freed women from patriarchal marriage, it also began a history of contempt for sexuality, especially the sexuality of women, which remains to this day as the unfinished agenda of Christianity.[12]

Irenaeus was reported to have died under the Emperor Septimius Severus, as had Perpetua in the year 202. During his time as Bishop of Lyons, as we have said, he had fought unceasingly against the Gnostics of southern France. He claimed a direct line to the apostolic church as part of the basis of his authority: Irenaeus knew Polycarp, Polycarp knew John, John knew Jesus. This is the kind of linkage that is necessary for authentic Christian teaching, according to Irenaeus. He posited Rome as a primary example, where the tombs of the great founding apostles, Peter and Paul, were even then being reverenced. He named the unbroken line of succession in Rome from the beginning – Peter, Linus, Cletus, Clement. Whatever the authoritative basis for this, it was to remain a powerful image for the remainder of Christian history. Every authentic Christian community should be able to trace a similar heritage of truth, and this truth was even more affirmed by the inter-communication among all these apostolic cities.

In all this, Irenaeus is more prescriptive than descriptive – he is laying down the foundations of orthodoxy, and describing a unity of authority that was far from the reality. From this apostolic succession, Irenaeus worked out a Rule of Faith, which was to be the one standard throughout the whole of Christianity. And finally, amid a welter of claims to scriptural authority, Irenaeus laid the basis for the New Testament canon. In so doing, he gave the churches their own sacred book, which he saw as the final chapter in the one long continuous story of salvation history. By the year 200 CE, the process was complete. Irenaeus had created a closed legalistic system, from which several other legitimate Christian strands had disappeared. Above all, women's leadership was no part of Irenaeus' story. The contribution of women lay on the other side of the ledger under the heading of heresy. By 200, Christianity was one of the major religions of the Roman Empire, and its main dealings were now with the Roman State.

The first language of Christian fidelity had been that of discipleship, the following of Jesus. This was an option open equally to women and men and celebrated in the rites of Christian initiation. This option remained basic for women, but the choices of how to live this discipleship became more and more restrictive. By the year 200 CE, the options of teaching, preaching, eucharistic presidency and any kind of public ministry had been removed for women. A second major language of Christian perfection, however, appeared in the option for martyrdom. There were always more men then women martyrs, but the very possibility of martyrdom presented believers with an awesome choice. The martyr, both female and male, witnessed to the transformation of the self by losing life in order to gain it. An added dimension to the public spectacle of the execution of women was the prurient interest in the ravaging and destruction of the bodies of women. This is common to both pagan and Christian accounts and, as we have seen, it was also central to

the martyrs' own thoughts. The images of suffering women become increasingly ambivalent in today's world. Pornography
delights in these images in vicious and profoundly corrupting
ways. Throughout history, we have examples of the sado-
masochistic pleasure derived from the images of suffering
women. Christian theology has prescribed suffering as particularly the lot of women in atonement for the sins of Eve. It is not
at all surprising that Irenaeus invested much energy in delineat-
ing the contrasting figures of Eve and Mary, impure and pure, as
key to understanding the Christian history of salvation.[13]

Many contemporary artists have tried to portray the suffering of women as a redemptive act in their depictions of the
Christa, that is in the crucified body of a woman Christ, a divine
woman. This is such an unusual portrayal that it has usually
evoked howls of outrage. It is a profoundly unsettling image.
The crucified, suffering, male Christ is so central to the Christian
theology of redemption that any tampering with it is seen by
many as blasphemy. In many ways, the violence of the image no
longer penetrates the imagination – the cross is often used as a
piece of jewellery, as well as a Christian symbol. When the crucified figure is a woman, however, the linkage with redemption
seems impossible for many. A woman cannot be an *alter
Christus*, another Christ, a *Christa*.[14] As we have seen, this symbolic transfer was obvious for those who watched the suffering
of the slave-girl, Blandina. For them, she took on the features of
the Christ she was imitating. To have a woman stand in for
Christ has been infallibly ruled as impossible by the Roman
Catholic Church, in its ruling against women priests. Throughout the history of Christianity, the suffering of women has been
a horrible reality. The unravelling of the causes and meaning of
this suffering and its significance for today is one of the purposes
of the present text. The history of Christianity for women can be
seen, in large part, as the history of Christian attitudes toward
women's bodies and women's efforts to live with integrity in
these bodies. The next chapter on virginal asceticism will add
another perspective to this ever-present reality.

CHAPTER 6

Deaconesses, Widows, and Virgins

*O Eternal God, the Father of Our Lord Jesus Christ, the Creator of man
and of woman, ... do thou now also look down upon this thy servant,
who is to be ordained to the office of a deaconess, and grant her Thy
Holy Spirit ...*[1]

*For if it were lawful to be baptised by a woman, Our Lord and Teacher
himself would have been baptised by Mary, his mother, whereas he was
baptised by John.*[2]

*In the Christian literature of the third-century church, the widows hold
a prominent place. They are consistently listed with the clergy. As
members of the church hierarchy, the widows are targets of the persecutions of the age ...*[3]

The desert is more ideal than real, a landscape of the mind.[4]

The main Christian centres of the third century were the Latin-
speaking cities of Rome and Carthage, and the Greek-speaking
cities of Alexandria, Antioch and Ephesus. Rome continued to
remain comparatively obscure, an imperial outpost, despite the
boost given by Irenaeus, but within another hundred years, it
will have attained the dominance that characterised it for centuries. Persecution continues but often arouses attitudes far from
the fervour of earlier times, when the faithful were 'really faithful!'[5] A whole new theological perspective begins to emerge
from Alexandria, particularly, and the role of the clergy begins
to assume the features that are still familiar into today's Catholic
churches. More and more insistently, the ascetical emphasis
comes to the fore, as the Christian model begins to move from
the martyr who renounces life itself to the 'virgin' who re-

nounces sexuality and carnality. Eventually, vast numbers of virginal women will present the church with a major challenge but, in the third century, it is women clergy who are the chief preoccupation of their Christian brothers. Far away, on the natural imperial borders of the Rhine, Danube and Euphrates, we begin to hear of the 'barbarian' stirrings, which will eventually bring about the downfall of the great Roman Empire. Already, in the third century, the martyrs' prophecy about the eventual winners is beginning to be verified.

After the Severan persecution, at the beginning of the third century, which saw the death of Perpetua among many others, there was comparative peace until mid-century. The urban middle classes in the imperial cities now figure largely on the Christian membership rolls. Christianity is growing in confidence and seems to be biding its time until paganism falters. There is still a strong revolutionary element, maintained mostly by the constant threat of persecution, but the urban middle classes are mostly conformist. They had a great deal more to lose than did the slave and women disciples of an earlier age and were, therefore, more interested in maintaining ties with the secular state. The martyr stories are still popular but the charismatic and radical edge of an Ignatius of Antioch or a Perpetua of Carthage seems to have disappeared. The church is organising itself on increasingly hierarchical lines and charismatic excitement is undesirable. Leaders are now fulminating against 'wicked' slaves who think that Christianity should bring them freedom. It is clear that the church of the third century has accepted slavery, with its whole apparatus of torture and cruelty. There is hardly a voice raised in protest. We hear of both masters and mistresses beating slaves to death in fits of temper, and the church prescribed five years of penance for this.

The renewed persecution of the Emperor Decius in mid-century produced a new flock of martyrs, but for the first time we hear of vast numbers trying to escape the consequences of their Christian faith, through bribery, lying, and the tried and true method of leaving town. Bishop Fabian of Rome and dozens of other bishops suffered martyrdom, but their colleague in Carthage, Cyprian, decided to retire to the desert for the duration. He explained his decision as an act of prudence, because the church would need strong leadership after the persecution. In his absence, the church of Carthage suffered all the rigours of the persecution on their own. By now, the emperors were intent on compliance, not martyrdom, and the faithful believers were often viciously tortured. When Cyprian returned, he was faced with a disobedient church, who accused him of cowardice and abandonment. Those who had remained to suffer, they said, now had access to the Holy Spirit, not cowardly bishops and the other *lapsi*, that is, those who had given in under torture. Cyprian turned to the Bishop of Rome, Cornelius, for advice and help. The resulting debate about the efficacy of ordination – even the ordination of cowardly bishops – and about the baptism of lapsed Christians and their restoration to the fold, went on for decades. If one could just run away and then return when the danger had ceased and be forgiven, what was the point of suffering? And what an insult to the martyrs!

We have few names from this persecution. We hear that many 'cowered with fear'.[6] In some cities there was almost total compliance with the authorities. We hear of Pionius and his companions in Smyrna, who refused to sacrifice to the Roman gods and were mocked by their 'Christian' companions for their intransigence. These companions seem to have included some women, including a visitor to the town, Sabina. She was treated as a nuisance – why could she not go and act the martyr in her own town?

After the Decian persecution, the church was seriously disorganised and frightened. The collapse of Christianity seemed a possibility. It was, in fact, providential that another half-century intervened before the final great persecution inaugurated by Diocletian. In the intervening half-century, the church regained its confidence and grounded it, partly, in increased clericalisation. Several councils held in the aftermath of the persecution emphasised this trend and gave the impression of widespread organisational efforts. The authority of the bishops was grounded anew in appeals to ancient tradition, not in the more fallible personal sanctity of the bishop himself. The roles of presbyter and deacon were spelled out and, in some areas, women made not the slightest appearance in this structure. But, as we shall see, this was not the whole story.

The Diocletian persecution was at once the most total, most systematic and most threatening to the church. When it was proclaimed in the early fourth century, on February 23, 303, it was almost welcomed as God's discipline for a church grown slack and complacent after almost fifty years of peace.[7] This was the final struggle of the empire to halt the spread of Christianity. The Christian response was again very mixed. Many suffered horrible tortures, and many died. But thousands fled, bribed their way out of difficulty, or temporarily apostatised. Hundreds of churches were burned and vast amounts of books and properties were seized. On May 1, 305, the Emperor Diocletian dramatically resigned, thus ending the persecution in the West; it lingered on for several more years in the East. On July 25, 306, the soldiers far away in York proclaimed Constantine as their leader, and prepared the way for one of the most crucial events in the history of Christianity. Before following Constantine to his ultimate triumph in Rome in 312, we return to the third century to trace a yet more momentous event – the progressive removal of women from the ranks of the clergy amid the growing misogyny of Christianity.

Rejection of the body

Third century Christians were preoccupied with the body and its relationship to mind and spirit. Docetists raised questions about the reality of the body of Jesus.[8] The Encratites were disgusted with the human body and urged all to renounce everything to do with sexuality. It was an age when even pagans were renouncing sexuality in disgust. Christian teachers, then, like Clement of Alexandria, were forced to address these issues for the sake of their congregations. He wrote about the necessity of marriage and love between spouses and children, 'the dearest relations of our life'.[9] As in every age, the vast majority of church members were married, but the voices of the married are not heard. Clement wishes the married to be sober in their lives, to avoid all pleasure and to bring up their children, knowing that this was an honourable task. But his praise of marriage, though genuine, is limited. The church was in a dilemma, having to challenge the widespread mystique of continence, or face its own ruin. Second marriages are frowned on, and the combination of old age and sexual activity seemed particularly repugnant to most Christian teachers. Since many women were widowed in their late teens or early twenties, the church was faced with many young, independent women for whom they had to find an ecclesial place.

Origen

Before proceeding to look at the deaconesses, widows and virgins of the third century, it is necessary to look at developments in theology. This is the period when the scientific basis for the study of scripture and the basic principles of Christian theology are formulated by the amazing Alexandrian scholar, Origen.

Origen was a devoted Christian. His father had died in the Severan persecution of 202 and Origen, who wanted to follow him to martyrdom, was saved, it is said, because his mother hid his clothing. Origen got his wish later and died in prison during the Decian persecution in mid-century. Origen succeeded Clement as head of the great catechetical school of Alexandria. We know very little about this school except its fame, but it must have been open to women and men students, because it is reported that Origen had himself castrated so that there would never be a hint of impropriety in his dealings with his students. Origen, in his encyclopaedic *Hexapla*, continued Irenaeus' task of determining the authentic version of the scriptures. He also engaged in a huge work of synthesis on Christian theology, starting, not from the words and deeds of Jesus, but from the pre-existing heavenly relationships between Jesus and the

Father. Even though he was subsequently declared heretical, Origen laid the basis for all later theology.[10] In Origen's work, the incarnate life of Jesus is de-emphasised, and the pre-existent Christ, the *Logos* of God, comes to the fore. With the focus now on heaven rather than earth, women, their voice and their contributions to Christianity, were even further removed from theological thinking and from concrete ecclesial life.

These developments in theology parallel and support the increased clericalisation of the churches. The clergy had to define their position and impose their authority on many fronts. On the one hand, wealthy Christian benefactors, both male and female, had to be convinced that their wealth and very welcome patronage gave them no power over the clergy. On the other, all the laity – and the gap between laity and clergy was now being strictly emphasised – had to learn to respect the clergy for the authority they had inherited at their ordination. More and more emphasis was being placed on the post-marital celibacy of the clergy, though, in the context of Encratic tendencies, sexual renunciation had to be treated delicately. Finally, the exclusive access of the clergy to the eucharistic presidency was now standard almost everywhere. As the male clerical roles were solidified, the continuing unnerving presence of women continued to present the churches with a major problem. If every woman were married, and allowed to re-marry after the death of her first husband, the whole problem could have been nicely put away. But Christianity offered women options other than marriage, and these options, paradoxically, always carried higher esteem with the clergy than marriage and motherhood. The taint of blood pollution attached to menstruation and childbirth continued to haunt Christian teachers. Though not officially forbidden in so many words, participation in the eucharist after sexual intercourse or childbirth or while menstruating was discouraged. Such activities, it was thought, excluded the Holy Spirit and rendered the person unworthy to approach holy things.[11] Besides, married women were presumed to be wholly taken up with household affairs. Origen complained of 'congregations full of chattering women, more concerned with household affairs than with worship'.[12] It was in this context of worldly distrust or 'divine discontent', as Origen put it,[13] that Christian teachers struggled with the theological place of the body, and essentially, therefore, with the public presence of women in the church. As discourse about Christ became more spiritualised and rarified, the physicality of believing Christians presented itself as a serious pre-occupation. In line with other third-century developments, the solution adopted by the church was institutionalisation. Women who were called widows, deaconesses, and virgins were now assembled into 'orders', and eventually, as we shall see, these 'orders' were assumed into the great monastic movements of the fourth century.

Deaconesses

There is no doubt whatever that in the third century – and later in some parts of the church – women occupied the two ecclesial ministries of widow and deaconess, with at least the deaconess being officially ordained. This is clear in the ordination prayer, quoted in part at the head of this chapter. The evidence for both these ministries is abundant, but it is scattered geographically and the terminology is often confusing.[14] Though the term 'deacon' is still used in a parallel sense for both women and men, nevertheless, the term deaconess now gains in popularity, as the role of the deaconess is more and more confined to service to women only. From New Testament times, the work of the deacon, female or male, is associated with the bishop. When Origen wrote about Phoebe in Paul's letter to the Romans, he understood her to be officially ordained for the ministry of the church. Later, in the fourth century, John Chrysostom, Patriarch of Constantinople, wrote of the same Phoebe: 'You see that these were noble women, hindered in no way by their sex in the course of virtue; and this is as might be expected for in Christ Jesus there is neither male nor female.'[15] These comments simply show that the notion of women exercising a continuous and officially ordained ministry in the church was a familiar and accepted one, at least in some parts of Christianity. The major testimony to deaconesses belongs to the third century and it comes from the work known as the *Didascalia Apostolorum*, a document from Christian communities in the Palestinian church. In this text, there is definitely an Order of Deaconesses and their position in the hierarchy is clearly spelled out. It seems clear that the institutionalisation of women outlined in this document solved two problems at once for the church. First of all, the married women who were almost totally secluded in the privacy of their homes, needed ministry. Secondly, the women who had taken the option of not marrying had to be organised under the control of the bishop. The third century Order of Deaconesses served both purposes well. The deaconess was directed to have special care for married women confined in pagan households. It was the deaconess who taught these women both before and after baptism. However, as the fourth century dawns, it is made very clear that deaconesses cannot baptise, as the quotation at the head of this chapter indicates. The deaconesses also ministered to the sick and the poor, and increasingly it is insisted that her ministrations are to women only.

Nevertheless, the deaconesses were considered to be definitely part of the clergy. By now a set of ecclesial images assigned each ministry its appropriate place: the bishop was in the image of God the Father; the deacon was the image of Christ; the deaconess was the image of the Holy Spirit; and the priests were in the image of the Apostles. This is the situation in the third century *Didascalia*, and is taken to describe the relative positions of the clergy during the celebration of the eucharistic liturgy. During the fourth century, the *Apostolic Constitutions*, a revision of the *Didascalia*, though still recognising deaconesses, confines them more and more to menial tasks. 'The deaconess does not make benedictions or perform any of the services for which elders and deacons are responsible. She simply guards the doors and, for reasons of decency, assists the elders in the administration of baptism.' But even now the deaconess is still officially ordained. The strictures are becoming more strident, however, as can be seen in the words of Basil of Caesarea, 'We will no longer permit the body of a deaconess, which has been consecrated, to be used for a carnal purpose.'[16] This indicates that the third-century trend toward the celibacy of the clergy is now being applied to women, and that any remaining deaconesses are necessarily virgins. Even the congregations are being sorted into different sections of male and female, and each section is to exchange the greeting of peace only among themselves, that is, men with men and women with women. It is the duty of the deacons to maintain these arrangements in the churches.

Deaconesses appear in the literature of the eastern churches right up until the twelfth century, but by the end of the fifth century, women performing the functions of deacons are completely absorbed into monastic life. The rapid growth of the practice of baptising children in the West, from the fourth century onward, deprived the women of another essential aspect of their ministry. From the time of the Council of Nicaea in 325, there is a continuous insistence that the deaconesses were never really ordained. The Council insisted that women were no longer to receive any imposition of hands from the bishop, and were henceforth to be numbered among the laity, not the clergy. Bishop Epiphanius of Salamis, who was one of the great misogynists of the age, takes pains to explain that the role of the deaconess was 'never part of the sacerdotal function and was instituted solely in order to observe the proprieties of the female sex'. Indeed, Epiphanius is engaged in a long correspondence about deaconesses with his brother bishops and defends his own reputation thus: 'I have never ordained deaconesses ... nor done anything to split the church.' And just in case his point is not clear, Epiphanius continues:

> Courage, servants of God, let us invest ourselves with all the qualities of men and put to flight this feminine madness. These women repeat Eve's weakness and take appearance for reality. But let us get to the heart of the subject. Never anywhere has any woman acted as priest for God, not even Eve; even after her Fall she was never so audacious as to put

her hand to an undertaking as impious as this; nor did any of her daughters after her ever do so. ... I come now to the New Testament. If women had been appointed to act as priests on behalf of God, or to perform official liturgical acts in the church, it must surely have come about that Mary herself, who received the privilege of carrying in her bosom the Sovereign King, God's Son, would in the New Testament have exercised the priestly office. But she did not judge such action to be right. She was not even trusted with the bestowal of baptism, since Christ himself was baptised not by her but by John ... Never has a woman been appointed among bishops and priests. But, someone will say, there were four daughters of Philip who prophesied. Yes, but they did not exercise the priestly office. And it is true that there is an order of deaconesses, but they are not permitted to act as priests, or have anything to do with that office.[17]

What is astonishing in this passage is the evidence of a lively conversation taking place in the church, not just about the diaconate, but about the priesthood. Women are making claims, based on New Testament evidence, and Epiphanius is rallying the troops against them. Further evidence of the continued insistence, by at least some women, on their right to inclusion in church ministry, is contained in the endless stream of legislation in East and West. A fourth century council at Nimes in modern France declared:

It has been suggested by some people that women somewhere or other seem to have assumed for themselves the ministry of levites (that is, deacons). This is against apostolic discipline and has been unheard of until this time. The practice is highly questionable and not allowed by ecclesiastical discipline. Any such ordination that has taken place is against all reason and is to be destroyed. All care is to be taken that no one presume in this way again.[18]

This edict from a remote Christian community shows the lack of communication between churches, but also the ongoing discussion about the ministry of women. By now, there is no

longer any need to return to New Testament proofs; 'ecclesiastical discipline' can be invoked to end all such discussion. By 390,
civil law had become aware of the deaconess and decrees that
sixty is to be the minimum age for admission to the order. The
law further instructs women to dispose completely of their
property before becoming a deaconess. At the end of the fifth
century, Pope Gelasius expresses his impatience with the
women of southern Italy. Some of these were, apparently, being
ordained, and were demanding inclusion in the church's ministry. The Pope pronounces this to be a 'lethal wound for the
church'. The sixth century Council of Epaon finally rules that all
hitherto consecrated deaconesses are to be cut off from the
church, and nothing is to be provided for them except the blessing of penitents.

Hence we see the role of woman deacon changing from a
graced charism in the early church, to inclusion in clerical 'dignity' in later centuries. Finally, ordained women are seen as
lethally wounding the church and are instructed to repent of
such desires. What is instructive is the continued demand of
women. We know nothing about such women except that they
continued to make their presence felt. It is clear, too, that it is the
initiative of women which kept the debate alive. By the fifth
century, there is no argument with them, no trading of biblical
quotations. Ecclesiastical discipline is invoked, but it has to be
invoked over and over again. One of the basic principles on
which this legislation is based is the old saw of Tertullian that
whatever is not explicitly permitted is forbidden. Much of the
spirit of Epiphanius pervades all further ecclesiastical legislation
on women's ministerial roles, right up to the present day. He insists that the role of women was always one of mere assistance
to priests, and tries to root this in New Testament teaching. His
approach is 'agressively masculine', to quote Jean Danielou,
who nevertheless goes on to agree with his distinction between
the 'real' ministry of the clergy and the mere assistance offered
by women. According to Danielou, the exclusion of women
from priestly ministry after Epiphanius, is now based firmly in

divine and apostolic authority. As Epiphanius pointedly says,
'The Word of God does not permit a woman to teach or lord it
over men.' From this meagre base, Danielou goes on to state de-
finitively what women are allowed to do: they can give instruction to adolescents and children as opposed to the official task of
teaching; they can assist the clergy in the preparation for baptism; nuns can engage in some instruction within their own
communities; and some spiritual direction can take place.[19] In a
revealing final word, Danielou suggests that the church has deliberately been opposed to conferring too definite a status on
women, so as to allow their initiative to develop according to
need.

Discussion on the inclusion of women in the official ministry
of the Roman Catholic Church has not advanced too much
beyond this stage. True, the arguments are rooted in a more
sophisticated biblical and theological base. The ignorance of
history which plagued the church of Nimes still seems to afflict
the churches of today. And finally, the current anthropological
arguments, so beloved by the present Pope, nevertheless all
seem capable of being reduced to Epiphanius' old comment
about women not being allowed to lord it over men.

Widows

While the debate over women deacons does not sound strange
in the church of today, the debate over the Order of Widows is
definitely not a current concern. As has been well said, the
Order of Widows died of its own ambiguities.[20] The first time
we meet widows in the pages of the first letter to Timothy, they
are divided into three groups: those who are completely alone
and destitute and therefore deserving of assistance, those who
still have families to care for them, and finally, those who are
'enrolled' on the church's official list of widows.[21] These last
must be over sixty years of age and must have been *univira*, that
is the wife of one husband. The enrolled widow must have
raised her children well and be known for all kinds of good
works, especially hospitality, including 'washing the feet of the

saints'. This last phrase clearly bothered later writers and it was interpreted in an allegorical fashion as washing the souls of the saints through good works.[22] It is clear from our sources, especially the *Didascalia Apostolorum*, that the church was never quite happy with the Order of Widows. We know very clearly, from endless repetition, what the widows are not allowed to do. They cannot teach or baptise, and the frequency of the admonitions indicates that this is, in fact, what the widows were doing. Without the express orders of the bishop they were not allowed to visit other houses for the purposes of eating, drinking, fasting, receiving gifts, laying on hands or praying – or, we might add, teaching or baptising. This very specific list from the *Didascalia* indicates that the widows were an active group going about their ministry in the Christian community, and whether they were usurping some of the prerogatives of the male clergy or, as most later male commentators suggest, bringing disrepute to the church, it is definitely the bishops' desire to get them off the streets. The most frequent admonition to the widows is to stay at home, pray at home, and act like the 'altar of God'. The fixity of the altar seemed the best image for the desired quiet, hidden, inactive life of the widow.

Confusion will probably always persist about the role of the widow. For a time, they were definitely considered, as the Order of Widows, to be a part of the clergy. The sources suggest that they were not ordained like the deaconesses, but 'instituted'. The *Didascalia* seems to present us with a picture of the Order of Widows at a time when the church is curtailing its activities on all fronts and advising them to make their ministry a totally spiritual and inactive one. There are several insulting comments about widows as 'gadabouts', lining their own purses. They are 'not widows but wallets', one source suggests. There always seemed to be some confusion between widows who needed care and those who did not. The famous list of Bishop Cornelius of Rome in the year 251 gives us some idea of the size and responsibilities of the Roman Church. There was 1 bishop, 44 presbyters, 7 deacons, 7 subdeacons, 42 acolytes, 52 exorcists, lectors and doorkeepers, 1500 widows and other distressed persons. This great number of widows probably belonged to the group depending on the church's charitable contributions, and there are some suggestions that many widows wished to be active in the church out of gratitude. But over and over we hear that all that is needed from them is prayer.

On the other hand, what the widows seem to want to do is preach and teach. Origen provides one of the clearest denunciations of this role:

> For it is improper for a woman to speak in the assembly no matter what she says, even if she says admirable things, or even saintly things, that is of little consequence, since they come from the mouth of a woman. 'A woman in an assembly': clearly this abuse is denounced as improper – an abuse for which the entire assembly is responsible.[23]

The teaching of widows is to be confined to the home, and even there is to be limited to very simple statements such as 'don't worship idols', and 'there is one God'. They are explicitly forbidden to tackle redemption, the kingdom of Christ, the incarnation and passion of Christ and anything to do with reward and punishment.

Doubtless there were widows who used the church's system of contributions for their own benefit, but it is also clear that the foibles of the few are played up to impose restrictions on all. There is a constant sense that this confinement of role is not palatable to the widows. One of the last roles left to the widow, that of visiting and 'laying hands' on the sick is finally also removed. The widows are accused of exacting payment for such anointing, but perhaps the real cause of the removal of the widows' ministry is seen in the peevish conclusion to the section on widows in the *Didascalia:* 'For you wish to be wiser and to know better not only than men but even than the presbyters and bishops.'[24] As the rights, duties, and privileges of the clergy are being more clearly elaborated, it is also clear that no encroachment on these rights is to be tolerated. The removal of the teaching role from women who were widows and deacons, signals also the removal of the last traces of charismatic teaching in the churches in any official sense. Church teaching now takes the form of the communication of intellectual truths couched in allegorical biblical language, and in the new scientific theological language formulated by Tertullian, Clement and Origen.

From the end of the fourth century, then, until the twentieth century, Christianity functioned with a wholly male ministry. It is clear that women made conscious efforts to prevent this from happening. We have no word from these women. As is usual with the church's 'enemies', their efforts are painted in the worst possible light. But there is no doubt that these efforts were persistent. It is clear also that there was some goodwill as well as aberrations on both sides of the debate, but the weight of contemporary social mores and ecclesiastical discipline won the day. The same Synod of Epaon which had decreed the death of the Order of Deaconesses, also legally ended the Order of Widows in 517. By then, the Germanic tribes had offered Christianity a whole new opportunity to evangelise in a totally different vein, and the *locus* of the Christian faith had shifted from the Mediterranean to the dark northern forests, where Celtic missionaries were spreading their own brand of the faith. The Celtic travellers were monks, and it is monasticism, in its many forms, which provided a place for women to continue to exercise their gifts of faith when the public clerical roles were denied them.

The legacy of the third century
Before proceeding with the examination of the roles of women in monasticism – indeed virtually the only history of women remaining to us comes through monasticism – it is important to turn once again for a last look at the historical losses to women in the third century ecclesiastical developments. The victors in the clerical debate were men, and these are the only voices remaining to us. Women, who represent half of Christianity, are the most significant group of historical losers. Telling the story of women Christians in the third century and thereafter is ham-

pered beyond repair by the loss of their voices. Almost everything we hear from the pens of male writers about the voices of
women is negative. The equation of women with Eve and
therefore with sin is partially responsible for this, but also the
growing evidence of hostility to the body serves only to devalue
women in their own persons, as being more equated with
carnality. This negativity has been emphasised by feminist historians, because it can be somewhat concealed behind the fairly
constant teaching of the churches about the spiritual equality of
women and men. Since the third century, especially, there is no
attempt to translate this spiritual equality into any kind of
structural form. In fact, the opposite happened. The lack of any
ecclesiastical structures testifying to this spiritual equality of
women and men, eventually led the churches to forget this basic
truth. Hence, later theologians like Augustine and Thomas, as
we shall see, could wonder why God had created women at all.

Many feminist historians have tried to reconstruct the actual
history of women in the third century of Christianity. Even from
our very meagre sources, it is clear that Christian women continued to create forms of Christian living that did not depend on
the biological relationships of the household codes. The vision
of co-equal discipleship in the gospels lingered as an inspiration
for women as martyrs, widows, prophets, deacons, teachers,
and liturgical leaders at least to the end of the third century. The
efforts of these women were directed at breaking through the
special restrictions of the patriarchal household, and this hidden
story contributes a very important chapter to the Christian history
of women. The sources illustrate that every effort of the clerical
establishment resisted this attempt at continuity with the biblical tradition. Eventually, it was only in the radical renunciation
of sexuality rather than in its transcendence, that the women
found some space to elaborate their own response to the
Christian gospel. This choice had positive and negative effects
on the churches, but perhaps the main loss to Christianity was
the postponement of the theological exploration of sexuality.

A special form of contempt for sexuality, and for women as

supposedly the more sexual, became the shadow side of the Christian tradition. So women's efforts to continue the egalitarian gospel tradition led eventually to a radical sexual asceticism. This choice allows some women a place to organise their own religious lives, but it condemns all other women to a kind of ignominious second choice, namely marriage. However, had the choice for ascetic virginity not been made, our knowledge of the history of women in Christianity would be practically non-existent. Hence, from this point onward, the only women for whom we have any evidence are virgins, those who, for whatever reason, renounced marriage. For almost seventeen hundred years, we hear practically nothing of the voices of married women. Their particular gift to the Christian tradition has been totally obscured.

Monasticism
Early in the fourth century, the Emperor Constantine had made Christianity a legitimate religion of the Roman Empire; by the end of the century, it had become the mandated religion. The advent of peace brought both negative and positive effects. On the one hand, the phenomenon of the 'baptised pagan' becomes a reality. As Christianity became the universal religion, and as the threat of persecution ceased, inertia and laxity seemed to take hold of many Christians. The corruptions of empire, power and wealth penetrate the Christian world and in the pages of authors like Jerome, we hear scathing critiques of unworthy clerics, greedy bishops and hypocritical ascetics. On the other hand, peace brings leisure for study, prayer and a deepening of the Christian commitment. One of the major resources for the latter was the monastic tradition, which dominated the fourth century in both its desert and urban dimensions. Monasticism was partly a continuation of gospel traditions already seen, but partly a prophetic protest aiming to restore the evangelical life of Jesus and his female and male followers. All credit the Egyptians, Antony and Pachomius, with the founding of the hermit and communal forms of monasticism respectively, but women

might be permitted to question this, as all historians also mention that one of Antony's last acts was the confining of his sister
to a convent. Unfortunately, our sources do not tell us the details
of the foundation of this convent, which obviously predates the
officially designated male founders. From the late third century,
women and men flocked to the desert in huge numbers, in an
unprecedented retreat from the world. Both women and men
lived as hermits in the Palestinian, Egyptian and Syrian deserts,
and both became part of community groups. The wilderness, the
desert, removed them from temptation, gave them space to
struggle with their own demons, and brought them nearer to
God. This was an alternative form of life, offering freedom and
entirely new social relationships. A new Christian elite was
coming into being which was to have enormous influence on the
future of Christianity.

Palladius, in his *Lausiac History*, regales us with tales of many
desert women whom he personally met in his tour of the monastic sites of Egypt. He describes one convent with four hundred
nuns, and a remarkable woman abbess, Amma Talis, who had
lived the ascetic life for eighty years. We hear tales of prostitutes
who repaired to the desert to do penance, and whose skins
turned black under the desert sun. He describes the extraordinary spiritual freedom of these women and the hospitality he
enjoyed without any sense of embarrassment at being a lone
man in the presence of so many women. Many of his stories are
plainly fictional, but many are verified from other sources.[25]

However, it is to urban monasticism that we now turn our
attention, and the city of Rome in particular. Here we meet an
extraordinary group of women ascetics, who can be counted as
the first community of nuns in the West.

The ascetic movement

We learn of the women's ascetic movement in Rome and the
parallel one in Milan from the pens, respectively, of Jerome and
Ambrose, writing towards the end of the fourth century. Despite
the eminence, intelligence and holiness of the women involved,

no word survives from their lips. A word of caution, then, is in order, as we read both the glowing praises of these women and also the often harsh and cutting criticism. Both Jerome and Ambrose and later, Augustine, wrote for their own purposes. All three were avid advocates of the ascetic life and, in particular, saw it as the God-given solution to the ecclesiastical problem of women. And the women who became the major pre-occupation for these men were the women who chose not to marry, or having been married, chose to live a life of virginity. We get the impression that there are huge numbers of such women in the cities of the Roman Empire and their option for life in independent communities as an ascetic sisterhood presents the 'fathers of the church' with unforeseen challenges. In the next chapter, we will explore the patristic response in their articulation of an anthropology, which continues to influence the life of every Western Christian. Here, we will look at the lives and choices of these women and try to penetrate to the reality of their daily lives through the very explicit agenda of the patristic authors.[26]

Marcella and Paula
The beginning of the ascetic movement in Rome is lost in the mists of history, but it seems to have been a spontaneous growth for some noble women, clustered in their great houses on the Aventine Hill. The general history of asceticism in the West was boosted by two specific events. The first was a series of visits to Treves and Rome by the great Bishop Athanasius, who was constantly being chased out of Alexandria into exile by a succession of emperors. Athanasius was recognised as one of the most avid promoters of the orthodox teaching on christology proclaimed by the Council of Nicea in 325. He was also an advocate of the ascetic life, and during his exile in Rome in 340, he stayed at the house of Marcella's mother. Secondly, Athanasius had also written a life of Antony, the first hermit, which later had such influence on the life of Augustine, and we are told that he taught the twelve year old Marcella the secrets of Antony's monastic way.[27] Marcella was a young widow when we meet her and she resisted all efforts of her mother to have her re-married. When one rich

suitor was presented to her, she is said to have remarked, 'If I wished to marry ... I would marry a man, not an inheritance.' Marcella is said to have lived a life of asceticism alone for a number of years and was then joined by several other women. These women were the 'mothers of the church' in the fourth century and it is appropriate to list their names in a history where so many have to remain nameless. They include Sophronia, Asella, Principia and Lea. Meanwhile another group of women met in a house close by owned by Paula, who was a relative of Marcella. These included several members of Paula's own family (whom we shall meet again) as well as Furia, Fabiola and perhaps, Marcellina, the sister of Ambrose of Milan. Paula and her group spent each day in Marcella's house praying, studying, reciting the psalms and learning from Marcella the principles of the ascetic life.

These women had been engaged in ascetic practices for about forty years before Jerome arrived in Rome in the year 382. Jerome, in his forties at this time, had pursued the standard career of wild youth, more sober student, and a kind of conversion in his twenties which led to a time as a discontented monk in the desert of Chalcis. Eventually, he was recognised as one of the premier scripture scholars in the West. He had accompanied Bishops Paulinus of Antioch and Epiphanius of Salamis to Rome. The redoubtable Epiphanius, whom we have already met denouncing women seeking ordination, was entertained in Paula's house. Through Epiphanius, Paula and Jerome met and thus began one of the great friendships of the early church. Jerome's reputation had preceded him. Pope Damasus summoned him to act as secretary and papal scripture scholar and Marcella invited him to give scripture lessons to the Aventine group of women ascetics. Jerome was delighted and, as he tells us, the 'lectures led to frequent meetings, through their meetings intimacy grew and their intimacy inspired mutual confidence.'[28] Jerome also taught the women to sing the psalms in Hebrew and to practise scriptural exegesis on their own. This must have been the high point of Jerome's life. He was an irascible character and personal disasters followed him everywhere. He was unable to sustain personal relationships and craved the presence of women even as he often ridiculed them mercilessly in his writings. His friendship with Marcella and Paula seems to have been one of the more steadying influences in his life. Eventually the 'intimacy' described above and Jerome's obvious preference for female companionship led to questions being raised in Rome about what exactly was happening on the Aventine. Jerome's tempestuous nature and sarcastic tongue did not help his cause.

In 384, Pope Damasus, Jerome's patron, died. The same year, one of Paula's daughters, Blesilla, died of starvation after only three months practising the ascetic life under Jerome's guidance. The wrath of the Roman clergy fell on his head. Blesilla had been widowed after only seven months of married life, and immediately Jerome moved in to persuade her to convert to the life of asceticism. She threw herself so ardently into the life that, he tells us, she conquered Hebrew in a few days. Three months later, she was dead. Immediately, questions were raised about Jerome's methods and his reputation was even further damaged by the cruel letter he wrote to Paula, Blesilla's mother, after the funeral. Jerome accuses Paula of sacrilegious tears and tells her that the profession of asceticism far outweighs the claims of motherhood.[29] Jerome was forced to leave Rome and he headed for Jerusalem, followed closely by Paula. Together, using her money and under her direction, they eventually set up double monasteries in Bethlehem and Jerome continued his biblical work. Without Paula's help, Jerome would not have had the money or leisure to complete his biblical translations and commentaries. When she died aged 57 in the year 404, her daughters, Eustochium and the younger Paula, took over the running of the monasteries. The key to Jerome's understanding of asceticism is contained in his letter describing Paula's departure from Rome:

> She reached the harbour, accompanied by her brother and other relatives, by her friends and of course by her children. Already the sails were swelling and the ship, guided by the

oars, was on the point of heading out to sea. On the shore stood little Toxotius [Paula's youngest child], imploring with childish gestures, and Rufina, her daughter, soon to be married, begged her with silent tears to linger until the wedding had taken place. However, dry-eyed, her resolve mirrored in her gaze, Paula conquered her love for her children by her love for God. She ceased to act as a mother in order to prove herself the servant of Christ. It was clear that she was struggling intensely with her sorrow, all the more admirably in that she had great love for her family.[30]

After their departure, Marcella's convent continued to occupy a central place in the life of the Roman church. The number of 'virgins' had increased and Marcella was their undoubted leader. She was addressed as mother and teacher by all. Dozens of letters arrived inviting her to come to Bethlehem, but she refused, thereby earning Jerome's taunt of being anti-semitic. Suddenly, news of the conquest and plunder of Rome by Alaric's soldiers reached Bethlehem. Every piece of literature from the ancient world describing this event showed its author to be overcome with shock and horror. The fall of Rome signalled the end of the world. Marcella's home was plundered and burned and she died shortly afterwards. Before her death, Jerome had dedicated to Marcella his commentary on Paul's letter to the Galatians:

The idea occurred to me that I might heal her grievous wound with the balm of the scriptures. I know her fervour. I know her faith. I know the fire with which her heart is always aflame. I know that she is superior to her sex, that she forgets everything that is human, and that at the ringing call of divine literature, she boldly crosses the Red Sea of this world …

Within a few years, the same Jerome was to write:

The love of a woman is accursed; it is always insatiable … It makes a manly soul effeminate and allows him to think of nothing but his obsession … Woman is classed among the greatest of evils.[31]

The teaching of Jerome and his contemporaries, Ambrose and Augustine, on asceticism and on women, will provide the content for the next chapter. Here some reflections are in order on the lives of these women. We know of them mostly through the writings of the 'fathers'. The writing of Jerome, especially, is laced both with a fanatical enthusiasm for asceticism and sarcastic vitriol against anyone who dared to question either his scholarship or his intentions. In many ways, he used the women for his own personal agenda. It was only with them that he found any solace. It is very difficult, therefore, to discern the details of the women's lives behind Jerome's fiery rhetoric.

Paula seems to have been his soul-mate, and together they are often named in a line of female/male friendship which starts with Thecla and Paul. Both Paula and Marcella are examples of the post-marital celibacy which was practised by many noble Roman women. One of Paula's daughters, Eustochium, is celebrated by Jerome as the first life-long Christian virgin in Rome. In an act of the most extraordinary trust, Paula seems to have entrusted the child to Jerome for intensive education in asceticism. Jerome consoles Paula in the famous twenty-second letter by saying, 'You have begun to be the mother-in-law of God.' There is no doubt whatever that Jerome and his contemporaries rated virginity much more highly than marriage, hence his delight when Paula forsook her family for him. An interesting comment by Palladius throws another light on the relationship between Jerome and Paula. Paula was, he says, 'hindered by a certain Jerome. For though she was able to surpass all, having great abilities, he hindered her by his jealousy, having induced her to serve his own plan.'

But Jerome did not invent the asceticism practised by these Roman women. That credit goes to Marcella. Under her guidance, the women learned to pray, to dispose of their possessions wisely, to live in utter simplicity, and to learn the art of governing their own lives. After Jerome's departure, they continued to sing the psalms in Hebrew, the only people in the West who could do so. They rejoiced in the companionship of women like themselves and were famous for their hospitality. We know that Marcella certainly engaged in the great theological discussions which were rocking the church at that time – many of them of Jerome's own making. Their lives continued to be lives of prayer and study and even the Pope consulted them when he ran into theological difficulties. There is no hint that all these women shared Jerome's contempt for marriage, but they certainly saw that life outside of marriage was the only route to the actualisation of their evangelical call.

Even though we do not have any words or teachings directly from these women, they speak to us across the centuries with their bodies. The virginal bodies of women offered to the world of the fourth century a powerful image of the advent of a new kind of woman. The writings of the male church teachers delight in presenting these bodies to us as wracked with penitential pain and gaunt from lack of normal womanly care. But the hints that are available to us from a variety of sources give us a different picture. We see powerful women intent on achieving a new kind of egalitarian living – the only fourth-century example of this particular dimension of the gospel. These were wealthy women and, as they disposed of their wealth, they offered to their household, including their slaves, the opportunity of gaining their freedom, or of joining them in the practice of the evangelical life. We hear that a younger contemporary of Paula's, Melania the Younger, disposed of eighty thousand slaves in this way. Most of these joined the ranks of freedpeople. Others rejected the offer of freedom and offered their services to others. But many joined Melania in her convent in Bethlehem, where they were near neighbours of Paula. Paula's own convent had three separate social and religious levels, but all the women dressed alike and joined together for meals and prayer. Moreover, all shared alike in the manual labour, which was an essential part of the ascetic life.

Olympias and Macrima
In Constantinople, the circle of John Chrysostom included several women deacons (in fact, he seems to have ordained half the

women in his family) and several women who founded convents. One of the most famous of these, Olympias, invited all her slaves and servants to join her in her convent. 'She called her whole household from slavery to freedom proclaiming them to be of the same honour as her own nobility.' As Jo Ann McNamara points out, some of these women may have had no choice but to join the convent to continue their employment. For those who felt called to the evangelical life, such freedom would indeed have presented them with a very rare opportunity of experiencing the freedom of the kin-dom of God.[32]

A final example of this new attempt at a continuation of the egalitarian life of the gospel is to be found in the life of Macrina, written by her younger brother, Gregory of Nyssa, as she lay dying. Indeed, Gregory tells us that she controlled the writing of the story. Macrina seems to have persuaded her mother to turn the whole household, including servants and slaves, into a monastic community. Another brother was the great Basil of Caesarea, who is acknowledged by history as a great monastic founder, but who was bullied into the ascetic life by Macrina. His later famous rule was probably based on hers. Gregory, Basil and a cousin, Gregory of Nazianzen, are remembered as the Cappadocian fathers who piloted the teaching on the Holy Spirit through the Council of Constantinople in 381. Macrina stated clearly that her model for the ascetic life was Thecla. In fact, we are told that when her mother was giving birth to her, she gave her the secret name of Thecla, in response to a dream. In this, she is trying to create a tradition of female leadership in the church.

It is obvious by now that the only women of whom we hear anything are the women who had left the conventional and recommended life of patriarchal marriage behind. Women in such marriages produced no models of holiness. The women ascetics of the fourth century had to create their own models from the traditions known to them and they appealed to these in support of their life choices. Thecla figures almost uniquely in this capacity. Of Macrina, it is written that she did not look to men for help, but desired to spend her life by herself, that is, without male control.[33]

Macrina had been taught scripture by her mother and she was also trained in philosophy. The family had been Christian for four generations, and possessed vast wealth and land-holdings, even though they had lost land repeatedly during times of persecution. Macrina regarded the family wealth as a sacred trust, and made the decision that, together with their household of servants and slaves, they would hold all things in common. All were to be treated as 'sisters and equals, instead of slaves and servants'. Macrina took her brother Basil in hand when he returned from university 'monstrously conceited and full of self-importance'. Macrina seems to sum up so many roles in her own person. She has been called the 'Christian Socrates', as she was virgin, philosopher, teacher, scripture scholar and monastic founder. She was a genius in a family of geniuses. Macrina's body, as she lay dying, had become almost transparent. But Gregory regards it with awe as the body of one soon to be resurrected in her transition to a new life.

Hypatia

Before leaving this description of the extraordinary possibilities available to some wealthy women ascetics in the late fourth century, it is worth remembering that not all women were equally blessed. It is to these women, however, that we owe some of the very few examples of the rich voluntarily dispossessing themselves of their riches. Male ascetics did likewise, but it is only the women ascetics who move on to the next step of trying to create an evangelical egalitarian lifestyle. The convent provided women with a safe place, for the most part, where they could allow their own genius to flourish. Outside the convent, women were not so lucky. We end this chapter with the story of Hypatia, a pagan philosopher who had gained fame through her teachings. Hypatia has been called a 'Christian martyr in reverse'. At the age of forty-five she was killed by being dismembered by a group of Christian monks in Alexandria in the year 415. Her body was then thrown in the gutter to await public burning.

Hypatia was killed because she was a teacher of philosophy and expected to be given the authority due all teachers in her milieu. She was said to be more learned than her father and her husband. She was loved by her students and she is said to have nurtured in them a love of diversity. One of these students later became a Christian bishop, Synesius of Ptolemais. She is said to have remarked that he was the only Christian she had ever heard with a hearty laugh. Her horrific death is a fearsome presage of what can happen to women teachers who would dare to claim authority in their own voice. The convent lent some kind of protective shelter, and this is one of the contributions of the tradition founded by the great Marcella in the fourth century.[34]

CHAPTER 7

The Life of Virginity

It was a woman who was the subject of our discourse, if indeed you can say 'woman,' for I do not know if it is appropriate to call her by a name taken from nature, when she surpassed that nature.[1]

The love of a woman is accursed; it is always insatiable ... It makes a manly soul effeminate and allows him to think of nothing but his obsession ... Woman is classed among the greatest of evils.[2]

Thus a long and careful tradition was built to deny the faintest possibility that women and men could live together without sexual tension.[3]

Their bodies became, for ascetic women, both the location and the symbol of the religious self.[4]

The period of the late fourth and early fifth century has generally been called the Golden Age of Christianity in reference to the extraordinary proliferation of male writers, referred to collectively as the Fathers of the Church. In the last chapter we looked briefly at the Mothers of the Church from the same period, though conventional history has never accorded them this honorific title. This chapter will explore how the Fathers regarded the Mothers, thus generating huge volumes of writing about women that have been foundational in forming Western Christian attitudes toward the human person. Human personhood has a history, and as the twentieth century nears its close, the teachings of the Fathers about the Mothers are still close to the centre of all debates about the notion of the human person. All those who have been influenced by Western culture have internalised this teaching. Even the most radical philosopher and theologian today in the West is still grappling with the legacy of Ambrose, Jerome and Augustine.[5] The same can be said of the so-called sexual revolution. Though their names may be totally forgotten, Ambrose and his friends are still dominating the conversation.

By the mid fourth century, the effects of the legalisation of Christianity, both positive and negative, were beginning to be felt at all levels. There is a new confidence and assumption of authority in the actions and writings of the leading bishops. Christianity is beginning to take on a splendour in its liturgy and public life that is almost gleefully described. As pagan life declines, so Christianity flourishes. Two centres of power, paradoxically, govern the thought of the late fourth-century church – the desert and the city. Our attention here will be focused on the city primarily, and on the almost total preoccupation with the urban monasticism of women which provides a backdrop of anxiety for every male writer of the period.

It cannot be emphasised sufficiently that the Fathers did not initiate the structures and practices of virginity exemplified by the women described in Chapter 6. The choices of the women for a particular way of life – here we will refer to it as the life of virginity – preceded the voluminous outpourings of the leading Christian men who tried to regulate and tame their lives. Contrary to the conventional thinking, throughout most of Christian history, these women were not following the example of Mary the Model of Virgins. This fictional and theological Mary was almost single-handedly created by Ambrose, as we shall see, as part of the programme of domesticating the spiritual lives of women ascetics.

This period saw one of the most active and vociferous public debates about the role of women in the church. Actually, the debate was often reduced to the question of what exactly God had in mind when he created women as an inferior species. For, with very few exceptions, the starting point of all discussion about women was that they were inferior and dangerous, as Paul, supposedly, had pointed out. The precise reason for the public discussion at this time was that, in choosing and living a life of virginity, women seemed to be acting above their nature, and

looked very close to being 'female men of God'. This disturb-
ance of the natural order was profoundly troublesome to the all-
male church leaders while, at the same time, they felt compelled
to laud the practice of asceticism. The quotations at the head of
the chapter give some indication of the depth and intensity of
the discussion. The writers whom we shall study – bishops except for Jerome – were profoundly ambivalent in their attitude
towards women but, without exception, what we are receiving
in their writings is the product of the male gaze. We see the
women, not as they saw themselves, but as the men saw them,
and as the men projected on them their own deep anxieties
about the nature and roles of women and men.

Virginity versus marriage
In this chapter we shall explore the doctrine of virginity as
found in these writings[6] as well as the doctrine of marriage,
which follows along as an unworthy handmaiden. Then the special features of the writings of our three main sources will be
briefly explored, because each has left his own specific legacy to
Christian theology and culture. There was little vocal opposition
to the practice of asceticism at this period, but we know of at
least two 'heretics', who dared to suggest that the contemporary
exaltation of asceticism was exaggerated at the expense of normative Christianity. Unfortunately, late fourth-century Rome was
neither the time nor the place for such musings. Finally, the
creation of the image of Mary, the Model of Virgins will be explored for its extraordinary influence on subsequent Christian
history, theology and spirituality.

   In all of this, the approach taken is frankly influenced by a
hermeneutics of suspicion. Conventional Christian history has
credited these men with the foundation of the life of virginal asceticism for women and their works have been interpreted from
this stance. As we now know, the lives of the women came first
and it is impossible to know what effect such writing had on
their choices at that time. The influence of these tracts on the
lives of later ascetic women is much clearer, as we shall see. But
even though everything we know of these women comes from

the pens of men, the tenor of much of the writing, as of much of the occasional praise and almost continual condemnation of women, would lead us to believe that women's choices and spiritual lives were not initially governed by the principles that inspired these writings. The point has to be reiterated that these men wrote from their own reactions to the women's choices and from their own disordered sexual lives. Therefore, their writings tell us much more about what they would have wished for women than about what the women were actually doing or thinking. As has already been said, the uniform starting point for their teaching was that women were of an inferior nature. If the women had not apparently risen above this nature to practise 'manly virtues', there would not have been a problem.

It is standard teaching that the option of not marrying was offered by Jesus to his followers, in imitation, it is said, of his own example. The practice of voluntary virginity was rare in the ancient world, though the 'virgin' was not unknown. In the scriptures, the general import of the virginal life was that of one who, like widows and other indigent people, was included in the group called the *anawim:* those who had no one to rely on but God alone. These are often the people who are chosen by God to carry on the plan of salvation. In their very social weakness is their strength, in God's eyes. The virgin, in particular, had no familial or social future and so, throughout biblical history, we see God providing a most spectacular future for such socially unattached and spiritually humble people.

There are some hints that young women and men – our written evidence overwhelmingly concerns young women – availed themselves of this choice and lived lives of sexual renunciation in their family surroundings. Total sexual renunciation was rare before the second century, but by the third century, it is clear that there are growing numbers of people called 'virgins' in the Christian communities. Clement of Alexandria was the first to devote a work to this practice but, in general, he advised marriage. Marriage was a serious familial and civic duty in the ancient world. It was said that every woman should have five children in order to keep the population on an even keel. We know very little of these third-century virgins and there was probably little to distinguish them from other young women.

It appears that most ecclesial lives of virginity were post-marital. There was an insistent propaganda in the early church against second marriages. This created a workforce of women ministers for many communities, but also forced the churches to deal with the presence among them of many very young women, often in control of large inheritances. Many women were widowed as early as late teens and since, in general, the menfolk did not become Christian as easily as the women, the church had to find ways to keep such riches at its own disposal. This proved no easy task.

Melania was widowed at the age of twenty-two. She set off for Egypt laden with all her silver and gold, and kept many monastic settlements going for years. Partly because of her post-marital virginity and consequent holiness, and partly because of her social standing in the Roman aristocracy, this 'female man of God' conducted her life with enormous freedom. Olympias, another heiress, was not allowed similar freedom in Constantinople. She was widowed at twenty after a little over a year of marriage. Shortly afterwards, she was ordained a deaconess so that her enormous wealth would remain at the disposal of the church. Her palace became a centre for the distribution of food and help to the poor, and a convent was built to house all her former dependants. We are told that Olympias contributed to the church at Constantinople ten thousand pounds of gold, a hundred thousand pounds of silver and properties all over Asia Minor.[7] Obviously, very few women had this kind of wealth, but such stories are not an infrequent background to the stories of the fourth-century practice of virginity.

By the fourth century, huge numbers of women were taking on the life of virginity. By now, a certain number of groups, such as the one around Marcella, had organised themselves, and there was a greater degree of stability and visibility to the life. For many, there was a public consecration, though Jerome, for example, never mentions this in connection with any of the women associated with him. Marcellina, sister of Ambrose, was consecrated to the virginal life by Pope Liberius at St Peter's around 352.[8] Ambrose was still a young man and a pagan at the time. Thirty years later, in the 380s, we have evidence of hundreds of virgins in Gaul, Milan, Spain, Rome, Palestine and Asia Minor, not to mention the deserts. But, in the cities, as soon as women begin to assemble in communities, the question of permanence and organisation is raised. This is where the bishops enter the picture and the patristic doctrine of virginity begins to be formulated. Here, we will give the general outlines of the doctrine and, later, outline some of the differences among the writers.

The doctrine of virginity

The doctrine of virginity is based on a series of formulae, some arising from the experience of the writers rather than the practitioners, and some rooted in the scriptures. One of the most common biblical foundations was the parable of the sower, where fidelity to the gospel is rated according to the receptivity of the soil to the Word of God. All the writers rate virginity at the top level – 100%, widows rate at 60% and wives at 30%. The criterion was the level of carnality evident in the person's life. Prostitutes, who were understood to be sunk in their bodies, were outside the scale. Next to them came wives, who were universally seen to have made a poor second choice. Their bodies were to be used for procreation only, but even here all the Fathers express great doubt about their salvation. Widows have escaped the body and are constantly urged not to return to marriage, as we have seen. Virgins, however, have gone beyond the nature of women and now lead angelic lives. Both astonishment and fear are evident in the writings describing this phenomenon. The virgins are the glory of the church, the new aristocracy of faith. In rising above their nature, they have placed themselves in a situation where the church leaders are forced to fear the consequences of their own logic. Without exception, they advocated the ascetic life of sexual renunciation, but then were forced to deal with the enthusiastic response of hundreds of women to this life. Female passivity was essential to their vision of the church and so the life of the powerful women virgins had to be tamed. All the writers exhibit great fear of free and independent women, and so, as the doctrine of virginity develops, the emphasis moves from freedom to obedience and submission. In men, it was said, the virtue of virginity elevates nature. In women, this virtue extinguishes nature. Women, therefore, were in need of a double redemption. The first, the choice of virginity raised them to the level of men; the second redemption, then, helped them to attain to the transformation offered to the perfect. For all these writers, the male sex is stronger, more rational, and closer to the divine. Women are inherently weaker, more prone to heresy, and always daughters of Eve.

Virgins, therefore, had to be secluded from the world. All meetings with men had to be eliminated, as also meetings with married women. Silence, obedience, modesty and penance are recommended over and over again as the essential guardians of the virginal life. Fasting was especially advocated as the tamer of lust. The whole of virginal asceticism, then, is geared to a breaking of ties with this world. This is the God-given cure to the carnality of women. Since the fall, the age of sexuality had reigned. Now, after the redemption, the age of virginity has arrived. Virginal women have become male and have learned to practice 'manly virtues'. In this way, they assure their eternal salvation because, in the next life, all will be male. Besides, having a virgin in the family guaranteed the salvation of all. The consecrated virgin is an example to all of the human being as she came from God's hands. Her body remains intact, without penetration of any kind. Her physical integrity has been maintained. Her flesh is holy flesh, just as God created it. This highly emotive teaching was also used to symbolise the pure intact church, unpenetrated by heresy. Virgins were likened to 'uncut meadows', 'untouched deserts', and the original 'virgin forests'.

The virgin is now also the Bride of Christ, and the Song of

Songs is plundered for imagery to describe the virgin's relationship with Christ, the Bridegroom. It is clear that most of this discourse is directed to women. The increasing insistence on the
celibacy of the clergy arises, partly, from the practice of virginity
by women. If the weaker and more despised sex can live like this,
how much more necessary is it for those who handle the Body of
Christ. The new prevalence of women virgins showed that a new
world was coming into being. 'The things of the resurrection
stand at the door.'⁹ The 'ugly scar' of sexuality was being healed,
and the ancient battle between the spirit and the flesh was being
won by the Spirit, in the bodies of women virgins.

But it was always a dangerous course. Women could fall so
easily. Women's bodies, seen through the projected sexual anxieties of men, were slippery with temptation. All signs of femaleness had to be erased from these bodies. Physical examinations
were initiated to assure that the bodies really were intact. This
emphasis on the physical was completely new in the rhetoric of
virginity. The 'flesh', which in Paul had stood for all that opposed the spirit, was now reduced to the physical flesh of the
ever-dangerous female. So this flesh had to be erased, as far as
possible. Food, wine, and even washing had to be curtailed, as
well as all normal human interaction. Such obliterated females
then could become the boundary stones of the church. Wherever
they went, they created sacred space. In the basilica, the place
for virgins was surrounded by a railing of pure white marble.
The public veiling of virgins was a great triumphal act for the
church, and we hear of bishops surrounded by hundreds of
chanting virgins as they process around their domains.

It is obvious from this teaching that the practice of sexual renunciation represented, for this generation of sexually fearful
and anxious men, the pinnacle of a kind of Christian perfection.
The practice of virginity seemed to solve, for them, the ever-present problem of women. There is no evidence whatever that contemporary women heard or implemented any of these teachings; it was later church leaders who saw these texts as the initial
basic structure of the life of virginity for women. They became

the normative understanding of this life and the experience of women henceforth was never consulted.

These writings inscribed the inferior status of women on the Christian consciousness and placed the vast majority of Christian women in the most appalling of double binds. On the one hand, virginity was lauded at the expense of marriage. On the other, most women were without any choice whatever in the matter. Their lives were governed by father and husband and strict obedience was demanded of them. The story of Ecdicia is a very good example of the dilemma such teaching posed for women.[10] Ecdicia was a married woman of some social standing when she felt called to the life of sexual renunciation. After some effort, she persuaded her husband to join her in this life and, for a time, their marriage was celibate. As the teaching on asceticism implied, Ecdicia had now freed her body from her husband's dominion. It followed, therefore, as had been the case with so many others, that her freedom also extended to their possessions. So Ecdicia began to share her wealth with the poor. Her husband, however, had been a somewhat unwilling partner in this enterprise, and he soon sought sexual release elsewhere. Ecdicia was distraught and wrote to Augustine for advice and support. Augustine's response is classic. These men lauded virginity, but then could not follow the logic of their own teaching. He placed all the blame on Ecdicia. Virginity, he said, gave her no rights whatever. Her one duty was obedience to her husband. Furthermore, the husband's sin was also to be laid at Ecdicia's door. In her lack of obedience, she had placed him in danger. The only course open to her was to return to her marriage, submit herself to her husband and beg his forgiveness. Nothing freed a woman from this submission; it was rooted in her inferior nature. It is time, therefore, to explore the teaching on marriage which was a direct result of the enthusiasm for asceticism which dominated this period of the church.

The doctrine of marriage
Marriage in the ancient world was regarded universally as a

civic duty in order to repopulate a world 'grazed thin by death'.[11] In this matter, young people had no choice. Their marriages were arranged for the benefit of both families, and the young woman passed from the authority of her father to the authority of her husband. It was universally believed, and repeated by the Christian writers, that this was the sole reason for a woman's existence. The dominance of the male in marriage, as elsewhere, was not in question. Under Stoic influence, there was also a widespread belief that intercourse in marriage was solely for the purposes of procreation. Too much softness and affection in marriage made a man effeminate, and repeated warnings about dewy eyes, sinuous movements and soft bodies kept men alerted to this possibility. The continued support of slavery within Christianity, however, left open a very wide door to marital infidelity, that is, on the part of the men of the household. The male heads of households owned the bodies of their slaves and there was no law against exercising this ownership in any way the master, or mistress, chose. Augustine continues to advocate flogging for disobedient slaves, and his own thirteen-year concubinage illustrates his sharing in the spirit of the age.

With the advent of ascetic enthusiasm, male Christian writers were faced with the task of defending marriage. This was obviously a difficult task for them. Clement of Alexandria, once considered to be more in favour of marriage than most, ended by saying that death would hold sway as long as women bore children.[12] Most writing on marriage aimed at damage limitation in what was considered a very poor second rate Christian way of life. The emphasis was on control, on not giving in to pleasure, on conscious control of sexual urges. Without exception, the male writers describe the 'horrors' of marriage, weeping children, heavy wombs, and always, for men, the dangers of becoming effeminate. And there was the constant anxiety about the uncontrolled and uncontrollable aspect of orgasm. As we shall see, this was one of Augustine's nightmares. All the patristic writing on marriage illustrates one thing with complete clarity: the married household as the basis of the Christian community

is no more. Marriage gives rise to anxiety, and rare are the references to the possibility of holiness in this state. Amazingly, apart
from encouraging men to be manly, there is no discussion whatever about the role of fathers in the marriage. The father is, without question, the head of the household, but his duty within the
home seems to be reduced to demanding obedience from all. In
this regard, Christianity seemed to present no challenge whatever
to fathers. The wife is endlessly admonished to complete submission and silence, to the extent that her position as wife seems
even more confined than in pagan times. Her submission is required, even to pagan and harsh husbands. Augustine speaks
with approval of his mother Monica learning to walk on eggshells,
so to speak, in order to escape the wrath of her husband,
Patricius. He also describes the women companions of his mother,
who frequently bore the marks of bruises on their faces and bodies. They are, he solemnly states, doubtless to blame for their
predicament. Women are made for submission, and any attempt
to change that opens them to the punishment they deserve.
Marriage, moreover, links them inevitably to this world and all
it stands for.

Augustine differed from his contemporaries in not seeing
marriage as an afterthought of creation. Jerome, Ambrose and
most of the other writers, considered marriage to be the result of
the fall – the fall being essentially a fall into sexuality. Augustine,
however, thought that sexual differentiation was an original
part of God's plan. What was new with the fall, for Augustine,
was his never-ending bug-bear, *concupiscentia carnis,* or in plain
language, lust. The marriage of Adam and Eve, he thought, was
based on friendship and did not include that 'hot little act' so
feared and despised by all the patristic writers. Apart from acknowledging the need for sexual intercourse for procreation,
Augustine never found a way of removing intercourse from the
realm of sin. In his own conversion, he found it necessary to renounce sexuality completely, and confined himself to a totally
male environment as far as possible. But throughout his whole
life he struggled with that 'inner corrosion' that was the result of

the fall. As we shall see, this was one of the primary sources for his doctrine of original sin and its handing on from generation to generation in the 'hot little act' of intercourse.[13]

Marriage, then, in the fourth century, while obviously remaining the lot of the vast majority of Christians, became a major source of anxiety for Christian leaders. Marriage took a man out of his normal sphere, and linked him to the inferior arena inhabited by women. Though Aristotle was not often quoted, his teaching that marriage was the union of one naturally in subjection and one naturally superior, easily sums up their approach. But, having confined marriage to the 'natural' sphere, all the resources of the church of this period went into promoting and regulating the 'super-natural' life of virginal asceticism. This was the arena of holiness and Christian perfection. Wives were forever confined to the 30% fulfilment of the Christian way of life. There seems to be no recognition whatever of the pain and torment of multiple pregnancies and the appalling, but normal, infant mortality. There is little or any sympathy for the battered women whom we meet in several sources. All of this is tied to women's lower nature, and her involvement with the natural world. It is not until the time of Martin Luther that we hear again of the possibility of holiness within marriage, and it is precisely his reversal of the rhetoric of virginal asceticism that makes such a discussion necessary in the church of the sixteenth century.

Ambrose

Ambrose was acclaimed as Bishop of Milan on December 7, 374. He was not yet even a Christian, but that presented no obstacle to the Milanese church.[14] Once he had acquiesced to the honour and completed the appointed course toward ordination, Ambrose became one of the most famous bishops in the Christian tradition, and is regarded as the first 'prince of the church'. He loved his position of power and used it successfully to challenge emperors, empresses and, in fact, the whole pagan world. One of the last battles of paganism for the minds and hearts of people was waged when Ambrose insisted on the removal of the Altar of Victory from the Senate house in Rome. It was on this occasion that one of the last pagan senators rebuked Ambrose's intolerance with his famous plea for religious tolerance: *uno itinere non potest perveniri ad tam grande secretum*, which can be loosely translated: 'if the mystery is so great, there must be more than one way of getting there.'[15] It was one of the last pleas for tolerance articulated in the Christian West.

Ambrose was an unabashed supporter of the life of virginity for women and made several distinctive contributions to the theological understanding of virginity. Until this period, both women and men practised a life of virginity 'in imitation of the flesh of Christ'. After Ambrose, imitation of the Virgin Mary was taught as the dominating motive for women. Thus, with the practice of clerical celibacy, the ideal of virginity for women and men became separated in the West. Ambrose taught that virginity in women was a virtue that transcended the course of nature. His esteem for virginity was all the more heightened by his very low regard for women. For him, the male sex was always stronger, better and, in fact, the principal sex. Women carried in their bodies the weakness of Eve, and thus had to endure the bondage, galling yoke, and slavery of marriage.[16] But this female weakness could be transcended by the practice of virginity. Mary had cancelled the debt of Eve for all women through her virginity. The virgins, therefore, led privileged lives and could revert to the innocent lives led by Adam and Eve before the fall. Ambrose wrote several texts advocating virginity and eventually had to defend himself against angry parents who accused him of stealing their daughters. Some parents even locked up their daughters to protect them from the lure of his preaching. In response, Ambrose encouraged the young women to disobey their parents and begin a life of virginity under his direction. We hear of an incident where a young girl, in response to his preaching, raced to the altar, tore off the altar cloth, and wrapped it around her head as a veil. We do not know the outcome of this particular incident, but, in Ambrose's church, such a girl would have been welcomed.

Ambrose's programme for virginity started with the utter necessity of seclusion, silence, fasting and complete separation from ordinary life. He abominated chatter, laughter and any kind of social gathering. 'Even to speak what is good is generally a fault in a virgin.'[17] Since virginity was a life above nature, there must be no pandering to this nature. Curls, especially, were antithetical to virginity. Weeping for the fault of being a woman was a recommended activity for all. Prayer was the key to success in this life, especially the recitation of the psalms, seven times daily. Ambrose recommended the diligent study of scripture, which presumes a certain level of education in his protegées.

Ambrose provided all future writers on virginity with a goldmine of imagery. He ransacked the scriptures for references, delighting especially in the nuptial images of the Song of Songs and the Psalms. Above all, Ambrose re-wrote the biography of Mary, the mother of Jesus, to make her a fit model for the practitioners of fourth-century urban asceticism. Mary became his main weapon in the promotion of the ascetic life. She is transformed into an aristocratic virgin of the fourth century and bears little resemblance to the Mary of the gospels. He was so successful, however, that it is the imagery worked out by him in fourth-century Milan which continues to furnish the Marian imagery for most Christians today. Ambrose concentrated on the physical aspects of the virginity of Mary. He delighted in praising her utterly intact body, and in so doing invented, almost single-handedly, the doctrine of the perpetual virginity of Mary. She was virginal before, during and after the act of giving birth. The virgin birth was central to his thought. He shows himself to be astonished that the bodies of Mary and Jesus were never stirred by lust. These bodies preserved their created boundaries, were never penetrated, and were never moved consciously or unconsciously by lust. In Mary, we see the taming of the female body. It was not a 'hot little act' which inaugurated the life of Jesus. Baptismal contact healed Christians, to some extent, from this ugly scar, but no such healing was ever necessary for the bodies of Jesus and Mary.

In this writing, we see for the first time the basis for a whole series of later Christian dogmas, ranging from infant baptism to the dogma of the Immaculate Conception. Augustine, as we shall see, developed some of these teachings in even more radical ways, especially the doctrine of original sin. It was the image of the utter bodily integrity of Mary that most moved Ambrose and was a powerful propaganda tool in his struggle with the Arian Empress, who was attempting to penetrate the virginal Milan church.[18] He emphasised especially – and for the first time in Christian history – the actual miraculous birth of Jesus. Nothing of the mother was broken, changed, or altered in this birth. He plundered the Hebrew scriptures for images of closed sanctuaries, enclosed gardens, ivory towers and houses of gold, which later generations of Roman Catholics will recognise as forming the basis of the Litany of Loretto. It was Ambrose also who struck one of the strongest blows in the long war of propaganda for clerical celibacy, in his insistence on the pure hands and bodies needed to come into contact with the pure eucharistic flesh of Christ. In this battle, he had one ingredient which had rarely been used, namely, the shaming of ordained priests into imitating the virginal lives of young women. Virgins were the public sign of the victory of the church against its main enemy, sensuality. 'How can sensuality recall us to Paradise, when it alone robbed us of its delights?'[19] The strictures on the life of those practising virginity were also applied, by Ambrose, to marriage. In his hands, marriage became an exceedingly gloomy affair. It was now seen, almost entirely, as an endless battle with this great enemy of sensuality. So sexuality was reduced to a purely utilitarian act of procreation, without any semblance of pleasure whatsoever. Such teachings have cast an endless anxious gloominess over the Christian attitude to sexuality in the West.

Jerome

Jerome was a contemporary of Ambrose, but they did not particularly like each other. Jerome was a 'fiery Dalmatian' and all his

writing is suffused with either his wild enthusiasm for sexual renunciation and those who practise it, or his violent anger against
those who dared to challenge his views. He was, perhaps, the
most learned man in the West, and could easily overcome both
Ambrose and Augustine with his exhaustive knowledge of the
scriptures. Unlike them, he was fluent not only in Greek, but
also in Hebrew. He had travelled widely, including a stint in the
desert of Chalcis, when he arrived in Rome in 382. Three years
later, he was expelled from the city, allegedly for a number of
unspecified immoral teachings and actions. There was, indeed,
much in Jerome's behaviour that raised alarm, not least his free
association with ascetic women, but it was more likely his bitterly
comic critique of the Roman clergy that sealed his fate. Anyone
who described the clergy as 'two-legged donkeys', or told one of
their number to 'hide your big nose and keep your mouth shut:
then you'll appear handsome and an excellent speaker',[20] was
not calculated to get clergy on his side.

Jerome had worked extremely hard during his three years in
Rome. Among other things, he re-organised the whole papal
archives in his capacity as secretary to Pope Damasus, translated
numerous Greek theological texts into Latin, and initiated the
enormous project for which he is best remembered, namely the
complete and definitive translation of the whole Bible into Latin.

Renunciation was the cornerstone of Jerome's teaching on
virginity, but unlike the writing of Ambrose which always
seems aloof and abstract, Jerome's writing on virginity jumps off
the page with emotion, whether excitement or anger. As we
have seen, Jerome mixed freely with many women ascetics in
Rome and these intense relations of friendship influenced his
whole approach to asceticism. Jerome hated the life of Rome, its
cruelty, pomp, displays of wealth, and the inevitable fawning on
power which was part and parcel of life around the papacy of
that time. Therefore, his teaching for these urban practitioners of
asceticism means the avoidance of everything that Rome stood
for. Nevertheless, Jerome knew that virginity was one of the
counsels, not a commandment. It is a choice that is made possi-

ble by the love of Christ, and Mary has made this choice possible for women.[21] But much of Jerome's teaching is forged in controversy, and it is in this context that he fell repeatedly into the trap of acting like a Manichaean, as his accusers implied. He urged the women to remove all traces of femaleness, to forget their maternal instincts, to shun marriage, and above all a second marriage. It would, he said, be like a 'dog returning to his vomit'. One essential aspect of Jerome's teaching on the life of virginity was its scholarly aspect. 'Sleep should overtake you with a book in your hand, and let the holy page receive your drooping face.'[22]

One extraordinary aspect of Jerome's teaching on the life of virginity distinguishes him from all the other Western writers. Jerome believed that, after undertaking the life of virginity, women and men became, in some sense, equal. The women became manly and practised manly virtues. Perhaps it was his own training in the East, where such an approach was fairly common, or perhaps it was his emphasis on scholarship for women, but Jerome presented himself here as one of the last Christian thinkers in the West to acknowledge the possibility of an egalitarian relationship between men and women. Certainly, this applied only to virgins, but it meant that the natural inferiority of women was not complete in his eyes. He spoke of cultivating a 'holy timidity' with women because, even after professing virginity, women and men remained sexual creatures. The paradox is that Jerome, having set his sights so high, turned ferociously on women whenever the experiment failed.

Jerome could not survive without the friendship – and the money – of women, but he knew from experience that he and they remained irreducibly sexual. Despite his obvious affection for the women in his Roman circle, they were a constant irritant to him, with the possible exception of Marcella and Paula. So, when his teachings were challenged as being extremist and anti-marriage, Jerome took it out on the women. His writing against Helvidius and Jovinian, as we shall see, lambasted women for thinking they could be the equals of men, even after a lifetime of ascetic living. And all this while his whole life and career was being made possible, both in Rome and Bethlehem, by his women friends. It would be instructive to know what they made of his rantings, but history preferred the outbursts of Jerome to any word whatever from these *mulieres sanctae* – holy women.

Augustine

Augustine found that he could live as a Christian only in an all-male world. He had none of the friendships experienced by Jerome, and confessed repeatedly that friendship with a woman was an impossibility. Augustine tells us in his *Confessions* that he had a compulsive need for sex. It is obvious, also, that during the thirteen-year relationship of concubinage with the woman he loved, they practised some form of contraception. In fact, he describes some of the practices of contraception with medical precision in his work on *The Morality of the Manichaeans*. Early in the relationship, when Augustine was only seventeen, they had a son. After that, their contraceptive practices seem to have been very careful indeed.[23] Augustine's conversion entailed for him the complete renunciation of sexuality. He believed that his baptism would release him from the sway of the 'things of this world', especially sexuality. But he was to be profoundly disappointed. What he came to call *concupiscentia carnis* dogged him all his life. From this time on, his ethical and ascetic thinking is haunted by the consequences of his nocturnal emissions. These led him to conclude that there was an evil at the core of human life, original sin, which tied the human to the earth and to the uncontrollable movements of sensuality in the body. Control was his watchword. It seemed to him that the will should be able to control all things human. But his wretched body betrayed him – even in his dreams.

An anxious sadness haunts the writing of Augustine. He sought for remedies in prayer, asceticism and study and, finally, it seemed to him that wisdom lay in the secular structures of the state. It was in this context that he advocated flogging for disobedient slaves and unruly peasants and finally called in the army against the Donatists, when all else failed. It was to be a fateful decision for subsequent Christian history, giving such strong patristic precedent for the use of violence for religious purposes. This sexual anxiety also indicated what his attitude to women would be. He would not even allow female relatives into his home, and he shunned all female contact, as far as possible. Hence also, for Augustine, women were necessarily subject to males, who in all aspects were superior. He instructed husbands to love their wives, but in the spirit of the scriptural dictum: 'Love your enemies.'

It is easy to see, then, how the practice of virginity seemed a heaven-sent solution to the problem of women for Augustine. And this was also the basis for his teaching on Mary. Unlike Ambrose and Jerome, who delighted in reflecting on the integrity of Mary's physical body, Augustine lauded her will. She alone, of all humans, was able to control her sexual feelings. In her there was no whit of *concupiscentia carnis*. Her body did her bidding. In her, through the power of her will, the ancient harmony of body and soul was recaptured.

One can easily imagine Augustine's horror, then, when Pelagius began to remind Roman Christians of the gospel promise of freedom of the will, in such passages as 'the truth will make you free'. Pelagius told them that they were not at the mercy of forces beyond their control. He urged Christians to move beyond their resignation in a kind of moral sleep, and waken to the freedom of grace freely offered to them. Augustine was appalled and devoted all his energies to the quashing of this heretical teaching. Pelagius was quickly dealt with, but one of his followers, Bishop Julian of Eclanum proved a worthier adversary. Julian was a married bishop, the son of a bishop and married, appropriately enough, to the daughter of a bishop. He was able to challenge his fellow-bishop at his most vulnerable point. For Julian, sexual desire was not corrupt, and anyway renouncing it did not seem to have done Augustine a great deal of good. Each Christian couple has the same sexual desire as God gave Adam and Eve. True, it must be controlled, but it is not corrupt. Julian was defending married sexuality. Augustine saw the need of defending the inherent corruption of married sexuality, because of the weakness of the will. And besides, it was precisely this weakness, rooted in lust, which passed on the inherent evil of humanity, the original sin, from one generation to the next. In this way, Augustine placed an element of lust and evil right in the very soul of humanity. One can only imagine some of his despair as he painted himself into an ever tighter corner. There seemed no solution. He knew, from his own experience, that asceticism was not the final answer.

Later writers, such as John Cassian, one of the founders of European monasticism prior to Benedict, were able to say that the struggle of flesh and spirit was good for us. Among other things, it taught us humility, and eventually matured the human person. For John, as for the monks of the desert before him, anger, pride, greed and resentment were far more dangerous enemies on the spiritual journey than lust. But it was Augustine's spirit which came to dominate Western thinking. It is depressing in the extreme to realise that Augustine's despair over his self-confessed unruly sexuality was to have such a negative influence on the Christian attitude to the body in the West. At the very least, it made marriage a nightmare for generation after generation of faithful believers, whom he would have called the *massa damnata*. Augustine's vision was distorted and drastically blinded by his own experience of his body. What a salutary lesson for all those laden with the responsibility of teaching others in any capacity.[24]

Opposing voices

Were there any voices raised in protest at this teaching? From the correspondence of all three men, we know that there were some, but the most challenging, and therefore the most strenuously resisted, were the voices of Helvidius and Jovinian. We know nothing of either of these men from their own pens; they appear to us only in the blasting anger of Ambrose and the utterly sarcastic fervour of Jerome. But even with this completely one-sided information, one might ask today whether it is Ambrose and Jerome who represent the essential Christian tradition or the 'heretics' they chose to condemn in such vicious language. The problem for both Helvidius and Jovinian was that they chose to suggest that baptism might be a more basic ground of decision about the worth of a Christian life than asceticism in itself. The fourth-century Christian community did not present a favourable audience for such musings.

Helvidius was a Roman Christian who, in response to what he considered to be exaggerated praise for ascetic virginity and Mary's exemplary role in its practice, wrote a book asserting that virginity was not superior to marriage. He further suggested that, according to the scriptures, Jesus had brothers and sisters, and that, therefore, Mary did not remain a virgin after the birth of Jesus. Pope Damasus asked Jerome to deal with Helvidius because the ascetic community in Rome was in complete disarray as a result of this book. Ambrose also attacked Helvidius from Milan. This was an excellent opportunity for Jerome to display his superior knowledge of the scriptures, and he knew that no one could match his erudition. Helvidius had suggested that the texts of the infancy narratives of Matthew and Luke pointed clearly to the normal marriage relationship of Mary and Joseph after the birth of Jesus. Jerome multiplied texts from the Hebrew and Christian scriptures to illustrate the utter ignorance of Helvidius on biblical matters, frequently addressing his opponent as the 'most ignorant of men'.[25] In this controversy, much of the standard traditional Roman Catholic approach to Mary's virginity finds its origin. Jerome 'proved' that the biblical word 'brother' meant relative (like most commentators then and since, he completely ignored the reference to the sisters of Jesus); further, he 'proved' that Joseph also was a virgin, because only a virginal spouse was suitable for the Virgin of Virgins. Jerome went on to re-assert the superiority of virginity over marriage because 'God was born of a virgin'. He hastens, as usual, to deny that he is belittling marriage, but nevertheless insists that the only worth of marriage is when it is lived in a spirit of virginity and produces virgins. Jerome presents marriage as one long sexual brawl with 'kettle drums, flutes, lyres and cymbals' drowning out the will of God. He suggests that married women are usually 'practically naked, dressed in flimsy clothing ... exposed to immodest gazes'. Against such descriptions of marriage, who would not choose virginity? Besides, in a theme common to Augustine also, he suggests that 'the world is too small for us' – there are already more than enough children. 'We do not deny that married women turn out to be holy, but we say that these women turn out to be holy who have ceased to be married women.'

Jovinian presented himself as an adversary some ten years later, again for both Ambrose and Jerome, who resisted him on differing grounds. Ambrose is wrathful and Jerome venomous as they set out to extirpate this latest questioner of asceticism from the community of the faithful. Jovinian seems to have been a wandering monk and his teaching gained prominence after Jerome's departure from Rome in 385. What caused the most anxiety in Rome was Jovinian's teaching that all the baptised, whether celibate, married, or widowed, gained equal merit before God, provided that they were living sincere lives. It was baptism that provided the real dynamism for a Christian life, not asceticism. He also suggested, on the same baptismal principle, that there is no difference between feasting and fasting, so long as the one who feasts does so with thanksgiving. Jovinian seems also to have denied the miraculous nature of the birth of Jesus, a point that was utterly essential to the ascetic programme of Ambrose. Other theologians of the time, including Jerome, were more muted in their teaching on the miraculous nature of the birth of Jesus, because it seemed to suggest that Jesus was not completely human, thus denying the teaching of the Council of Nicea. But it is this Marian doctrine which Ambrose defends and his passionate and towering anger ends in the excommunication of Jovinian by Bishop Siricius of Rome.

The whole affair would probably have ended there had not some of Jerome's friends sent him copies of Jovinian's writings after the fact, asking for a more detailed defence of ascetic prin-

ciples. It was suggested that he 'exterminate' the heretic with
'evangelical and apostolic vigour'.[26] Nothing could have
pleased Jerome more as he saw in this affair an opportunity to
defend his own teachings and behaviour. Jovinian had listed all
the married patriarchs and holy people in the scriptures in defence of marriage, and had then addressed the Roman ascetic
women: 'Be not puffed up; you and your married sisters are
members of the same church.' Jerome's defence of virginity, in
response to this, results in one of the most vicious condemna-
tions of marriage in the whole of Christian literature. Quoting
Paul, he says, 'If it is good not to touch a woman, it is therefore
evil to touch her. The only opposite to good is evil.' He compares
marriage to eating *stercus bubulum* – bull shit – when one cannot
tolerate the good grain of virginity. When the evangelists speak
of the 'abomination of desolation', they are not speaking of
brothels, says Jerome, but 'swelling wombs, wailing infants, and
all the works of marriage'. Jerome's writing only descends from
there, as he exhaustively demolishes almost every biblical reference to marriage in both Old and New Testaments. And eventually, it emerges that what he is really condemning is the being
of women. 'No one knows better what is a woman than the man
who has had to endure one as a wife.' Jerome's deeply rooted
misogyny comes to the fore here and all of Rome was shocked
by the crudeness of his language and the coarseness of his
thought. His former friends tried to remove all copies of this
two-volume diatribe, but it was widely popular. Jerome was
asked to explain himself, but he refused to back down on the
question of the inferiority of marriage to virginity, quoting current church custom in his own defence: 'What kind of good is
marriage which prevents us from receiving the Body of Christ? I
know that at Rome it has been the custom that the faithful always receive the Body of Christ ... but I appeal to the con-
sciences of those who receive communion on the same day after
coition.'[27]

It was partly in response to this controversy that Augustine
wrote his work *On the Good of Marriage*, probably the first positive Christian thesis on marriage. But it is obvious that this is a

difficult task for Augustine. He also continues to assert that virginity is an intrinsically superior state to marriage, but that the virgins should not, therefore, be puffed up, and no individual virgin should consider herself superior to a married woman. Christian love should dominate all. But Augustine's own personal experiences and his own sense that, for him, Christianity and sexuality were incompatible, prevent this work from being the vigorous defence of marriage that was required. He had deliberately removed himself from all womanly contact and, as a result, his defence of marriage sounds strangely abstract. Nevertheless, in his insistence on the three goods of marriage as fidelity, permanence and procreation, he laid the basis for centuries of subsequent Christian teaching. Since Augustine's notion of 'fidelity' was a quality of the institution of marriage, and not a quality between persons, he influenced the lack of emphasis on a personal relationship within marriage until the present day. Besides, with Augustine's insistence on the headship of the male and the natural inferiority of the female in marriage, as elsewhere, the concept of an equality of personal relationship would have been impossible for him. His fragmented view of human personhood, especially the personhood of the woman, has had untold influence on Christian attitudes in these areas ever since.[28] From this arose his assertion that only men were created in the image of God. Women, as the 'corporeal sex', were not. Nevertheless,

> The woman together with her husband is the image of God, so that the whole substance is one image. But when she is assigned as a helpmate, a function which pertains to her alone, then she is not the image of God, just as fully and completely as when he and the woman are joined together as one.[29]

The period of church history from 350 to 550 was truly a Golden Age in the extent of its powerful writing, so influential on all later ages of Christianity, especially the Roman Catholic tradition. Indeed, it was believed that the 'Fathers' had so brilliantly encapsulated the Christian tradition in their interpretation of the scriptures, that it was no longer necessary to study scripture. An examination of any Catholic document from that time to the most recent official papal or episcopal statement will illustrate this point in its extensive citing of patristic sources. But this golden aura was gained at the expense of women, marriage, and especially the position of wife and mother. It was also tragically gained at the expense of children, who for much of later Christian times were seen often as needing strict and often harsh discipline, to counteract in them the effects of original sin.

From this time on, married women disappear almost entirely from the Christian story. Their lives had been proven to be more in line with nature, and therefore not fit subjects for theological reflection. One model for women, however, emerged from this period, and that is the model of the Virgin Mary. It is obviously a double-edged model for married women and impossible of imitation. Nevertheless, Mary, the perpetual virgin, assumed from this time forward an indelible place in the spirituality of centuries of women, as 'our tainted nature's solitary boast'. The alienating effect of this virginal image, accompanied with the institutionalised fear of women following on the growing emphasis on priestly celibacy, goes without saying. It remains for us to pull together briefly the fourth-century contribution to Marian devotion, in the context of the monastic and ascetic enthusiasm of the period.

Marian devotion
Devotion to Mary was a late arrival on the Christian devotional scene. There was no biography, no grave site, no relics – as had eventually focused Christian devotion on the martyrs. The appearance of Mary in the gospels had been ambivalent, as we have seen, and her presence in the apocryphal literature is more polemical (in the Gnostic cause) than devotional. Mary had played a foundational but minor role in the biblical theology of Irenaeus of Lyons. In his theory of recapitulation, Jesus undid the sin of Adam and 'the knot of Eve's disobedience is dissolved by Mary's obedience'.[30] This Eve/Mary comparison becomes one of the favourite Marian themes in every subsequent generation. Carnality and purity, sin and grace, disobedience and

obedience, dealings with devil/serpents as opposed to dealings with angels, sexual involvement as opposed to virginal integrity – all these themes were lovingly played and replayed down the centuries. In fact, this theme provided a kind of straitjacket within which women were confined. Women were either Mary or Eve, and, since so few women, by definition, were Mary, the imagery of Eve provided one of the main lenses for the theological analysis of the role of most women in the Christian dispensation.

So the themes of the virginity and obedience of Mary are already theologically in place when we reach the fourth century. There is, as yet, no devotion to Mary, partly because of the centrality of christocentric doctrines, and partly because of fear of the dominance of pagan goddess imagery all over the ancient world. The ascetic debates were to change all that. As we have seen, the life of virginity preceded any re-evaluation of Mary. Initially, virgins did not live their lives in imitation of Mary; it was Mary who was re-invented on the model of the ascetic virgins of the fourth century. And this almost entirely fictional re-invention became the dominant image of Mary and provided the basis of much Roman Catholic mariology. It was Ambrose who set the stage in his writing on the integrity and intactness of Mary's body. As we have seen, Mary served both his political and ascetic purposes, and he also supplied the language and imagery which still dominates devotion to Mary. His re-invented Mary has all the desired features of a model Milanese or Roman nun, few of them having any relation whatever to the biblical testimony to Mary:

> She stayed at home all day and rarely ventured forth. She shunned the company of men. She worked like a honeybee. She prayed to God, constantly, and let no bad thoughts take root in her heart. She was never bold or hard-hearted and always kept her voice low.[31]

The one biblical passage that appears in all the patristic writing is Mary's *fiat* in the Annunciation scene. Here is the key to womanly obedience to the will of God. This image of Mary and its summing up of all that is contained in the word 'feminine' remains central in all spirituality based on the life of Mary. She was retiring, demure, submissive and silent.

Jerome's addition to the imagery of Mary came, as we have seen, from his controversies with Helvidius and Jovinian. In his ascetic writing, he rejoiced in portraying Mary as the exemplar of virginity, adding, as was his wont, a studious element to his picture of Mary. His theological additions, however, still dominate Marian dogma. Mary was a virgin before the birth of Jesus and remained a virgin after the birth – that is, she was a perpetual virgin. Jerome, the biblical scholar, was always a little more cautious about emphasis on the miraculous nature of the actual birth, but this also became part of Marian teaching. Jerome also added the image of the virginal Joseph, thus differentiating Eastern and Western mariology. The East, to this day, sees the biblical brothers and sisters of Jesus as children of Joseph by a former marriage. As Jerome's enthusiasm for his subject developed, he had to re-explain the brothers and sisters of Jesus as relatives. Augustine, with his wonted emphasis on conscious control of one's sexuality, introduced the notion of Mary's vow of virginity. Virginity did not happen to Mary by accident; it was consciously willed by her. He based this on Mary's question to the Angel: 'How can this be, since I am a virgin?' (Lk 1:34)

There is no doubt that this developing picture of the Virgin Mary, exemplar of the life of virginity, served to tame the lives of actual virgins. The emphasis was on submission, not liberation, on male/female differentiation, not on any egalitarian principles. The virginity of women was also subordinated to the celibacy now more and more advocated for the clergy, though not necessarily practised by them. Universally required celibacy was still six hundred years in the future. The virginity of men was said to be in imitation of the flesh of Christ; that of women, in imitation of Mary. This very handily prevented women from ever again making claims to manly virtue, as had been common in early monasticism. But perhaps the most significant result of this Marian development was the sexualising of the notion of virginity as a primarily physical characteristic. It was the bodies of women that represented the greatest danger to the church, and so it was the utterly intact body of the virgin that would redeem them. The theological distortion of all this is plain today, but the imagery, spirituality and emotion associated with these teachings still wield enormous influence.

Had it not been for the re-invention of Mary, the Mother of Jesus, perhaps much of the excitement of the ascetic movement would have disappeared from history. As it is, the submissive image of the exemplary virgin has completely overshadowed the powerful and extraordinary lives of the virginal women who preceded the creation of her image. Needless to say, it also distorted, for centuries, the imagery of discipleship, which is key to the biblical testimony to Mary. But Mary entered the Christian landscape and her place in the later Christian life of the West was assured.[32] The council of Ephesus in 431, in naming Mary as *Theotokos*, the God-bearer, amid extraordinary scenes of joy and high emotion (mostly choreographed by Cyril of Alexandria for his own purposes), placed Mary on an even more permanent footing in the dogmatic and imaginative life of Christians. Since Marian dogma and imagery is so important to the developing story of women, we will be following it throughout. Enough has been said so far to illustrate the inevitable shape of the story of women from the fourth century forward. Most of the remainder of the story will concern 'virgins', and the Christian story of married women, wives and mothers will tragically fail to create the smallest dent on the developing tale.

This summation, of course, concerns the history of women as written, not as it actually happened. The fourth century patristic theological choices, however, have removed the 'female men of God' from the consciousness of the vast majority of believing Christians the world over. The restoration of these and all women to history and consciousness is the major task of feminist history writing and, as the story continues, that will be our serious task.

CHAPTER 8

The Abbesses

In the same way, she [Radegund] sent great men to give salutary advice to the illustrious kings so that the country would be made more salubrious both for the king and the people.[1]

After the example of the primitive church, no one was rich, no one was in any need, for they had all things in common and none had any private property. So great was her [Hilda's] prudence that not only ordinary people but also kings and princes sometimes sought and received her counsel when in difficulties.[2]

No woman began a career of sanctity without the substantial material resources necessary to acquire a reputation for charity. Nobility and wealth were the first requisites.[3]

Dating from the fifth century, the Wisigothic Sacramentary gives instructions for the ordination of abbesses. In the prayer it is stated that before God there is no discrimination of the sexes and that women, like men, are called to collaborate in the spiritual struggle.[4]

The sack of Rome by Alaric and his Gothic army in the year 410 seemed to the citizens of the Roman Empire to herald the end of the world. In many ways, this was true. The Greco-Roman classical world was passing away. The unthinkable had happened. Everyone looked around for scapegoats. The pagans blamed the Christians' lack of reverence for the ancient gods. The Christians accepted this criticism, to some extent, turning the blame inwards to bewail their lack of fidelity to the laws of the Christian God. Between the years 413 and 418, Augustine laboured on his massive philosophy of history, *The City of God,* in an attempt to come to terms with these momentous events. Whereas the citi-

zens of the Roman Empire, both pagan and Christian, had regarded the Empire as central to God's plan for humanity,
Augustine now downgraded all human institutions and posited
that, henceforth, Christians would be *perigrini*, exiles and aliens
on the earth, always longing for their true home in heaven. The
City of this world was now an alien place; Christians were called
to turn their attention to the new city, the City of God, and to
make sure that all peoples had a chance to enter their true home:

> The Heavenly City, while on its earthly pilgrimage, calls
> forth its citizens from every nation and assembles a multi-
> lingual band of pilgrims; not caring about any diversity in
> the customs, laws and institutions whereby they severally
> make provision for the achievement and maintenance of
> earthly peace.[5]

Augustine had more foresight than perhaps he knew.
Christianity was already beginning to be home to peoples and
nations quite unknown to most Romans, and to adapt practices
and beliefs that would have horrified the staid and solemn
Roman believers. In the succeeding centuries, two great new
cultural groups would be host to the Christian tradition and
their adaptations of the preceding Jewish and Greco-Roman
traditions would create the world of Western Europe. These
traditions are, of course, the Germanic and Celtic, used here in a
very broad sense for a huge variety of cultural and religious
groupings. Regretfully, it has to be our primary purpose to explore the roles of Germanic women in this phenomenon, and to
attempt to restore to conscious memory the very significant involvement of women in the Christian foundations of the
Western World.

The Barbarians

The period under review here comprises the fifth to ninth centuries, centuries of breathtaking turbulence across the face of
what we now call Europe. Successive movements of peoples,
called by the Romans 'barbarians' because of their general ignorance of the Latin/Roman culture, swept through Europe, each

group to some extent disrupting the previous one. The Goths, Visigoths, and Vandals were succeeded by the dreaded Huns. As these moved into the area known today as Germany and the Netherlands, the Angles and Saxons were pushed westward to Britain, and the Franks to the regions of Gaul. Previously, the Celts had traversed Europe to settle in the western parts of Britain and in Ireland. Eventually, the Vikings, Lombards and Normans would continue the disruption but, by the year 1000, Europe was beginning to take on the tribal features still familiar to us today. The widespread, but highly centralised Roman Empire gave way to much smaller units constantly at war with each other. In fact, the main occupation of most of the occupants of this quagmire of races and tribes was war. No wonder Christians were to feel like aliens in this world. Eventually, however, the new tribes were evangelised and a wholly new kind of Christian emerged. It is one of the great ironies of history that the monasteries, which played such a central role in this evangelisation, were also instrumental in preserving for future ages the heritage of Greek and Latin pagan classical literature.

When we explore the historical sources for the next five centuries, we are a long way from the 'Golden Age of Patristic Literature'. The tribes, almost without exception, handed on their laws, customs and stories through lively oral traditions. It was the Christian influence of the monasteries which eventually transcribed this lore, altering it in the process to provide some continuity with Roman written law. This was not entirely an imposition, as the tribes hankered for the respectability which Roman culture could bestow. The blending of the cultures happened over centuries and eventually resulted in the flowering known to history as the High Middle Ages. Our attention now turns to the Christianising of the tribes, and, in particular to the indispensable role of women which has been almost universally ignored in this process.

The task of extracting information about women becomes even more complicated in this era. Present-day historians are tiresomely obtuse in their persisting attempts to make women's role an auxiliary one, even when dealing with material that puts women in the forefront of the evangelisation of Europe. The sensational and the miraculous now take centre stage. One of the contributions of this extraordinary period of Christian history is the tactility of the peoples' faith. The Germanic peoples needed to see, hear and touch the presence of God. Heaven was peopled with the same kind of aristocratic warrior class that was familiar on earth. The inter-connecting web of human relationships that kept the tribes intact, was expected to be continued in the next world. The monastic communities of women and men who extended hospitality, healing, and care in this world, were expected, through their founders and holy members, to continue this care from beyond the grave. In this context, we encounter one of the greatest contributions of this era – the art of hagiography.[6]

Hagiography
The new Christian peoples needed new saints who would be recognisable to them, almost part of their own families. The writing of the lives of these saints took on a very predictable format, replete with extraordinary births and sensational conversions, followed by wealthy and hospitable foundations and miraculous interventions on the people's behalf, and finally edifying death-bed scenes. The saint who continued to work miracles from beyond the grave was especially esteemed and many sites of pilgrimage resulted from such beneficent holy ones. There is no question of canonisation for centuries yet, but the people found their own way of honouring the holy ones who made life more liveable for them.

The purpose of such writing was didactic and evangelising. The stories provided concrete examples of the working of God's grace in people's lives. Obviously, it is almost impossible to pin down actual historical details behind these texts, where the miraculous is accepted by all without question, but even the stories reveal a great deal to us about the lives of men and women who were considered to be holy by their contemporaries. The hagiography of women saints will most concern us here, but first we will turn our attention to the earliest evangelising tales of the Franks, Angles and Saxons.

One of the first hints we get of a new form of non-Roman Christianity is in the life of Martin of Tours. After living as a soldier, Martin was baptised, moved to Gaul and attached himself to Bishop Hilary of Poitiers around 360. Martin lived as a hermit and within a decade his fame as a holy man had spread and, with some opposition, he was consecrated bishop. Martin was a new kind of bishop, about as far removed from Augustine, Ambrose, and indeed his Gallic contemporaries, as can be imagined. Martin made a choice for a life of poverty and gloried in appearing uncouth and un-episcopal. He rode on a donkey, dressed like a peasant and lived in a monastery rather than an episcopal palace. Martin spoke his mind to everyone, thus ignoring centuries of Roman rhetorical training and the polite discourse which had been expected of every educated Roman, pagan or Christian. Martin battled devils, spoke familiarly with angels and saints, foretold the future and read peoples' hearts. He exorcised demons, healed the sick, ordered hailstorms to cease and engaged in head-on battles with pagans and their rituals. Here was a new kind of evangelisation for a new people, unfamiliar with the sophisticated theological and biblical argumentation of another place. It is astonishing to think that Martin is a contemporary of the 'Fathers' of the Golden Age, but for the next five centuries, it is Martin's kind of Christianity that will prevail. Christianity has moved from the city to the country, from the palace to the monastery, from the south and east to the north and west, and from the Latins and Greeks to the Germans and Celts.

Rome had fallen to Alaric in 410, but the Empire struggled on until 476. After this date, there was no Roman emperor in the West until the Franco-Roman alliance produced Charlemagne in 800. The Eastern Roman Empire continued until 1453, surrounded on all sides, from the seventh century on, by the flourishing Islamic kingdoms. To all intents and purposes, the West was on its own for about four centuries. This period has been called the

Dark Ages, and often treated accordingly. As feminist historians have discovered, however, it is when the 'normal' structures of human living break down that women come into their own. This is definitely the case in this period. The stories of the episcopal ordination of Brigid and the later monastic abbesses have been considered best forgotten. Conventional Christian history – and historians – have little room for women bishops and powerful abbesses. Before dealing with the abbesses, however, we must meet a few powerful wives, namely, Clotilde, Bertha, and Ethelburga.

Clotilde

The Goths, through their patron saint, Ulfilas, had been evangelised into an Arian form of Christianity, and Arianism seemed to gain the allegiance of many barbarian tribes. Hence the relief when Clovis, grandson of Maroveus the founder of the Merovingian dynasty, finally became the first barbarian to adopt Catholic Christianity. Rheims was the centre of this particular branch of the Franks, and Clovis took up residence there as their king around 481.[7] It is Gregory of Tours, the composer of the hagiography of Clovis, who credited him with making France the 'eldest daughter of the church'. Unfortunately, Gregory and all subsequent historians have falsified the story of the evangelisation of the Franks. It was, in fact, Clotilde, the Burgundian princess who became Clovis' wife, who brought Catholic Christianity to the Franks.

Clotilde's is one of the first Christian examples of the kind of womanly influence we shall meet often throughout succeeding centuries. She moved from Burgundy to be married to Clovis, thus causing, in her own person, the blending of two cultures, two languages and two faiths. Over and over again, we see aristocratic women performing this function right through the so-called Dark and Middle Ages. They are often shuttled hundreds of miles from their own people in order to create beneficial marriage alliances, and are expected to make a success of this single-handedly. Obviously, such women have to be much more adaptable than their menfolk, and in the cases under study here, this adaptability served the Christian cause well.

Gregory of Tours tells us something of Clotilde's efforts to convert her husband and her household from paganism to Christianity. She persuaded her husband to allow her to have their first son baptised, but he died shortly afterwards. For Clovis, this proved the weakness of the Christian God, compared with his traditional pagan gods. Despite this, Clotilde had their second son, a sickly child, baptised, and as he continued to cling to life, she intensified her efforts to convert Clovis. Eventually, in the heat of battle, when defeat seemed assured, Clovis turned to the Christian God and was victorious. He began secret instructions with Bishop Remigius and eventually he was baptised, together with 3000 of his followers and a good number of his family. Clotilde accomplished what none of the clergy, Arian or Catholic, could seemingly bring about.

We are left in the dark about what kind of Christianity it was that could be so instantly assumed, but such stories abound at this period. What Clotilde needed was a combination of profound faith, nerves of steel and good luck. The God of the Christians had one main function in the life of a warrior king, and that was the persistent proving of his superior prowess in battle. One defeat could turn the tide of a nation's history, so one can only imagine the persistent encouragement and ingenuity required of Clotilde.

One result of his conversion was that Clovis received some recognition from the Eastern Emperor in far-off Constantinople. Clovis began to act like a 'new Constantine', and built a new church of the Twelve Apostles as proof of his new and exalted Christian status. Like Constantine, he built a new capital for himself in Paris, and, again like Constantine, he began to preside at church councils. He compiled and promulgated the famous Salic Law and took on all the characteristics of a Christian king. A new tradition was founded, and it is more than time to remember Clotilde's part in it.

Bertha

Both the Frankish historian, Gregory, and the Anglo-Saxon, Bede, contribute to the evangelising story of Queen Bertha of Kent about one hundred years later. Bertha was a Catholic Christian Frankish princess when married to the pagan Ethelbert of Kent sometime in the 570s. The marriage contract included a promise from Ethelbert that Bertha could practise her faith freely. She was accompanied to Kent by a private chaplain, Bishop Liudhard, and a small retinue of clergy. We are told that her husband gave her a church, 'built in ancient times while the Romans were still in Britain, next to the city of Canterbury, on its eastern side.'[8] Meantime, far off in Rome, Pope Gregory the Great was taking his fabled walk through the Roman slave market, and questioning the origin of the fair-haired young slaves he saw there. When he was told that they were Angles from Britain, he famously replied, 'Not Angles but Angels.' This, as suggested by Bede, has always been considered to be one of the main motives for the subsequent evangelising mission sent by Gregory to the court of King Ethelbert and Queen Bertha in 596. As Richard Fletcher points out, however, other sources imply that a request had come from Kent for help in evangelisation – and who would have been the source of this request, but Queen Bertha.[9] Bertha, after all, was the great-grandchild of Clotilde, and would have known of the female family tradition. At any rate, a letter exists from Pope Gregory thanking her for her part in the conversion of her husband. The arrival of Pope Gregory's envoy, Augustine of Canterbury, in 597, and his subsequent success in the Kentish mission is well known, but his fame has all but obliterated the memory of the woman who initiated the project. We are told that somewhere around Christmas Day, 597, King Ethelbert and ten thousand Englishmen were baptised. Pope Gregory wrote to congratulate the king, comparing him to Constantine – it is obvious that the Pope is intent on Romanising the English church, which after all, used to be part of the Roman Empire. Gregory compared Bertha, in his letter, to Helena, the mother of Constantine, and assured her that her fame had spread as far as

Constantinople. Canterbury now became a royal, Christian, and, to some extent, a Roman city. And, like their Roman imperial and royal Frankish predecessors, the Christian King and Queen of Kent began to write down and enact a new legal system for their people.

Ethelburga

Some thirty years later, a Christian princess from Kent, Ethelburga, together with her chaplain, Paulinus, went to Northumbria for her marriage to Edwin, the pagan king of the area. Edwin was a powerful warrior king and his gods had served him well. The mission was successful and Edwin was baptised on Easter Day, 627. The king founded the episcopal church of York, and Paulinus became its first bishop. But Edwin's conversion owed as much to household events and wifely persuasion as did that of Clovis and Ethelbert. It involved the safe delivery of Ethelburga's daughter and victory in battle. As a result of the victory, the daughter was baptised, and Edwin began instructions with Paulinus. The Pope of the day, Boniface V, wrote to both king and queen, praising her and encouraging him to join the faith 'of all the human race from the rising to the setting of the sun'. The Pope was being a bit premature in this seventh-century assessment of the state of Christianity, but he added to his persuasive powers by sending gifts of gold-embroidered robes for the king and a silver mirror and ivory comb for the queen.

* * *

In these three stories, we see the influence of three Christian princesses who were powerfully influential in introducing Christianity to their respective realms. That their stories have survived at all is amazing, but their influence has never been given the credit it deserves, from either a personal or historical perspective. History has come to be written as though the male actors functioned in a vacuum, but with this evidence, the point can easily be made that the Christianisation of Europe was effected by the faith of Christian women, who persisted in their faith in the most unpromising circumstances. The nature of this

Christianity remains a bit of a mystery, as does the Christianity
of the thousands who were baptised around their monarchs. We
are on a little firmer ground when we explore the next group of
women whose stories have survived from this 'dark age', the
abbesses. Here, we will confine ourselves to two, Radegund and
Hilda.

What kind of Christianity?

Before exploring the lives of these women, it is necessary to stand
back in order to gain some sense of the nature of Christianity as
practised by these new converts. With the collapse of the
Empire, organised religion also collapsed. It continued to survive in a fairly haphazard way, at the behest of local rulers,
urged on, as we have seen, by their wives. The sources for the
history of Christianity during this period are sparse. The information available to us describes an aristocratic Christianity,
which saw the faith as a servant of the state even more, perhaps,
than as a new way of life. War was the main occupation of these
tribes, to such an extent that violence was seen as natural and inevitable. Eventually, the monastic enclosure provided a haven
from violence for many women and men, especially for the sur-
plus females of the aristocratic houses. The form Christianity
took in these centuries, then, the way of being human that it offered its members, was as a means of surviving chaos, disruption, violence, pillage, hunger and rape. The fact that one lived
under a Christian king was no guarantee that life would be that
much different for most people. Eventually, however, some of
the more vicious forms of life were tamed by Christianity, and a
new web of relationships was built up between rulers and ruled.
The rulers owned the land and everything on it – including the
clergy, the churches and the monasteries – and, in return for
army service, agricultural work or prayer, they promised protection to their people. This new form of government was called
feudalism. Those who gave their services to the rulers were
called 'serfs', and took their place alongside the other slaves
who were war booty. Monasteries, since they were built, owned

and governed by aristocratic families, were run on the same principles. The same was true, to some extent, of the diocese. Our sources are even more sparse here, because the rulers were not going to allow powerful bishops to survive in their realms. For most of the population, Christianity was represented by the ministrations of the local monastery.

So the Christian gospel was being preached and heard in a wholly new setting, one that was little conducive to living a holy life. In order to carry out its functions, the church needed to be as powerful as the rulers. Hence, it needed land, wealth, armies and a host of servants to keep the institution thriving. Theoretically, all this wealth and power was to be at the service of the gospel, and the theory was never quite forgotten. In practice, however, wealth and power were often accumulated for their own sake, so that by the end of the seventh century, the church owned more than one quarter of the farmland of Europe. Bishops, abbots and abbesses received tithes from their holdings, and dispensed food and care to the needy. But the church now functioned as a big business and needed armies and warriors to defend its possessions. The system, though it may not look very 'Christian', did in fact work in that setting. The population grew healthier and infant mortality seemed to decline. The one major exception to this new web of relationships was the Jews. Throughout this period, pogroms increased and violence against the Jews became an accepted way of proving one's Christian faith, and also gaining new riches.

The great theological and liturgical symbolic structures of the patristic period were now scaled down to the bare minimum. Grace, salvation, conversion and the sacramental life were seen as concrete realities, to be bought and sold, touched and felt. The Christian God was required to prove his presence, power and ability to dispense gifts. In this setting, mass conversions are understandable. The people, in fact, did not have a choice. It is one of the great paradoxes of this period that this tribal form of Christianity was, at exactly the same time, being diluted by the practice of individual confession and spiritual direction introduced by the Irish monks. By this means, the notion of individual conscience and individual responsibility was being introduced, though this was, indeed, a very slow and gradual process. In the Dark Ages, God was seen as far removed from this earth and its cares, just like the kings and emperors. God, like his royal representatives on earth, had to be approached through a whole series of courtiers and representatives. No serf would think of approaching the ruler directly; similarly, no ordinary believer would think of approaching God directly. The monasteries and their holy inmates fulfilled the functions of intermediaries. Hence the value to any monastery of having a holy founder, holy members on earth and, especially, holy and sainted members in heaven. Lives of saints, and stories of their successful mediation abound at this period. Eventually, the numberless local saints give way to the holiest and most powerful of all intermediaries, the King's mother, the Blessed Virgin.

The sacraments of baptism and penance (as it came to be called) were re-designed as the main weapons against paganism. These were the tools used to enforce the transfer of loyalties from the old pagan and rural gods and superstitions to the new and more powerful God of the Christians. Confirmation, now completely separated from baptism and any initiation process, was used to bring each individual into contact with the bishop. After confirmation, people were numbered, named, registered and accountable. This development, of course, took place over centuries, and often the collection of tithes was more important than any spiritual outcome. It took several more centuries to sacramentalise marriage. Only the marriages of the nobility were regularly noted and celebrated publicly to ensure that lines of allegiance and inheritance were clearly known. The marriages of ordinary members of the population have left little record as to their nature, though it is likely that they were much more stable and enduring than aristocratic marriages. It would be difficult to name even one aristocratic Christian marriage, known to us from the sources, that was monogamous. Clothar, grandson of Clovis, had at least seven wives and even more concubines, as had Charlemagne, two hundred years later. Charlemagne refused, for dynastic reasons, to allow his daughters to marry, but he encouraged them to have as many concubines as they desired. The male/female relationship in concubinage was unambiguously sexual, and the offspring had no claim whatever to be considered legitimate. Hence another common cause of the use and abuse of monastic hospitality, by dispatching thence any unwanted children.

This was a layered society, the basis of an intensely hierarchical structure in the church. The lord and lady of the manor had the keys to the estates' storerooms. Likewise, bishop, abbot and abbess had the keys to the storehouse of God. The bishops, in particular, after the Cluniac and Gregorian reforms, became the administrators of both the spiritual and temporal things of God. The local priest was often an unlearned serf, one of the people, owned and married off at the lord's behest. Many church documents suggest that the least they should be able to do was recite the Pater Noster and the Creed. This was definitely not a society with well-run seminaries. In fact, the seminary as an institution is still almost one thousand years in the future. There are continuous attempts all through this period to impose celibacy on the clergy, with the intention of wresting power from the aristocracy and ensuring that church property would not be passed on by way of inheritance.

Most monasteries had libraries and we know that some bishops also prided themselves on the numerous books in their possession. But for most, life was too busy for reading. Practical learning was what was needed, not theoretical or historical lore. Parents passed on what lore they possessed, but the only centres of learning were the great monasteries. Here, as we shall see later, a nun like Hroswitha of Gandersheim could study all the Greek and Latin classics as well as many of the patristic writings. From around the seventh century, preaching manuals abound and contain endless moral exhortations and spectacular stories of saintly exploits. In general, the most popular form of preaching was the narrative of the lives of the saints. Christ was portrayed as an aristocratic king and conqueror who, like all kings, demanded the people's undivided allegiance. There is little sign of any biblical spirituality, and even the commandments are reduced to exhortations against family feuds, magic and superstition, sex during Lent or on the Sabbath, and resignation to one's lot in life.[10]

Monasticism

In the midst of this turbulent world, Celtic and then 'Benedictine' monasticism offered a genuine alternative. Here we will focus on the Benedictine variety, because of its long-lasting influence, and especially because whenever we speak of women's monasticism, it is the Benedictine tradition to which we refer.[11] In comparison, the sources for women's Celtic monasticism seem virtually non-existent. To this day, writers on the Celtic monastic tradition manage to convey the impression that, apart from Brigid, it was a totally male world.

Benedict lived from 480 to 547 and, though there has always been a great deal of controversy about his authorship of the rule that has always borne his name, we can safely proceed to acknowledge the centrality of this way of life to Western Christian identity. The Benedictine tradition for women has always been given a secondary role in monastic history, including, apparently, by Benedict himself.

The key to Benedict's system was moderation. The nun or monk was to work toward personal holiness through a balanced life of prayer, work, study, community life, good diet, separation from the world, and imitation of the life of Christ. It was designed as a stable, regular life, open to beginners in the spiritual journey. Unlike his Celtic brother founders, Benedict did not expect or desire any heroic feats of holiness. His way of life was to be common to all, and its one goal was conscious awareness of the presence of God at every moment of the day. The abbot/abbess functioned as a parental figure, and each member of the community engaged in a daily examination of conscience (a Celtic borrowing) and frequent revelation of the state of one's soul to one's director. Within the walls of the Benedictine monasteries, the liturgical 'work of God,' *Opus Dei*, progressed, day in and day out. Here, the liturgy was restored to its former beauty, with all the embellishments of music and chant – and even dance, as we know later from the Abbey of Hildegarde of Bingen. The liturgical calendar with its round of festivals was restored, and the availability in monasteries of scholarly resources added depth and meaning to these celebrations. It was about as far removed as possible from the normal violent life outside the walls.

We have seen something of the greatly undervalued role of wives in the evangelisation of Europe. It is time now to turn, first in general, then in particular, to the role of women. It is important to emphasise again that we are dealing here with aristocratic women, because they are the only people for whom we have sources. We are dealing, for the same reason, with nuns who, for a variety of reasons, have left the ordinary world for the life of the monastery. The lives of the vast majority of ordinary women and men are totally lost to us. We can assume, from the endless warfare, that most men grew up to fight – whether they liked it or not. The lives of women remain to us only in 'old wive's tales', a phrase used here with the utmost respect for an historical source rarely given the respect it deserves.

The monasteries of women played a role in the Dark Ages somewhat akin to the house-church of early Christianity.[12] The monastic institution served spiritual, educational and healing needs as well as acting as a safe house and providing general 'social work' services. Women entered these convents for a variety of reasons. Some entered voluntarily at the age of consent, which at this period was around the age of twelve. Later, in the thirteenth century, fifteen was the established age. But we know that some entered even earlier. Hildegarde of Bingen, being the tenth child of her family, was offered as a tithe to the local monastery at the age of five. The unmarried daughters of the nobility who lacked marriage dowries were often consigned to monasteries for reasons of safety as well as economy. The monastery also offered shelter to women in trouble for a variety of reasons, including women suffering from physical disabilities. Some, of course, entered in response to a perceived call from God, and often these women experienced the greatest difficulty. They had to defy their parents and refuse to enter into marriage arrangements. One of the main interventions of bishops on behalf of women was to come between the young woman and her family in these, often bloody, confrontations.

A dowry was essential for entering the monastic life. Economic survival was always a cause of distress in women's monasteries. Women had access to far fewer financial resources than men, and as enclosure became more and more the norm, women's monastic communities had to be entirely self-sufficient. One can see the advantage of being visited by grateful pilgrims and anxious suppliants. Inevitably, nuns were graded according to the size of their dowries and family endowments, so that the social hierarchy outside the convent prevailed inside as well. A widow was universally preferred as abbess. It was assumed that she would have had experience in running a household and in dealing with men, whether secular or ecclesiastical lords.

Every monastery of women was dependent on men for sacramental and liturgical ministry, and such relationships were often hostile in the extreme. There are endless stories of verbal battles and actual military encounters between abbesses and bishops, and even of nuns studying canon law so that they could outwit their ecclesiastical opponents.

The life of the convent was, at its best, a prayerful round of work, liturgy, meditation, *lectio divina,* and study. All convents had bakeries, breweries, scriptoria, guest-houses, farms and tenants, and, in fact, functioned like small towns.

All monks, female and male, took vows of poverty, chastity and obedience, as well as stability. The vows were designed as a framework for living the *vita apostolica* and the imitation of the life of Christ. The vow of poverty meant that all things were held in common and that individuals owned little but the clothes on their back. Each year, on the feast of Martin of Tours, November

11, all Benedictines were given a new set of clothing, and the old ones were given to the poor. Dowry and endowment supplied the economic needs of most monasteries and the temptation to welcome only the wealthy must have been overwhelming. Many sources tell us that families left bequests to feed and clothe their own daughters during their lifetime. After death, the money went into the community coffers. Men had much more access to income, particularly later, when most monks were ordained priests. The Cluniac monastic reform introduced the celebration of Masses for the dead and this innovation added enormously to the wealth of male monasteries. It was well known that simony, the buying and selling of holy things, was forbidden, but donations were always welcome.

The vow of chastity entailed a solemn renunciation of the right to marry and engage in sexual relations of any kind. In male monasteries there was always fear of homosexuality, but lesbianism, since it did not entail the spilling of male seed, one of the foundational issues in sexual ethics, was not seen as a crime against nature. Endless stories narrate sexual horrors in monasteries, but one visitation record from the twelfth century gives the lie to much of this – at least in one bishop's domain. Bishop Eudes Tigaud visited the monastic institutions in his diocese in 1249 and reports that 90% of the monks and nuns were faithful to their vows of chastity. He remarks that women are more easily detected in chastity aberrations than men, not only because of pregnancy, but because, of necessity, they are less mobile than men and cannot escape the consequences of their actions. This, of course, refers to a much later period, but whether observed or not, the ideals were the same in the sixth century.

The vow of obedience entailed the renouncing of one's will in order to recognise and submit to the will of God in the Rule, and in the voice of the abbot/abbess. Many breakdowns in obedience happened as a result of poor leadership, or when two rival families were competing to place their own daughter or son as monastic superior. The abbot/abbess was in a powerful position, having well-nigh absolute control over the lives of all in the monastery. A system of episcopal visitation was instituted to offset any abuse of such power. The role of the abbess entailed great skill in what we would call human relations, given the motley nature of those living under her authority, and the abbesses whom we shall meet in the course of the next few chapters do, indeed, demonstrate their authority in brilliant ways.

Radegund

We return now to Radegund, who was seen for centuries as the model nun. She was a Thuringian princess, captured in battle by the Franks in 531 at the age of seven, together with her brother. They were the only surviving members of their family and were given as booty to the vicious King Clothar, son of Clovis. Clothar reared Radegund to become his bride, having killed her brother in her presence to scare her into submission. They were married in 540. Clothar was a polygamist several times over and Radegund practised a kind of passive resistance in the marriage, refusing to co-operate in his excesses. In an attempt to escape the situation, she begged the local bishop to consecrate her as a deaconess. On his refusal, she consecrated herself and ran away to one of the royal country villas, which she turned into a hospital. When her husband tried to recapture her, she escaped to Paris where Bishop Germain gave her a warmer welcome. As can be imagined, this was no easy decision for a bishop, earning as it did the wrath of one of the most powerful rulers of the Franks. Eventually, Germain persuaded Clothar to free Radegund from the marriage and a convent was founded for her at Poitiers. Radegund refused the role of abbess and lived the rest of her life in a hermitage attached to the walls of the convent. She died in 587. She outlived her husband by twenty-six years, but remained in close contact with the royal family. We have two accounts of her life, one by her convent friend Baudonivia, the other by her admirer, the poet-Bishop Venantius Fortunatus.

The Rule that Radegund adopted for her convent was one that Caesarius, Bishop of Arles, had written for his sister. One wonders again if this is another case of false attribution. The convent he eventually had built for her was a strongly fortified edifice and he insisted on complete claustration for the nuns, in part for their own safety. These precautions, understandably, appealed to Radegund as, for her, the monastery was most definitely a sanctuary of peace. Her biographer and friend, Baudonivia, tells us that Radegund was so insistent on peace and quiet in the cloister that she commanded a bird to stop squawking and shattering the evening's peace. The life was strictly communal, and even gifts of food from one's family had to be shared with the whole community. We are told that Radegund participated fully in the daily work of the community, taking her turn in the kitchen, carrying wood and water, cleaning the latrines and even polishing her sisters' shoes. This humble behaviour of a former queen did not fail to attract beneficial attention to the convent of St Croix at Poitiers. All convent officials were elected democratically and the abbess was advised to meet daily with her sisters for consultation and advice. It was standard monastic exhortation to suggest that the least of the sisters might come forward with the best idea. Despite these democratic ideals, however, the abbess was usually the highest born member of the community, since it was likely that this arrangement assured the greatest stability.

Even though Radegund was not the abbess of Poitiers, she, the former queen, continued to wield enormous influence in the community. It was she who organised the huge relic collection for the community, which was the envy of all. It was also Radegund who used her royal connections to request a relic of the true cross from Constantinople. This would definitely assure the future of her convent as a centre of cult and pilgrimage. Her friend, Venantius Fortunatus wrote the famous hymn *Vexilla Regis prodeunt* for this occasion and huge pomp and circumstance accompanied the arrival of the relic at Poitiers. Thus, one source of revenue was assured for the convent. Radegund also had miraculous help in maintaining the convent provisions. We are told of a jar of wine that was never empty. Such stories of food and drink multiplication are common for abbesses, and in-

creased both the pressures on convent hospitality and also gifts
as an expression of gratitude. Radegund cared for her visitors in
lavish ways. Their feet were washed, fresh bedding was prepared, huge banquets were served, and wonderful liturgies celebrated. Radegund washed and dried the faces of the sick with
her own hands. All this served to add to the convent's fame and
reputation.

We are fortunate to have two biographies of Radegund, significantly by male and female authors. Venantius Fortunatus
emphasises what he considers appropriate virtues in a woman,
namely humility, hatred of her femaleness and endless attempts
to erase all signs of it through horrific mortifications. This male
evaluation of what constituted a woman's holiness was to be an
ongoing feature of male writing. Baudonivia, on the other hand,
portrays Radegund as a strong, emotional woman, who as well
as caring for the needs of the monastery, kept her eye on the affairs of the kingdom. Within the convent, she is presented as ap-
proachable, delighting in teaching all and explaining the scriptures even to the most timid. Radegund assumed the role of
peacemaker, both within and outside her community. She instructed her sisters to pray unceasingly for the stability of the
kingdom. While she acted as a loving mother to all, Radegund
did not tolerate any resistance to the regular life of the
monastery – even from animals. Baudonivia recounts the tale of
the poor mouse who was about to bite the thread with which
Radegund was sewing sacred vestments. Its sacrilegious jaws
were closed forever before any harm was done.

When Radegund died, there were over 200 nuns at Poitiers.
Gregory of Tours arrived to perform the funeral rites and found
the nuns ravaged with grief at the death of their founder and
patron. 'We gave up our parents and friends and country and
followed you.' There follows a delightful description of life
within the convent at Poitiers:

Here we found gold and silver; here we knew flowering
vines and leafy plants; here were fields flowering with riot-
ous blossom. From you we took violets: you were the blush-

ing rose and the white lily. You spoke in words bright as the
sun, and as the moon against the darkness, you burned as a
lamp with the light of truth. But now, it is all darkness with
us ...

Well they might mourn, not just from affection, but from un-
ease as to what lay ahead. They had lived well on the royal riches.
But Radegund's fame assured that after her death her cult
would develop quickly. Several miraculous cures occurred at
her funeral. She was very quickly venerated as a saint, and her
feast is still celebrated in many parts of France on August 13.
Radegund, who was queen, scholar, deaconess, hermit, miracle
worker, founder and peacemaker, soon became the model for all
nuns in the West.[13]

Hilda

Radegund was almost an exact contemporary of the great
Columba of Iona, who was so instrumental in evangelising
Scotland and the north of England in the spirit of Celtic
Christianity. Columba died in 597, the year when Roman mis-
sionaries were dispatched to Canterbury. About twenty years
later, as we have seen, in 619, Bishop Paulinus accompanied
Ethelburga north from Kent to be the bride and evangeliser of
King Edwin. He was eventually baptised into the Roman form
of Christianity in 627. Thirty years later, Edwin's great-niece,
Hilda, became the first abbess of the double monastery at
Whitby, where the eventual confrontation between the two
forms of Christianity occurred. When Hilda died in 680, she was
succeeded by Aelffled, the daughter of King Oswy, the founder
of Whitby. So Christianity, in the north of England was very
much a royal affair. Hilda is one of about twenty royal nuns
named in the pages of Bede's massive history, and her story
stands out among them all. Nevertheless, following the pattern
we have seen, we have no word from Hilda herself and Bede
tells us exactly what he thinks we ought to know.

Hilda received knowledge of the faith directly from

Paulinus, and was baptised on that famous Easter Day of 627 when King Edwin accepted Christianity. Eventually, after becoming abbess of Hartlepool, she was frequently visited and assiduously instructed by the great Aidan of Lindisfarne. So Hilda was well prepared to take on the task of abbess of Whitby or Streanaeshalch, as it was then called. She was already known all over Britain as one of the 'ornaments of Northumbria', not only for her extraordinary knowledge, but also for her charity, meekness and humility. It is no surprise then that, under her leadership, Whitby became a great centre of learning. At least five bishops and endless numbers of theologians and scholars credit Whitby as their *alma mater*. Hilda's zeal for learning led her to build a vast library at Whitby and eventually she is famed for encouraging Caedmon, the first English poet, then but a cowherd on the abbey farm.

It was Hilda's good fortune to live at a momentous time in the Christianising of Britain. There was unlimited scope for a woman of her talents and fortunate background, such as later Christian women have rarely enjoyed. As was the case before among the Franks, the conversion of a king did not automatically guarantee the survival of the faith. Stable environments, such as those provided by Hilda's double monastery, were an essential feature for the rooting of the new faith among the populace. The course of Christianity had not run smoothly in Edwin's kingdom. He himself was killed in battle in 633, and the sons of his former rival, Oswald and Oswy, took over the kingdom. During Edwin's life, these young men had fled to the Irish/Scottish province of Dal Riada and come under the influence of Celtic Christianity. They both became kings of Northumbria, first Oswald and then Oswy. It was in their reigns that Hilda's fame as a very able and holy abbess spread all over Britain or, as Bede put it, 'the splendor of her light' lit up all of Britain.[14]

Bede tells us that, in imitation of the Celtic Church, Hilda was guided principally by the scriptures in the setting up of her monastery. The old egalitarian ideal of equality between women and men seemed to return for a while in this well-run double monastery. We know hardly anything of the details of living at Whitby, but such joint efforts were extremely beneficial to women. The double monastery was almost always headed by a woman, perhaps following the earlier *agapetae,* who used the example of John taking Mary 'into his own household' as model for their lives.[15] During the early centuries of Christianity, as a result of the widespread practice of virginal asceticism, the separation of the sexes seemed to have been overcome. Female and male ascetics lived together, sometimes even sharing the same quarters, in the firm belief that the angelic life of virginity would prevail. The practice seems to have been widespread, even though roundly denounced by Jerome, Augustine and others for its obvious dangers. Such experimental living arrangements continued, however, to be very attractive to women in monasticism. It allowed for the leadership of women, as Mary obviously would have taken precedence over John, and also provided on-site sacramental and liturgical services for the women and relieved them of much hazardous ecclesiastical negotiation. Hilda seems to have chosen to continue a monastic existence deriving from the *agapetae* tradition. The one certain fact about Whitby is its emphasis on education and scholarship. The study of the scriptures was central, not only in theory, but Hilda insisted on the actual living out of the scriptural injunctions to lives of poverty, humility and service. There is no small likelihood that Whitby was intended by Aidan, Oswy, and perhaps Hilda herself to serve as a seminary for the training of local clergy in the Celtic way of Christianity.

Whitby also seems to have been a centre for what we might call today pastoral catechesis, and Hilda's encouragement of the cowherd-poet, Caedmon, was probably designed toward this end. Hilda herself took on a good deal of the instruction both within and in the environs of the monastery. Besides, kings, princes and scholars came to Whitby from far and wide to benefit from her learning and the opportunities provided there. In the great synod of Whitby in 664, Hilda needed all her learning and diplomacy to maintain her reputation for holiness while defending the losing Celtic side. The matter of moment was the date of Easter, with the Celts following their ancient dating system, and the Romans trying to impose a formula that would never allow the Christian Easter to fall on the same day as the Jewish Passover. In fact, this was just the tip of an ice-berg of differing perspectives between two ecclesiastical traditions. The issue, at base, was the power of Rome and the eventual Romanising of the whole of British Christianity. The Roman tradition was rooted in the power of the bishop and his episcopal see rather than the role of the abbess/abbot and the monastery. This was an issue rooted in the past, but definitely looking toward the future.

In Northumbria, the debate also took on a very personal and political dimension. King Oswy, trained in the Celtic style during his youthful exile, was married to Eanfled, who had been taught and baptised by Paulinus, in the Roman style. As Bede tells us, it sometimes happened that the king was celebrating the resurrection while the queen was still observing the Lenten fast.[16] To complicate matters, the famous Wilfrid of Lindisfarne defended the queen's side while Colman, Aidan's successor, defended the Celtic way. Wilfrid, having started out observing the Celtic way of monasticism, set up by Aidan at Lindisfarne, was regarded as a traitor. One visit to Rome had changed him and he had succeeded in turning Oswy's sons to his way of thinking. Indeed, it was a case of the younger generation against the older. Hilda, a lover of Celtic monasticism, had moved in the other direction, having started out in the Roman style. So when King Oswy summoned all to the Synod at Whitby, the issue of Easter, though important then, simply served to conceal many other agendas.

Kings, queens, bishops, abbots and scholars attended this great synod on Hilda's home turf. The result was a foregone conclusion. The Roman side won, but the haughtiness of the young Wilfrid and his obvious contempt for all things Celtic gained many enemies, both for himself and the church he represented. Wilfrid is reputed to have insulted the Celts by telling them that they were 'stupidly contending against the whole world'. Wilfrid invoked St Peter as his authority and challenged Colman to find a Celtic authority of superior worth. To everyone's intense disappointment, the Celtic side gave in gracefully, perhaps under the leadership of the abbess/host, Hilda. Colman and many of the Celts went into voluntary exile rather than publicly challenge the Roman way, but one gets the impression that they continued to observe their native ways till they died. Fifteen years later, we hear of an attempt by Hilda to depose Wilfrid, now the Abbot/Bishop of Lindisfarne. We do not know the exact details of this particular debate, but the pomp and ceremony of Lindisfarne under Wilfrid contrasted sharply with the gospel simplicity adopted by Hilda for her territory. Besides, Wifrid had an ally right at the heart of Hilda's community because Oswy's widow, Eanfled had joined the monastery after her husband's death. She had been preceded there by her daughter, Aelffled, beloved of Hilda, and her successor as abbess.

In recounting the story of Hilda, one feels a real sense of loss in knowing virtually nothing about her own thoughts and beliefs. We can only be impressed that in such contentious times, even those who disagreed with her continue to speak of her only with the greatest respect. Bede was one such, having no love for the Celtic way of Christianity. Another Synod under Aelffled in 706 succeed in reconciling all the warring parties. Hilda had died in 680, still teaching on her death-bed. The monastery was destroyed by invading Danes around 867, was rebuilt in the twelfth century, and eventually ruined during the monastic dissolution in 1540. The ruins are still impressive, even though little remains of Hilda's old home. It is a fitting tribute to the grace of her tenure that one of the recent archaeological findings from her time is the remains of some harps. A contemporary poem seems to sum up much of what we can learn, if only by implication, about the life of Hilda. The words are put into Hilda's mouth as a homily:

Trade with the gifts God has given you
Bend
your minds to holy learning you
may escape the fretting moth
of littleness of mind
that would wear out
your souls.
Brace your wills to action
that they may not be
the spoils of weak desires.
Train your hearts and lips to song
gives courage to the soul.
Being buffeted by trials, learn to laugh.
Being reproved, give thanks.
Having failed, determine to succeed.[17]

CHAPTER 9

Women as Monastic Missionaries

Leoba arose from prayer and, as if she had been challenged to a contest, flung off the cloak which she was wearing and boldly opened the doors of the church. Standing on the threshold, she made a sign of the cross, opposing to the fury of the storm the name of the High God.[1]

It is not expedient for that sex to enjoy the freedom of having its own governance – because of its natural fickleness and also because of outside temptations which womanly weakness is not strong enough to resist.[2]

Consciously or unconsciously, they swept women out of their way as they re-organised their official world.[3]

The right to self-development and social responsibility which the woman of today so persistently asks for, is in many ways analogous to the right which the convent secured to womanhood a thousand years ago.[4]

Throughout the ninth and tenth centuries, there were two periods of intense ecclesiastical reform, first the so-called Carolingian, originating in the imperial court of Charlemagne, and secondly, the Cluniac, originating in the exempt monastery of Cluny. Conventional histories usually greet these reform moments with enthusiasm and relief as bringing only benefit to the Christian church. Such ecclesiastical reforms, however, are rarely good news for women. As the third opening quotation above indicates, official ecclesiastical reform tends to sweep women aside.

These two reform movements are particularly significant for the history of women in the Christian context, as they laid the foundation for the further removal of women from the position of partnership, envisaged by Galatians 3:26-27, to the malign position of temptress and endangerment to the institutional

Christian church. It is particularly ironic and tragic that it was in the centuries immediately preceding and accompanying these reforms that women in the monastic setting reached the highest point of partnership and shared authority in their position of abbess. These women acted publicly and often spectacularly with power and authority, often as abbesses of double monasteries, and just as often with what Joan Morris has termed 'quasi-episcopal' power.[5]

The ninth century, then, sees the deepening of the great male weariness with women's ecclesial partnership, and this eventually reveals itself in some of the most misogynistic writing in Christian history. Instead of missionary partner and pastoral collaborator, monastic women are reduced to virtual invisibility through the imposition of cloister. As the religious and political need for clerical celibacy is voiced more strongly, and as increasingly monks are ordained as clerics, the public role of women is reduced to one of temptress. Much of this discussion ignores the very existence of the vast majority of women, but some brief glimpse of their lives can be gained through the spate of ninth century writing on marriage. This is the period when ecclesiastical reform begins to reach out to this most intractable of human institutions, and bishops become marriage counsellors as they try to sort through the amazing diversity of marriage custom and practice.

This chapter, then, will explore both the high points and low points of women's ecclesial involvement in these centuries. Of necessity, the story is hugely hampered by the availability of sources. The voices of women themselves are almost universally absent and silent. Their lives have to be cobbled together from the relevant fragments of canon law, synodal decree, royal and imperial annals and monastic rule. These sources are abundant, but their concern is not with women. Nevertheless, from a rereading of these documents, from the occasional male biography of significant women, such as Leoba, and from some amazingly tenacious devotional traditions, such as that of the cult of Frideswide, founder of Oxford, we can glimpse the lives and influence of some early medieval women. Very occasionally, too, we find something from the pen of women. Even here, the voice is shrouded in cultural and spiritual pre-supposition, but the writings of women such as Dhuoda and Hugeberc, open for us a broad spectrum of womanly involvement far removed from the institutional preoccupations of the ecclesiastical reformers.

Germanic Christianity

The centuries from the death of Pope Gregory in 604 until the Cluniac reform at the beginning of the tenth century have always been considered as something of a liability to the Christian church. These were centuries of turbulence, with warring princes, nomadic tribes in search of land and, as a consequence, the use of the papacy as a pawn by Eastern Goths, Byzantine Emperors, and Frankish and Lombard princes. The theory of the papacy was not in doubt, but the actual occupants of the See of Rome were reduced to virtual helplessness. For the papacy, the worst lay ahead, as we shall see, after the collapse of the Carolingian Empire at the end of the ninth century. Before the papacy had worked out, in the person of Pope Gregory VII, that moral authority was the only reliable basis for its ecclesiastical and social dominance, it had become the plaything of whatever faction ruled Rome. In many ways, these were indeed Dark Ages, but the seeds of Western Christian culture were sown here. Even more appositely for the history of women, this was, for a time, an age of unprecedented and unmatched female influence.

The focus of interest for this period is the land of Northern Europe conquered and occupied by the Germanic tribes whom we have already encountered. The chain of monasteries, founded by Columbanus and other Celtic missionaries, together with the growing Benedictine influence, still served to bind Europe together. Both Celt and German treated their womenfolk with much greater respect than their Mediterranean neighbours, and Christianity offered these women new and unforeseen opportunities. Many historians call this church the *Adelskirche*, or church of the aristocracy, for several reasons. First of all, the nobles are the only ones to leave any kind of written sources, but also because most Christian missionaries worked on the 'trickle down' theory. This was a belief that if the nobles were converted, the people would follow. Since the people did not have much choice in the matter, this evangelising method proved somewhat successful. On the other hand, the 'threshold between the world of secular nobleman and that of the noble prelate was not difficult to negotiate'.[6] The event of conversion was seen as a reciprocal event: both missionary and aristocrat stood to gain. As we have seen all along, the contribution of women in this task of evangelisation was indispensable. Aristocracy and wealth preceded gender in the evaluation of women and the Christian vision of shared ministry still held sway, to some extent, in practice in the Adelskirche. As long as the monastery, as opposed to the celibate episcopacy, was the main *locus* of Christian mission, the role of women was acknowledged and promoted.

The church of the aristocracy presents us with a unique picture of ecclesiastical life. Germanic princes, though often fervent Christians in their own and in their contemporaries' estimation, believed that they owned the church in their domain and had a right to govern it. When they endowed monasteries and churches and then placed family members as abbots, abbesses and bishops, they knew that they still retained the use of and profit from this land. Giving land and riches to the church was a very shrewd way of assuring that that land remained exactly where it was. This period, then, sees an abundance of lay rulers in monasteries and dioceses. Many of these rulers were women, and when they ruled, it was assumed that they had authority and power over all in their territories, monks, nuns and clergy included. Often too, noblewomen chose to join the communities, and it was automatically assumed that they would become the ruling abbess of their chosen and endowed community. These aristocratic women were no strangers to power and the tasks of administration, and they easily assumed the symbols of authority recognised by their societies. Hence the description 'quasi-episcopal abbess' for their role. These abbesses dressed and acted in an episcopal style and, apart from the ordination of priests, seem to have assumed easily all other episcopal tasks.

Quasi-episcopal Abbesses

Joan Morris elaborates on the history of these women, and, though subsequent research has clarified the picture somewhat, her account still shines with the record of these women.[7] Titles unheard of before or since were used to describe Abbess Ebba of Coldingham and Abbess Etheldreda of Ely. Both were called *Sacerdos Maximus*, a clearly episcopal designation. Such women are shown wearing mitre and ring and using the episcopal crozier as of right. Both these monasteries flourished for centuries until destroyed by the Vikings in 866. Similarly, the canonesses of Clerkenwell had rights over eleven counties around London and sixty-four parish territories within the city, together with all tithes and revenues. They were responsible for hiring, firing and remunerating the clergy.[8] For centuries, canonesses were distinguished from nuns in a monastic setting. The canonesses are, in fact, a bit of a mystery, but they seem to be a kind of Western descendant of the women's diaconate, and likewise forerunners of the Beguines of the thirteenth century. These women lived a more public life than women in monasteries. The canonesses were usually attached to a cathedral or principal church. They engaged in ministries of charity and teaching and were involved in the celebration of the liturgy. Their vows of celibacy were temporary, not permanent, and they took no vow of poverty. This state of life often seemed particularly suitable to royal and aristocratic women who could continue to administer family estates while pursuing the spiritual path of their choice.

Similar institutions flourished on the continent, such as the Royal Abbey at Jouarre, Chelles and Faremoutier, the last mentioned having been originally founded by Columbanus. These abbeys functioned like small states for centuries, with the abbess having the right to strike her own coinage for use on their vast domains. The Abbess of Jouarre insisted on her right to exempt status for centuries, that is, the right to owe allegiance directly to the pope and not to the local bishop. Needless to say, this provoked endless disputes. After one abbess was excommunicated for refusing to obey the local bishop, her successor conveniently found new 'ancient' documents proving the monastery's right to exemption. She was reconfirmed in 1225. Jouarre continued to have a disputatious time of it right up to the end of the seventeenth century when Bishop Bossuet finally prevailed against them and took over the abbey. Jouarre was destroyed during the French revolution, but has now been rebuilt and continues to function as an abbey.[9] Similar stories pertain to monasteries such as Quedlinburg in Germany where the abbesses had control of the 'whole town, its people, churches, hospitals, clergy, canons and canonesses and all other religious orders'. Here, the abbess was even called Metropolitana, and held the jurisdiction of a bishop.[10] Morris' book is rife with such examples, and serves, at the very least, to challenge contemporary affirmations about traditional teaching on women's divinely ordained submissive and private role, and their non-ordainable status.

It is important to keep repeating that the sources for this period simply skim the surface of life in these turbulent centuries, and describe only the life of the aristocracy. But, as historians continue to observe, later memories and saintly cults are rooted in some substance. We may never know the exact origin of some of these traditions, but the tenacity of the memories testifies to women of very powerful influence.

Frideswide

Such is the memory of Frideswide (680-727), the monastic founder of Oxford, whose memory and veneration survived even the attempts of Henry VIII to destroy its very traces. Frideswide seems to have presided over a double monastery at Oxford in the early eighth century. She was the daughter of the local king, Didan, and her story follows the now familiar one of complete resistance to her family's attempt to marry her off for dynastic reasons. She fled into the local forest near Oxford and when her suitor pursued her, he was struck blind. Hence, says her biographer, 'the kings of England were in dread of entering or lodging in that town since it is said to bring destruction'. Thus the origin of a very useful tale to keep royal interference away

from Oxford.[11] Frideswide healed her former and now repentant suitor, and proceeded to found her monastery at the site of
the present Christ Church, from the proceeds of her inherited
royal wealth.

Frideswide's story is full of the miraculous – she seemed to
be especially skilled in curing 'women's problems' – and is also
linked to a whole woodland mythology about the 'Green
woman'. She is said to have predicted her death on Sunday,
October 19, 727, but had her grave dug on the Saturday, so that
no one would have to break the sabbath laws. The continuous
celebration of her feast throughout the centuries is astonishing.
Chaucer mentions her feast-day and we are told that Catherine
of Aragon visited her shrine in 1518. During the Dissolution, the
shrine of Frideswide was destroyed in 1528 – perhaps as revenge
for the ongoing kingly fear of blindness. In 1562, however, a
black marble slab was installed in the floor of Christ Church,
now the Anglican Cathedral of the Oxford Diocese, and this can
still be seen. In the Latin Chapel of this same cathedral, the
events of Frideswide's life are illustrated in the windows. Each
October 19, her memory is celebrated at Oxford by both 'town
and gown', and her name is memorialised in several other
churches and schools in the area. Unfortunately, the story of
Frideswide is not otherwise well known despite the fact that she
is the one 'whose leadership was the initial heartbeat of ecclesial,
academic and civic life in Oxford'.[12] The fairly lengthy comment
by the well-known medieval historian, Richard Southern, is
worth quoting in full:

> And yet, out of this turmoil and disaster, there emerged in an
> incredibly short space of time a new literature, poetry, history,
> sculpture, architecture, and missionary activity abroad – all
> of them closely connected with or emerging from the early
> religious communities founded by the saints of that time like
> S. Frideswide … The second point, equally extraordinary
> and unexpected, is that women played a very large part in
> these new creations. I say it is extraordinary because it was
> pre-eminently a time of war, violence, and feuds – the worst

possible time for women. And yet women, like Frideswide, emerged as organisers of joint male and female communities under the government of women, holding up the religious life of the community, administering large tracts of country, and encouraging complicated social and scholarly enterprises; responsible for large-scale enterprises to an extent never again possible for women in European history until the present day.[13]

The ancient and beautiful site for another monastic foundation dating from this period is familiar to many people from its use as one of the settings for the movie, *The Sound of Music*. This is Nonnburg (Nuns' Mountain) in Salzburg, founded in 700 by the Abbess Erentrude on the site of an old Roman fortress. From Nonnburg, the daughter abbey of Eichstatt in Bavaria was founded under the patronage of St Walburga, and it is from this venerable site that the Benedictine sisters of the United States took their origin, over one thousand years later, in 1852.

Walburga

Walburga's life spans most of the eighth century (710-799). She was an Anglo-Saxon princess from the south of England, sister of the great missionaries Willibald and Wunnibald and niece of the Apostle of Germany, Boniface. The story of Walburga links us with an astonishing network of family relationships which set the groundwork for the conversion of the Saxons in Germany, considered to be kinfolk. Walburga serves also to introduce us to the great Abbess Tetta and her remarkable double monastery at Wimborne in Wessex.

When Walburga started her religious life in Wimborne, at the age of ten, there were already five hundred nuns there, all engaged in a remarkable regime of prayer, study and eventually training for the great missionary enterprise ahead – nothing less than the conversion of Germany. Volumes could be written on these women but, unfortunately, we have space for only a few short words on one or two, with a little more time on the great

Leoba, perhaps the most famous graduate of Wimborne, and the writer, Hugeberc, who chronicled in her own hand some of the missionary travels. One of the amusing stories repeated in many places of the Abbey at Wimborne, tells of a group of young nuns dancing for sheer joy on the grave of their deceased and very strict novice-mistress. It is said that, after their celebration, the grave sank several inches and needed a miracle from Abbess Tetta to restore it to its proper dimensions.[14]

Walburga spent about thirty years at Wimborne before joining her brother, the missionary Wunnibald, at the monastery in Heidenheim in Bavaria. On his death in 781, she inherited the monastery and ruled it as abbess for the next twenty years. Walburga was a wise and learned abbess, noted for her healing powers, and particularly for her gift for taming wolves. After her death, her bones were moved several times, but finally were interred in the Church of the Holy Cross in Eichstatt, where they still rest. Walburga has always been known as one of the myroblyte saints, that is one of those from whose remains a healing oil flows.

Hugeberc

The only one of this throng of holy women from whom we have anything written in her own hand is Hugeberc, Abbess of Hildesheim, and this writing, called the *Hodoeporicon*, is one of the first travelogues in the German language. Hugeberc tells us that she began her writing on the summer solstice of the year 778. Her relative, Bishop Willibald (brother of Walburga whom we have already met), had travelled widely, and when he visited Hugeberc in her double monastery, he recounted stories of his travels. These were recorded by Hugeberc and remain today as one of the chance survivals from that distant age. It takes the form of a guide for pilgrims to the Holy Land, including almost every possible shrine on the way, but it also records the main details of Willibald's life and his missionary activity in Germany.

The act of writing has always been seen by the Christian church as a rare and audacious act for women, and so it is no surprise that Hugeberc becomes one of a long line of Christian women writers who make a point of belittling her own work. This was an act of survival. Women chose to discredit themselves in order to deflect the attention of a patriarchal church. Hugeberc, then, introduces herself as an 'unworthy sister of Saxon origin, last and least in life and manners'.[15] In fact, like a contemporary designer of crosswords, she hid her name in a cryptogram, which was deciphered only recently.

Like most travelogues, the book itself is not of absorbing interest, but does give us an extraordinary insight into the experiences of young Anglo-Saxon men travelling through Saracen countries, and their mutual curiosity about each others' lives. What is of absorbing interest, however, is the revelation in her writing by Hugeberc of her self-confidence, her scholarship, her astute judgements on Willibald's behaviour, and the vivid example of the ease of relationships that prevailed at this time between the Anglo-Saxon women and men who had left their homes to evangelise Germany. What is also remarkable, and is, in fact, remarked on by many historians, is the interest taken by women in book-making, in recording for posterity the events going on around them, and in the historical relevance of their location in that place and that time. She tells us that she 'writes for posterity', despite the fact that 'as a weak woman' she does not judge herself to have the necessary experience or skill. Meanwhile, this woman is abbess of a double monastery and more than likely administering estates such as we have seen in the lives of other quasi-episcopal abbesses. Nevertheless, the act of writing, of giving voice as a woman, is still seen as a dangerous enterprise.

Towards the end of her account, Hugeberc describes the investing of another Willibald with the 'sacred authority of the episcopate' by Boniface, and the founding of the monastery of Eichstatt on land donated to Boniface. Here, missionaries were trained 'with gentleness and sympathy' to work all over Germany. Eventually, God's word was preached successfully through the land of Bavaria which was 'dotted with churches, priests' houses and the relics of the saints'. The result is a charming but fairly idealised picture in the light of its subsequent history. 'From these places antiphons now resound, sacred lessons are chanted, a noble throng of believers shout aloud the miracles of Christ and with joyful hearts echo from mouth to mouth triumphant praises of their Creator.'[16]

This missionary picture of Hugeberc paints Bavaria as a kind of aristocratic monastic heaven. From her account, however, one would not guess at the importance of women missionaries to the whole enterprise. It is in the life of Leoba and her Anglo-Saxon companions that we gain some sense of their importance to the greatest German missionary of them all, Wynfrith, later called Boniface. There was a tradition that Anglo-Saxon women, who were married as political pawns to kings of hostile conquered tribes, were given the name of 'peace-weavers'. The women missionaries who set off courageously about the task of evangelisation deserve a no less honorific title.[17]

Boniface

First of all, however, Boniface must claim our attention. He is one of the fortunate few from the past whose memory has survived in some detail because his voluminous correspondence fortuitously survived. Like Paul before him, the name of Boniface tends to eliminate the memories and labours of his predecessors and co-workers. When Boniface entered the German mission-field in 716, it was an arena that had been successively evangelised previously by Irish, English, Spanish and Frankish missionaries. Boniface worked tirelessly and with extraordinary commitment, but his agenda differed substantially from his predecessors and even his co-workers.[18]

Wynfrith was born in Wessex in 680, and though we know that he spent almost forty years in England, the details of his early life are sketchy and contradictory. At any rate, his biographer, Willibald, describes him, from the start, as a totally committed Benedictine monk trained in the monasteries of Exeter and Nursling, though some of the details do not sound

Benedictine. Whatever the details of his origins, it seems that, from the beginning, the eyes of Boniface were fixed on Rome. He is said to have intensely disliked the Irish monks, but he did learn from them the missionary value of the monastic foundation. It was Pope Gregory II who gave Wynfrith his missionary commission and his new name, Boniface. Now he was a Roman Christian monk and, in 722, he was consecrated a missionary bishop, with a kind of roving responsibility, again directly by the Pope. Within the Frankish dominions, there was no possibility of a missionary functioning without official approval, so the following year Boniface visited the court of Charles Martel. From the time of Clovis, the Merovingian kings had reigned fitfully, but a new aristocracy had been created on the basis of land ownership – land rewarded, in fact, for service to the king. Charles Martel was one of the strongest of this new feudal aristocracy and it is he who is credited with stopping the northward march of Islam at Poitiers in 732. This battle has always been seen as one of the key events of European history as it drew the line between Islam and Christianity, while at the same time creating one of the first momentary experiences of 'European' unity against what was seen as the common enemy. Eventually, the remaining descendants of the Merovingians were packed off to the monastery of Monte Cassino and the foundations of the new Carolingian dynasty were laid.

Since this family had no dynastic claim whatever, Pippin, its founding father, appealed to the Pope to sanctify his *de facto* power through the mystique of divine kingly anointing, thus making it *de iure*. Pippin was eventually consecrated king – perhaps by, or in the presence of Boniface – and a whole new theology of divinely ordained kingship was born. The king reigned as the representative of Christ, thus altering both the perception of Christ and the king for centuries to come. The anointing of the king was similar to the sacramental anointing of the bishop and a new royal liturgy was created on the model of the anointing of King David. The famous *laudes* – liturgical acclamations – were sung to the king: *Christus vincit, Christus regnat, Christus imperat,*

Christ conquers, Christ reigns, Christ rules supreme. A new cosmic order was thus created with the Frankish monarchy seen as receiving its power directly from God – *dei gratia rex* – king by the grace of God. Eventually, the king's chapel, the capella, became the centre of ecclesiastical and liturgical reform.

After being formally taken under the protection of Pippin's son, Charles Martel, Boniface spent fifteen years labouring in the central German mission field of Thuringia and Hesse, a land of pagans and minimally evangelised Christians. Through Boniface and his companions, Christianity was pushing ever further east. As he travelled, Boniface set up a string of monastic foundations, one of the most famous being that of Fritzlar, built from the wood of the great pagan Thunder Oak. This had been the centre of pagan worship and the great oak had been felled by Boniface in a pointed Christian symbolic act. Finally, in 744, his most famous monastery was founded at Fulda. Throughout his missionary labours, Boniface had to rely on his old English friends, to whom he wrote unceasingly, often in quite a whiny tone. Even more important, however, was the patronage of the king, from whom endless gifts of land came for the monastic foundations. One of these new monastic foundations was at Tauberbischofsheim, and the first abbess was Leoba, a kinswoman of Boniface.

Leoba

Leoba was born in 700, probably in the south west of England. On her mother's West Saxon side, she was related to Boniface. As was conventional in the biographies of great figures, her birth was preceded by her mother Ebbe's dream of a great bell clanging in her bosom. This was seen to forecast the future of Leoba (the beloved one) and she was sent to the Abbey of Wimborne at an early age. In her late twenties, Leoba wrote a letter to Boniface, the only piece of writing surviving from her own hand. Her parents were both dead and it seems that Boniface was her one surviving relative: 'Dear brother, please shield me with your prayers from the darts of the enemy. And please would you correct the unpolished style of this letter and send me a few words of your own as an example? I long to hear from you.'[19] Despite her convent life, the woman Leoba needed protectors in that society, but it was another twenty years before Boniface requested her presence in Germany, as a comfort and support. Eventually, a party of thirty nuns set out from Wimborne for Germany, led apparently by Leoba. We know the names of several others, but the only one of whom we know more than a name is Walburga, the eventual Abbess of Heidenheim.

Leoba's biographer, Rudolf, describes her as a female Boniface, together worthy descendants of Benedict and Scholastica. She was said to be unusually learned, holy and full of kindness, but since this is the standard formula, it is difficult to get any clear idea from these praises of what she was really like. Her indomitable character appears more clearly, indirectly, in a number of stories told about her miraculous and administrative powers. It seems that Leoba's monastery became a training school for women missionaries. Again, we meet the emphasis on reading and therefore on book production. Leoba herself is described as a prodigious reader, even having young nuns reading to her while she slept, and catching them immediately if they slackened their pace. She insisted that her nuns took plenty of sleep, because 'lack of sleep dulled the mind, especially for reading'[20] It is clear, then, that *lectio divina*, the ancient monastic practice of slow meditative reading of the Word of God, played a significant part in the monasticism of Leoba. More time was given by her to reading than to manual labour, but she did work with her hands because she had learned that the one who 'will not work should not eat'. 'In her conduct there was no arrognace or pride; she was no distinguisher of persons, but showed herself affable and kindly to all. In appearance she was angelic, in word pleasant, clear in mind, great in prudence, Catholic in faith, most patient in hope, universal in her charity.' Such praises go on for pages, but it is in the incidental details of the miraculous stories that we seem to get closer to her real character.[21]

There is one extraordinary tale about the poisoning of the

water supply for the whole town. Apparently a beggar girl who sat at the gate of the convent receiving food every day 'from the abbess's table', 'committed fornication', concealed her pregnancy and when the child was born, disposed of it by throwing it into a pool by the river. At dawn a village woman, coming for her water, saw the dead baby and, 'filled with womanly rage', blamed the nuns for the double evil of murder and poisoning. Her outburst deserves to be quoted in full, revealing as it does both the mingled awe and contempt for the nuns among the village women:

> Oh what a chaste community! How admirable is the life of the nuns, who beneath their veils give birth to children and exercise at one and the same time the function of mothers and priests, baptising those to whom they have given birth. For, fellow-citizens, you have drawn off this water to make a pool, not merely for the purpose of grinding corn, but unwittingly for a new and unheard-of-kind of baptism. Now go and ask these women, whom you compliment by calling them virgins, to remove this corpse from the river and make it fit for us to use again. Look for the one who is missing from the monastery and then you will find out who is responsible for this crime.

Leoba called her nuns together and discovered that only Agatha was missing, and she had left with full permission to visit her parents. She was summoned home, and all the nuns were soon assured of her innocence. Then a whole series of penitential prayerful exercises was ordered by the abbess, including the singing of the whole psalter with arms extended and thrice daily processions around the monastery. Eventually, in horrific detail, the culprit is revealed: 'that wretched little woman, the dupe and tool of the devil, seemed to be surrounded by flames, and, calling out the name of the abbess, confessed to the crime she had committed'. We do not know what happened to this poor woman who was blamed totally for her condition, but 'the nuns began to weep with joy', and the reputation of Leoba certainly suffered no harm.

The other tale is of the great storm that turned day into night
and terrified everyone. After sheltering their animals (an interesting detail), all the people rushed to the church in despair for
their lives. Leoba went to them and promised that no harm
would come to anyone. Meantime, in their presence she prayed
as 'the roofs of the houses were torn off by the violence of the
wind, the ground shook with the repeated shocks of the thun-
derbolts, and the thick darkness, intensified by the incessant
flicker of lightning which flashed through the windows, redou-
bled their horror'. Eventually, the whole crowd rushed upon
Leoba, lost in prayer, and one of her nuns begged her: 'Arise,
then, and pray to the Mother of God, your mistress, for us, that
by her intercession, we may be delivered from this fearful
storm.' And then, in the words quoted at the head of the chapter,
Leoba marched out and succeeded in stilling the storm. At this
sign of God's attention to Leoba's prayer, 'unexpected peace
came to his people and fear was banished'.

As a result of such incidents, according to Leoba's biographer,
'Many nobles and influential men gave their daughters to God
to live in the monastery in perpetual chastity; many widows also
forsook their homes, made vows of chastity and took the veil in
the cloister.' Here again, we see the delicate economy of the
monastery at work. The nuns had to prove themselves by learning, charity and miraculous deeds, and then the blessings followed, not only in the conversion of the people, but also in the
influx of new members, accompanied by new patronage and
new wealth. For most monasteries, the burden of hospitality
was huge, and without such a constant renewal of resources, the
women's monasteries especially could not have survived. As we
shall see, restrictions on women's public activity sounded the
death knell of monasteries such as Leoba's. Besides, as Rudolf
makes abundantly clear, it was part of Abbess Leoba's task to
cultivate the great and powerful. Later, after the death of
Boniface, Leoba became a very close friend of Hildegarde, the
wife of Charlemagne, and the Emperor himself 'loaded her with
gifts'.

Around the year 753, Boniface and Leoba met for the last time. It is a tender scene as he commands his monks to care always for Leoba with reverence, reaffirming his wish that, after death, their bones should rest side by side, 'so that they who had served God during their lifetime with equal sincerity and zeal should await together the day of resurrection'. He then gave her his own cowl, begging her to continue the great missionary work. Boniface himself had not been idle in the intervening years. His biographer presents him as the single-handed restorer of the German church, but that is the task of biographers. It is clear that Boniface was not always liked, as he strode roughshod over the work of his contemporaries and predecessors. Between 742 and 747 he had held five church synods for the reform of the German church in an effort to stimulate the zeal of the Frankish bishops. Earlier in 738, Charles Martel had invaded Saxon territory and had treated the people with incredible savagery. In a preview of Charlemagne's butchery of the Saxons, Martel offered them baptism or death. In 744, Charles Martel's son, Pippin the Short and father of Charlemagne, repeated these actions and reported: 'Christ being our leader, many of them were baptised.' We do not know Boniface's reaction to these events, but it is likely that the baptising was done by his men.[22]

Boniface seems to have foreseen the events of his murder in Frisia, for he wrote through a friend to King Pippin for exact details on how the king should inform him, while he was still alive, 'about my disciples, what favours he will do to them afterwards'. He tells the king who his replacement should be – Bishop Lull – and says that he will die happier in the king's favour. In 753, Boniface set off for Frisia, but on June 5, 754, he and his party were set upon by a gang of predators and slaughtered. Boniface tried to defend himself by holding up a book, but the blade penetrated it and he was killed. The book may still be seen in Fulda. Boniface was immediately hailed as a martyr. Leoba survived him for over twenty years, which she spent administering her monasteries and keeping in close contact with Lull. This work took precedence over the needs of Charlemagne's wife, Hildegarde, who would have liked to keep her at court. 'But,' says her biographer, 'Leoba detested the life at court like poison.' She seems to have replaced Boniface as the counsellor of all: 'And because of her wide knowledge of the scriptures and her prudence in counsel they [the princes and bishops] often discussed spiritual matters and ecclesiastical discipline with her.'[23]

The monastery at Fulda was forbidden territory to all women, but Leoba was granted permission to come there to pray close to the grave of Boniface. With an eye on propriety and on the increasing suspicion of women, Rudolf describes the precautions taken on such occasions so that no monkish temptation would result. Towards the end of her life, when Leoba was already 'decrepit through age', Queen Hildegarde sent for her one last time, and 'although Leoba was not at all pleased, she agreed to go for the sake of their long-standing friendship'. As usual, Leoba detested her time in the court at Aachen and despite protestations, left as soon as she could. Queen Hildegarde, 'embracing her friend rather more affectionately than usual, [she] kissed her on the mouth, the forehead and the eyes and took leave of her with these words: "Farewell for evermore, my dearly beloved lady and sister; farewell most precious half of my soul … Never more on this earth shall we enjoy each other's presence."'

A short time later, probably on September 28, 780, Leoba died. Despite Boniface's request, the monks of Fulda were reluctant to re-open his tomb, so Leoba was buried to the north of the altar. Later, her remains were moved to St Peter's church, in order, it was said, that the tomb could be freely visited by female pilgrims.[24] In many ways, the death of Leoba signalled the end of an era. She was one of the last of an extraordinary group of Anglo-Saxon nuns whose labours created the Europe we know today. From the great monastery at Wimborne, thirty nuns had moved to the German mission-fields, where they had laboured side by side with the monks. This era was now over, as even the apologetic voice of Rudolf, Leoba's biographer, makes clear. Henceforth, nuns and monks would begin to be separated, as legislation about the enclosure of nuns was multiplied. While some form of enclosure is essential to all monastic life, and was always seen, besides, as a necessary protection for women in such turbulent surroundings, now enclosure is recommended as a protection for men from the wiles of women, and as a necessary imposition on women, whose weakness and immorality endangered all.

A new era of separation

How and why did this come about? As we have seen earlier, almost all periods of ecclesiastical reform spelled the diminishment of women. Such reforms tended especially towards the grounding of institutional clerical life, and from this period onward, the emphasis was placed almost exclusively on separation from women as one of the most necessary ingredients towards this end. Again, we need to back-track in order to trace this development.

Charlemagne had succeeded his father, Pippin the Short, in 768. Charlemagne was a man of destiny, reigning from 768 to 814, eventually claiming the title of 'Supreme Ruler of the Christian Church'. His first task was to expand and secure his dominions, and then to create a Christian commonwealth. In a series of brutal campaigns, the Frankish kingdom was expanded to include all of what we would call Western Europe and beyond. Paganism was not tolerated in this vast domain, and it was again the Saxons who bore the brunt of Charlemagne's cruelty. In 782, he tired of Saxon resistance, and perhaps following the advice of Abbot/Bishop Lull, the successor of Boniface, he massacred 4500 Saxons and enslaved the rest. For two more years, Charlemagne continued to push east, imposing Christianity wherever he went. In 784, the pope called for three days of thanksgiving to celebrate Charlemagne's evangelising victories and Abbot/Bishop Lull wrote celebratory verses. The 'Saxon Capitulary' was published outlining the means for the Christianisation of Saxony. Refusal of baptism, cremation, and eating meat in Lent all became capital offences. Attendance at

Sunday worship and the baptism of infants were imposed on
pain of death. Tithing was imposed and marriages within certain degrees forbidden.

Even though allowance must always be made for the difference between legislation and its fulfilment, these enactments
forecast a new era. This was not a Christian environment which
needed the ministry of women – indeed, they were seen as needless obstacles. These laws were designed not only to impose
Christianity, but also to destroy the whole Saxon culture, and
even the most intimate rituals of family life.[25] Many of the missionaries to Saxony in the years after these draconian measures
came from Fulda. In a strange twist of history, Saxony itself,
within a century, became a powerhouse of Christian life. One of
the few voices known to us who wished to temper such cruelty
and imposed Christianity was that of Alcuin, another Anglo-
Saxon monk from York, who had become Charlemagne's
Minister of Education. On Christmas Day 800, Charlemagne
was crowned Holy Roman Emperor by Pope Leo III, at the time
an act of treason against Irene, the reigning Empress in the East.
For the next century, starting with the *Admonitio Generalis* of 789,
a flood of reforming legislation laid the foundations of the
ecclesiastical organisation of Western European Christianity.

The aim was to create a Christian society with legislation
rooted in the Ten Commandments – in itself a significant choice.
There seems no hint whatever that anyone was interested in the
poor man of Nazareth or in the spirituality of the beatitudes.
Such an approach would have been quite simply inconceivable
in the Carolingian world. Charlemagne was the spokesperson
for Christ the King of Kings, and the chief bishop of his Empire
was the Bishop of Rome. Everyone knew the source of power
and authority. The Carolingian Reform divided society into a
variety of groups and ordered the appropriate contribution of
each to the Christian commonwealth: clergy to pray, soldiers to
fight, and the serfs to work the land and be ready to contribute
their military service when called upon. Benedict of Aniane, the
great tenth-century abbot, was delegated to organise monastic

life, and the concerns of women were addressed principally by increasingly stringent legislation about their enclosure. The powers of bishops were increased and, in a shrewd move, they were made responsible for the carrying out of this imperial legislation. The laity were only minimally involved. They were not active participants in this reform, except by way of obedience and tithing. Nevertheless, there are signs of growing literacy throughout the ninth century, and some elements of the legislation demand increased Christian involvement from all: 'And we command that no one in our whole kingdom shall dare to deny hospitality either to rich or poor, or to pilgrims; that is, no one shall deny shelter and fire and water to pilgrims traversing our country in God's name, or to anyone travelling for the love of God or for the safety of his own soul.'

Nevertheless, this is the period when monasticism for women began to decline. Boniface had moved from being a brother monk to the role of a father-bishop. Through his example, the episcopate was more and more influenced by the demands of the monastic vows, especially the vow of chastity. Demands for clerical celibacy grew louder. At the same time, monks began to be ordained to the priesthood and the old easy monastic association of male and female, especially in the work of evangelisation, disappeared. By 850, only 17 of a possible 170 monastic foundations for women continued to survive. Growing from the Carolingian reforms, bishops seemed to relish their new power. All the mid-ninth century legislation with regard to women seems to focus on two main aims: first, to separate women and men into their respective monasteries; and secondly to subject all of them to episcopal authority. The bishops, however, could not over-ride centuries of Benedictine tradition and remove the power of the abbot; the subjection of the abbess to the bishop was an easier task. Women religious always needed the minstrations of the clergy for sacramental purposes, and this necessarily entailed negotiation with the local bishop. It is clear that bishops wearied very quickly of the burden of women – the simplest solution seemed to be to render them invisible through the 'glorious prison' of monastic enclosure. These Carolingian reforms and the subsequent reforms stemming from the monastery of Cluny did not advance the cause of monasticism, but of the clergy.

The clericalisation of monastic life was extremely disadvantageous to women. In successive legislation, the tone and language change from one of protective incarceration to one of denigration. As monastic life is clericalised, daily Mass becomes more and more a feature of the monastic routine. For centuries, the monastic round of chanted prayer had made no distinction between male and female. Women seem to have participated fully in this liturgical setting. From Carolingian times forward women are forbidden to 'serve at the altar'. At the Council of Paris in 829 women are ordered not to touch the sacred vessels because, even in the act of cleaning, the hands of women pollute what they touch. Women are further forbidden to light candles or ring bells, or conduct prayers for the remembrance of the dead. In this way, not only are women removed from service at the altar and replaced by male acolytes and sacristans, they are also deprived of the financial benefits of the remembrance of the dead. Henceforth, Masses for the Dead would be solely the responsibility of the clergy and they alone would reap the substantial rewards. Women begin to be seen as feeble dependants instead of the active partners of an earlier time. Earlier in the ninth century, another source of income and involvement had been removed from the nuns when they were forbidden to educate young boys. They are perceived more and more to be a burden on the clergy and on their brother monks. As bishops and abbots begin to be bound more and more together through clericalisation, the abbesses are removed and often excluded completely from Synods and assemblies, even where the affairs of women are discussed.

Throughout the ninth century, there is a growing sense of the church as a male club and it is no surprise that misogynistic literary and legal attacks on women re-appear. The growing suspicion of women obviously reveals more about the attitudes of the reformers than it does about the lives of women. Women are blamed for every catastrophe that occurs to them. Even though

monasteries are repeatedly attacked in the coming years by
Vikings, Lombards, Normans and others, society's assessment is
that the women are the cause of their own downfall. It was the
common opinion of ninth century bishops, voiced for us by
Bishop Amalarius of Metz, that women, left to themselves,
would run amok. From this period, then, all religious women
are ordered into highly structured Benedictine monasteries.
This spells the end, for centuries, of a diversity of opportunity
for women. Where formerly there were still canonesses attached
to cathedrals, and smaller monasteries attached to family farms,
now all women are submitted to the Benedictine rule, but under
the authority of the bishop.

Nuns can no longer govern their own affairs, and there is no
opportunity left for any co-operation between male and female
monasteries. Women are dependants, and dangerous ones at
that. Far from being partners in a great missionary and ecclesial
enterprise, they are now seen as tempters and obstacles to clerical institutional life. The ninth century reformers had destroyed
what Jo Ann McNamara calls the 'third gender'.[26] Throughout
the centuries, women and men had co-operated in the Christian
enterprise in a variety of ways. After the fourth century, as we
have seen, this co-operation depended on the practice by both of
the life of virginity. Through the institution of the double
monastery and later of the missionary monastic house, women
and men continued this activity as partners. Now, with increasing clericalisation, this partnership was destroyed and would
not re-appear until our own day. Prior to the ninth century and
the Carolingian reforms, there was little distinction between the
monasticism of women and men, and the roles of abbess and
abbot. Now as abbots became more powerful, often adding to
their monastic roles that of the episcopate, the role of the abbess
was vastly diminished. For centuries, the most important topic
in church legislation for women was that of enclosure. From
now on, monks and nuns, men and women lived in different
worlds. The double standard was institutionalised. For women,
the convent had become a 'glorious prison', to be exchanged
only for the tomb.[27]

Before leaving this chapter, some remaining threads need to be assembled into the texture of eighth, ninth and tenth century life for women. These include a look at one mother's advice to her absent son, and a brief glimpse into the growing body of opinion about Christian marriage.

Dhuoda

First then, to Dhuoda, as she writes her motherly advice to her absent son. In the chaos that followed the death of Louis the Pious, the son of Charlemagne, it was very easy to find oneself on the wrong side, as his feuding sons fought bitterly over the remains of the empire. In such situations, it was customary for members of the nobility to send sons to court as hostages to guarantee loyalty. Quite fortuitously, a document has been preserved from Dhuoda of Septimania written for her elder son William in the court of Charles the Bald. Eventually in 843 at the Treaty of Verdun, the old empire had been divided between the three surviving sons: the East, that is Germany went to Louis the German; the West, namely France to Charles the Bald; and the central part, that is Lorraine and the Lowlands to Lothar. In the previous year, 842, Dhuoda had written her handbook, *Liber Manualis*. She had been married to Bernard, one of the nobles of Louis, in 814, in the imperial chapel in Aachen. Her sons were born in 826 and 841. Her husband, Bernard, found himself on the wrong side after the death of Louis and he was executed in 844 for treason. In this context, the fate of her sons, whom she likely had not seen since infancy, was of decisive importance to her own survival.

Dhuoda's decision to write a public document was highly significant. She was exceptionally literate, having read the writings of Augustine and Pope Gregory I among others. She was, apparently, a voracious reader and through her learning, wished to share in the education of her sons. Her work gives a very accurate sense of the universal feeling of dread at the fall of the empire, and she expresses well that her only hope lies in the immutable God. The writing of Dhuoda is, like all women's writing known to us, full of self-deprecation but, at least in her case, there is a real historical reason for it – the whole world is 'turning to dust,' she says.[28] She is well aware that writing is a 'perilous public contest' not usually entrusted to women, because Eve, the first woman who dared to teach, taught only to sin. Hence assuming the role of teacher is a life-threatening responsibility for women. Nevertheless she writes for her son, William, and it is clear that she intends her book to be read publicly. She writes as counsellor and political adviser lest her son be absorbed by the treachery at court. The reason she can assume any authority is because she is a mother. Her 'burning heart' will add fire to her words and she calls on the special skills available to all mothers. She picks up the theme of the 'troublesome little puppy' from the gospel story of the Syro-Phoenician woman (Mk 7:24-27), where the woman persists with her requests, despite being rebuffed by Jesus. She knows she is undeserving, she says, but 'God likes the underdog'.

Her words are addressed to 'my beautiful and lovable son, William' and to his 'little brother, whose name I do not know'. With these poignant words, we are allowed a glimpse back over a millennium into the life conditions of women of Dhuoda's class. She seems to have been lucky in having a library of some kind available to her. Her advice to her son is conventional: find a good counsellor, love God, find suitable companions, but the whole work is full of her own very real piety. 'Both of us must search for God, my son; in his will we take our place, we live and move and have our being. Unworthy and insubstantial as a shadow, I seek him in order to be strong.' In conclusion, she gives him a list of family dead, and supplies him with her own epitaph. 'I already feel as if I were enclosed in a tomb.'

Formed of earth, here in this little earthly mound,
Is the earthy body of Dhuoda thrown.
Infinite King receive her.
For the earth has received her fragile clay
Into its depths
Gracious King, pardon her ...

O indulgent God, order perpetual light
To be lavished on her with the saints at the end.
May she receive the 'Amen' after the funeral rites.[29]

Dhuoda is one of the very few mothers from whom we have any direct word throughout the whole history of Christianity. Her proud stature and courage as well as her deep mystical piety, shine through her constant self-diminishment. We know nothing else about her.

Christian marriage

Throughout the ninth century, the Christian bishops began to try to impose some order on the marital practices of the nobility. Charlemagne himself had had at least eleven women in his life, some legal wives, some morganatic, some concubines and several other assorted relationships. He never allowed his daughters to marry for dynastic reasons, but encouraged them in an assortment of non-legal relationships whose offspring he would not have to recognise. No bishop, not even the pope of the time, would have dared to challenge the 'Supreme Guardian of Christianity'.

One of the major tasks facing the bishops was the definition of marriage itself, entwined as it was in customs of Roman, Celtic and Germanic cultural practice. Although the Romans had tried to insist on a free exchange of consent as the essence of marriage – in an effort to limit abductions – this was not a consent that involved the woman, but rather her father or guardian. Until the ascetic movement of the fourth century, it was universally accepted that all women would marry. Then, the patristic writers saw the practice of virginity, and eventually chaste marriage, as the ideal solution to their firm belief that sex interfered with communion with God. This chaste marriage ideal perdured, though the church had a signal lack of success in the creation of a sexually pure clergy. The notion of a chaste marriage was especially attractive to women, as we have seen, and provided them with an opportunity to escape the demands of patriarchal marriage and pursue their own spiritual path. Such a marriage was based on a brother/sister relationship and did not include the customary domination of conjugality.

By the ninth century, bishops were faced with several thorny situations where members of the nobility were using the fact of a chaste marriage as a reason for dissolving politically undesirable unions. The notion of chaste marriage for the clergy had been most desirable for a number of reasons – it placed the marriage of clergy a step above ordinary marriage and, above all, ideally, there were no offspring to claim a clerical inheritance. Gradually the old definition of Augustine began to be explored again – marriage is a combination of fidelity, sacramental union and offspring. This definition served also to restore the original hierarchy of domination of spirit over flesh, men over women. The major and seemingly insurmountable obstacle here was that this definition threw the marriage of Mary and Joseph – the preferred model for centuries – into extreme doubt. What about the biblical dictum that the 'two shall become one flesh?' The debate went on for centuries with learned and holy men on both sides of the argument. Eventually, it was more or less concluded that there could be a double theory of sacramental marriage: one kind of sacramental marriage involved only consent and the social pact; the other, also sacramental by the twelfth century, involved the copulation of the flesh.[30] Thomas Aquinas added his own metaphysical refinements to this theory a hundred years later, but by then interest had focused again on the virginity of Mary rather than on her marriage.

Several famous marriage problems occupied the ninth-century bishops to such an extent that they felt they had to excuse their interest in sexual matters:

> We bishops say this not because we want knowingly to reveal or ignorantly to make known the secret places of girls and women, which we know nothing of by experience; but because it is written, 'The thing I do not know I will diligently investigate', we will keep before our eyes what we see written in the teachers of the church, so that if anyone caught at such things comes to us, asking in penitence for the judgement of just judges, we can judge her without error.[31]

The case in question here concerned the marriage of King Lothar, the grandson of Charlemagne, who had married Theutberga for political reasons and now wished to divorce her because she was childless. To this end, he accused her of pre-marital incest with her brother which, in the spirit of the times, would have rendered her incapable of marriage. The local bishops, including Hincmar of Rheims, convicted Theutberga, but she appealed to Pope Nicholas I, who reversed the decision after Theutberga had proven her innocence. For over a decade, Lothar kept the bishops busy as he tried to come up with other reasons for a divorce. He had, in fact, gone back to his lover Waldrada, despite taking Theutberga back in a very public ceremony, on the pope's command. Theutberga had been forced to make a false confession of incest, under pain of death. Contemporaries wondered why she wished to remain with such a brutal husband, when retirement to a convent would have been such a simple way out of the dilemma. She wrote to the pope: 'If I am forced farther, know that I will say what they want, not because it is true, but because I can do no other ...' Eventually, Lothar's behaviour became so despicable that his long-suffering queen initiated divorce proceedings herself, on the grounds of a supposed previous marriage between Lothar and Waldrada and her own sterility. She is reported to have told the pope that she would rather live among the pagans than have to look at Lothar's face again. Eventually, Lothar died in 869, thus solving one dilemma, but facing the bishops with exquisitely delicate problems for centuries.

These questions are so complex that they would require several volumes for an adequate treatment. Suffice it to say that the ninth-century bishops bequeathed two definite attitudes to later generations. First, they were convinced that, once a valid marriage had been formed (two in one flesh), all the effort on earth should favour its perpetuation. Secondly, they were absolutely convinced that marriage itself was secondary to a life of celibacy. For these reasons, the life of women changed dramatically. First of all, monasticism, a lay form of life open to real partnership be-

tween women and men, became clericalised. Monks were ordained to the priesthood, celibacy was eventually imposed on
all, and women were necessarily removed from the equation. In
fact, women became the enemy, as we have seen, and their complete enclosure in either the convent or marriage seemed the
only solution that would assure the safety of the clergy. On the
other hand, women in marriage were deprived of the option of a
chaste marriage and were driven almost by force into the marital
bed. The hierarchical dominance of a patriarchal marriage was
reinforced. The ongoing efforts to impose celibacy on the clergy
required the invisibility of women. The options of women for a
spiritual life were enormously diminished and, as we shall see,
any public activity by women in the future would require very
strong backing, usually that of a heavenly vision. Henceforth,
the efforts of women were directed at remaining single as this
was the only area of choice remaining where they had any hope
of disposing of their own lives in freedom.

CHAPTER 10

The Point of the Story: Joan and Hroswitha

Then turning aside out of abhorrence of Pope Joan whose image with her son stands near Saint Clement's, the Pope, dismounting from his horse, enters the Lateran for his enthronement. And there he is seated in a chair of porphyry, which is pierced beneath for this purpose, that one of the younger cardinals may make proof of his sex; and then while a Te Deum is chanted, he is borne to the high altar.[1]

I [Hroswitha] am the Strong Voice of Gandersheim.[2]

Despite all attempts to kill her off, Pope Joan keeps cropping up in our own times. People believe in her and go on believing in her because they want her to have happened ... Yet this appeal can distract from the fact that Pope Joan is much more than a wonderful story.[3]

She [Hroswitha] is the first known dramatist of Christianity, the first Saxon poet, and the first woman historian of Germany. Her dramas are the first performable plays of the Middle Ages, her epics are the only extant Latin epics written by a woman, and, finally, she is the first medieval poet to have consciously attempted to remold the image of the literary depictions of women.[4]

Story is the subject of this chapter. First of all, there is the ever-recurring story of Joan the Englishwoman who became pope in the middle of the ninth century, at a time when the fact of a woman pope would seem to have been the least scandalous aspect of the papacy. Even the most sympathetic observers label this papal period a 'pornocracy', and this epithet has nothing to do with Joan. Her story continues to fascinate, not least because in that time and place it is so believable. Secondly, there is the great Hroswitha of Gandersheim, that spinner of tales, who

227

from her convent tackled the literary image of women and re-
wrote the story of women's lives. She lived and died one hundred years after Pope Joan, but the tragic drama of the papacy
still continued. Each woman is linked with earlier chapters of
the history of women. Joan is said to have studied at the
monastery of Boniface in Fulda, and Hroswitha's life at Gandersheim continues the great saga of the women who found shelter,
stimulation and education in the monastic foundations of an
earlier age. The stories of both women tease and frustrate us
with lack of precise detail, but we know enough of the age in
which they lived to gain some sense of certainty about their
lives.

By any standard, the ninth century was one of utter disaster
for what is today called Western Europe. In successive waves,
the Vikings, both the Norse and Danish varieties, the Muslims,
and the Magyars harassed any settlement accessible from the
sea or by river. Paris was destroyed in 843, 856 and 861, and in
881 the Vikings even penetrated as far as Aachen. From the 830s
on, the Muslims devastated central and southern Italy sacking
the Papal States, including Rome itself in 849, and destroying
Monte Cassino in 882. Northern Italy and Germany were fairly
safe from Vikings and Muslims, but did not escape the ravages
of the Magyars. Spain, of course, had been under Muslim sway
for decades, but the *reconquista* had made something of a start
under Alfonso III. For over a century, there was complete chaos
in the ecclesiastical sphere. Abbeys and episcopal sees were destroyed and emptied of their possessions, and most remained
vacant for decades. It certainly was no great help that in the
midst of these recurring disasters, the sons and grandsons of
Charlemagne were constantly at war with each other, despite
several attempts to achieve what they called *fraternitas.* The
whole of the former Carolingian Empire was laid waste, but
eventually, as had been the Western pattern, the Viking and
Magyar predators became settled Christian colonisers.

It is not at all surprising, then, that during this period the affairs of the papacy were not going well, nor is it surprising that

several historians simply leave a gap in their papal lists between Nicholas I (858-867) and Leo IX (1049-1054). Rome had been under imperial control since 824 and all papal elections had been authorised by the emperor. Roman records for this whole period are sparse, but a new kind of record makes its appearance. From as early as 865, Rome began to rely on documents known then and now to be forgeries, but accepted in the intervening centuries as the official basis of Roman ecclesiastical power. These documents charted, supposedly, the foundation of the independent Papal States. The first was the Donation of Constantine, presented as a gift of land from the Emperor Constantine to Pope Sylvester in the fourth century. The specifically ninth-century contribution was the group of documents known collectively as the *Pseudo-Isidorian Decretals*. These documents were used by successive popes to attempt to establish a centralised papal government but, in the turbulence of the time, they were an utter failure. Pope Nicholas I had used these documents to assert his claims to absolute power against obstreperous archbishops, such as Hincmar of Rheims, but had failed conspicuously. Eventually, even this failed claim and its supporting documents was to have resounding results in the papacy of Gregory VII, but in the meantime, papal claims to power simply made the papacy more attractive to the highest bidder.[5] There is no point in relating the endless tragic and corrupt tales of the misfortunes of the papacy, but perhaps the beginning of the real trouble was the papacy of John VIII. He had Pope Formosus, a previous opponent, dug up, vested the putrefying corpse in full papal regalia, and put him on trial. Formosus was, of course, condemned, and his body given to the people of Rome. John himself was murdered in 882 and the best that can be said for the following years is that most popes lasted but a few months. The papacy was owned by three feuding Roman families, the Crescentii, the Tusculans and the Theopylact, who treated the See of Rome as their personal plaything.[6] Women played no small part in these events, both as mothers, mistresses, wives and lovers, but two women, in particular, must claim our attention briefly. These are Theodora, who had first come to Rome in 890 with her husband, Theophylact, and her daughter, Marozia. Their aim was to found a new imperial dynasty, based in Rome, and the papacy was the obvious *de facto* starting point. Theodora contrived to have one of her own men elected as Pope Sergius III in 904 and, as a reward, he was given Marozia, her fifteen-year-old daughter, as his mistress. Eventually, they had a son, John. The next three popes were Theodora's appointees, the third being her lover, John X. Despite his means of accession, this John managed to defend Rome from the Muslims, but by now Theodora was dead and Marozia had taken up the family cause. She was said to be beautiful, cold and intelligent and very free with her favours.[7] She set out to create a hereditary papacy, the first step being to make her own son, John, fathered by Pope Sergius, the next pope. This involved murders, lay popes, military sieges, two or more popes reigning or competing together, teenage popes and joint popes with Marozia herself. The line continued on and off right down to her great-grand-son, Benedict IX, who became pope as a teenager and died in his early thirties. It was Cardinal Baronius, one of the most loyal chroniclers of the papacy, who labelled this period a 'pornocracy'.

As these events rocked Rome, a new imperial dynasty was taking shape in Germany, the Ottonian. Successive German emperors made trips to Rome in order to attempt solutions to the papal turmoil, but as soon as they returned to Germany, events took up their now normal disastrous course. The forgeries, which had tried to provide the papacy with a juridical base, were now of some limited use. This was, however, the period of the proprietary church, that is, the church owned as a feudal possession by the king or emperor. In France also, under Hugh Capet, the church and its possessions were taken over. Episcopal sees were sold to sons and daughters and episcopal dynastic successions were set up. We even hear of a five-year-old being appointed as Archbishop of Rheims. Since each pope and bishop routinely cancelled all acts and ordinations of their predecessors, one can only imagine the utter chaos of the church. Under such circumstances, it is very difficult to maintain any pretence of a clear apostolic succession.

Pope Joan

Into this context, we can place the story of Pope Joan, the Englishwoman, and, as already mentioned, in such a context the accession of a woman pope would seem to be not the worst problem to assail the papacy. It is the story of Pope Joan, though, which to later historians seems the most extraordinary of this extraordinary age. Joan's papacy is dated from 856 to 858, coming between Pope Leo IV and Pope Benedict III. After Benedict came Nicholas I, whom most historians acknowledge as the only pope of any stature between Gregory I, who died in 604 and Leo IX (1049-1054). Joan's story is quickly told, but its significance has continued through the centuries for both opponents and proponents.[8] Joan was an Englishwoman, apparently part of the wave of Anglo-Saxon missionaries who became part of Boniface's German mission. She is said to have been born in Mainz and to have studied in Fulda. All report that she was extremely intelligent and thirsted for education. As we have seen, ecclesiastical reforms always tended to restrict the educational opportunities of women, and so it is no surprise that we read of Joan's decision to pass herself off as a man and head for the ancient centre of education, Athens. She had a male companion, reputed to be both tutor and lover.

In Athens, Joan soon outshone all others in the breadth and brilliance of her learning. Eventually, she returned to Rome and became the most sought-after teacher in the city, holding her lectures in the school where Augustine himself had taught centuries before. 'And for as much as she was in great esteem in the city, both for her life and her learning, she was unanimously elected Pope.'[9] Joan, whom all still thought to be the male, John VIII, eventually became pregnant 'by the person with whom she was intimate'. Her surprise delivery happened while on a journey from Saint Peter's to the Lateran, and 'she brought forth a child between the Colosseum and Saint Clement's Church'.

Here, the accounts begin to differ. Some say she died at the spot and was buried there; others that she was attacked by the enraged crowd and executed by being tied and dragged behind the horses. Others, yet again, have her banished to a convent to repent of her crime of deception. Her child is also given two different life stories, from instant death to survival to become the Bishop of Ostia, south of Rome.[10]

There is silence about Joan for perhaps four hundred years, but then the historical chroniclers, especially the Dominicans, begin to acknowledge her existence and the fact of her papacy. Both Peter Stanford and Joan Morris trace the manuscript evidence scrupulously, and while acknowledging the gaps, end up giving the story their cautious acceptance. Officially, of course, it is simply dropped from the record, or treated as a quaint survival from a very strange era. Apart from the manuscript evidence, three other pieces of evidence point in the direction of the veracity of the story. The first is the existence of the famous chair, still in the Vatican Museum, which was intended to prevent such a thing ever happening again. This chair, the *sedia stercoraria*, is said to have been invented so that, after election, all future popes should have their maleness tested, as was claimed to have been witnessed by the author of the first quotation at the head of this chapter. A variety of quaint and unconvincing explanations has been given for the continued existence of this chair, but none is as convincing as that of the eye-witness, Adam of Usk, and the other chroniclers. One constantly gets the impression from these accounts that the papacy could survive any kind of mayhem, corruption, illegality, but that another womanly deception could not be tolerated.

Secondly, there is the well-attested gallery of popes in the Cathedral at Siena, where eye-witness accounts describe the bust of Pope Joan in her proper place in the papal roster until the end of the seventeenth century. She is no longer there, and as Peter Stanford remarks, in his account of his visit there, little memory of Joan survives.[11] Catherine, one of the most famous Sienese women of any generation, seems to have captured for herself all the attention. Finally, there is the frequently described alteration in the papal route from Saint Peter's to the Lateran. From the time of Joan, it was said, all papal processions avoided the *vicus papissa,* the street where she is said to have given birth. As Martin of Poland narrates: 'And because the Lord Pope always turns aside from that way, there are some who are fully persuaded that it is done in detestation of the fact. Nor is she put in the Catalogue of the Holy Popes, as well on account of her female sex as on account of the foul nature of the transaction.'[12]

As this quotation indicates, it is the successful duplicity of Joan that has haunted the chroniclers rather than any immorality in her actions. For evidence of the latter, there was a great deal of choice in the popes preceding and following her. It is clear then that, whether they approved of her or not, the historians known to us accept the story of the woman-pope right down to the Reformation. Even such a well-known logician as William of Ockham (1280-1349), though he disapproved of Joan's papacy, did not challenge its veracity. With the advent of the Reformation, the story of Joan provided the opponents of the Roman Church with magnificent ammunition to embarrass the Catholics. And they used it gleefully. It is only at this time that Roman theologians and historians, in their efforts to defend the papacy, decided to relegate the story of Joan to the category of fiction. Till the sixteenth century, Joan, though by no means lauded, was allowed the validity of existence. Now, the heavy-weights of the Roman Church were arrayed against her.[13] As Joan is confined to the stuff of legend, the diatribes against her become more misogynistic, and her death becomes more and more gruesome. For centuries, the Reformers are blamed for concocting the story in order to embarrass the papacy. By the nineteenth century Joan is made the heroine or villain of a whole series of novels and dramas and this has continued right down to our own day.

One eighteenth century drama makes the story of Joan the stuff of farce:

The Holy Father groaned and shouted,
The fear in the crowd was quite undoubted;
Who could help him? Was there none?
Suddenly the Pope ... gave birth to a son.[14]

By the late nineteenth century, Joan's life had been turned into a romance that was also, despite the humour, decidedly anti-clerical. A card-game was even invented around the story, and eventually a tarot-card of Joan was added to the usual deck. In all of this, the old theme of Joan's womanly deception kept resurfacing. In the 1982 play by Caryl Churchill, *Top Girls,* Joan is made to comment about her downfall: 'I forgot I was pretending.' In 1995, a musical celebrated Joan with a large-scale production in Chicago. Here, she has become a model for contemporary women in business who experience the 'glass ceiling', and often have to resort to unconventional methods in order to pursue their goals.[15] The closing number, 'A Thousand Years from Now', charts a course for women's advancement, 'one step at a time, one day at a time', to the topmost echelons of power in the manner of Joan's extraordinary life.

Unfortunately, the remaining gaps in the evidence prevent a definitive decision about Joan's remarkable life. From what is available to us, the facts of the case can hardly be disputed. It is clear that no one really denied her papal life until after the Reformation, even though, as a woman pope, she was accounted a heretic and worse. Joan's story continues to fascinate, if only because it raises questions about and relativises the absolute maleness of the papacy and the ordained clergy. The remarkable thing is that such a story should survive for so long, that such thoughts were possible in the ninth century and after; that the notion that an education could open every conceivable door to women was in the air in this most turbulent time. Joan's story has a particular poignancy today as the utter and essential maleness of the Godhead, the Christ and the ordained clergy takes on the aura of infallibility. How necessary such stories as Joan's are in order to remind today's Christians that there is nothing absolute about the accepted version of hierarchical Christianity.

Joan's two-year papacy serves to keep alive the question of women's full inclusion in the Christian tradition at all levels. The efforts to quell the story serve only to illustrate the importance of her brief witness.

Hroswitha

The life of Hroswitha of Gandersheim brings us up to the first millennial mark, but apart from her writings, we know hardly anything about her. Like most women, her life has to be cobbled together from stray clues in her works and educated guesses about her probable place in the tenth-century scheme of things. Hroswitha's very existence, though, indicates the difficulty of assessing early medieval events even from the most official sources. She was a canoness one hundred years *after* Benedict of Aniane, in the Carolingian reform of the early ninth century, had legislated canonesses out of existence. She obviously had access to a library, fairly unique for her day, which contained not only the patristic writings, but also the pagan classics. Her dramas re-write the plays of the Latin dramatist, Terence. She was a member of a community in the free Abbey of Gandersheim, whose abbess had her own law-courts, her own army, and had the right to mint her own coins, and who also sat, in her own right, in the Imperial Diet. And all this after the reforms of Boniface in the eighth century, those of the Carolingians in the ninth, and the Cluniac reform of the early tenth century, had tried to shove women aside in their efforts to promote the power and authority of the institutional church.

The Cluniac reform deserves some attention. Benedict of Aniane, appointed by Charlemagne in the early ninth century to reform the monasteries, had laid the foundations of monastic life for decades. But that does not mean that the reform actually worked in practice. What he did accomplish was the instilling of the theory that the work of monks was prayer and liturgy. To do this, they needed sufficient property and income to keep them independent. The Benedictine rule was the only rule to be followed, and an attempt was made to have monastic life so stan-

dardised that every monk followed exactly the same routine of
prayer, work, meals and sleep in every monastery of the empire.
This did not materialise in Benedict's day, but the idea had been
planted and a tradition established. In a feudal society such as
that of the Carolingian and later the Ottonian empires, the aristocracy, who owned the land by God-given right, also understood themselves to own everyone and everything on their land,
including monks, monasteries, bishops and bishoprics. Most of
the efforts of subsequent monastic reforms served to try to win
ecclesiastical independence from this situation.

Women counted for nothing explicitly in these reforms. For
the most part, they were left to fend for themselves. As we have
seen, most of the reformers' attention was aimed at separating
women from men, and in so doing, successive reforms deprived
women of their traditional sources of income. Women were enclosed, could not teach, or engage in any liturgical activity or indeed in any activity that took them from the monastery. Instead
of being independent, they became a dependant burden on the
clergy, and were then blamed for their burdensome existence.
The important reforms of the famed Abbey of Cluny were, likewise, little concerned with women. The monastery of Cluny was
founded by the pious William, Duke of Aquitaine, in 910. He
stated explicitly that this was to be an exempt monastery, that is,
subject only to St Peter, i.e. the Pope, and not to any local bishop.
The first Abbot was Berno (910-927) and he set the model of a
strict Benedictine community, where most manual work was
eliminated so that the monks could spend their time at prayer –
their principal task. Cluny was fortunate in having a succession
of abbots – Odo, Majolus, Odilo and Hugh – whose combined
tenures in the abbacy lasted for hundreds of years. These were
extraordinarily long-lived men. All continued the rigorous discipline and struggled successfully to keep Cluny free from both
ecclesiastical and aristocratic control. It was from Cluny that the
word spread that monks prayed, not only for themselves but for
remission of sins for the whole world, and especially for the
dead. There, the feast of the Holy Souls was instituted, and in an

age where the devil was very real, Cluny became a powerhouse of prayer and, of course, prosperity. Donations flooded in, and petitions from other monasteries to join the reform. In this way, Cluny grew into something like an order, with hundreds of monasteries attaching themselves for the privilege of following the Cluniac routine. Cluniac churches became models of Romanesque architecture, where nothing was spared for the glory of the house of God. For two centuries, Cluny was the spiritual leader of Europe. Reform-minded dioceses would accept only Cluniac bishops, and even the Bishop of Rome needed some connection with this centre of reform, as the papacy of Gregory VII, Urban II, and Paschal II attests. The abbots of Cluny imposed their leadership also on kings and emperors. By the twelfth century, however, Cluny was in a state of decline, leaving only its magnificent churches and abbeys to witness to its former greatness, when it numbered about 1000 monasteries extending throughout Europe from Spain to the Holy Land.

As Cluny gained its freedom, women's monasteries were being made more subject to local bishops. Bishops gained supervisory power over the election of abbesses and sometimes handed the convents over to reforming monks. Throughout the following years, monks and bishops were free to do what they liked with women's monasteries, all in the name of reform. The right of canonical election was taken from the nuns, and often their very property was taken from them when a local lord wished to befriend a local bishop. Thus begins a period of intense denigration of women, which only intensifies through the centuries as the push for clerical celibacy accelerates. Eventually, the nuns could not even depend on the aristocrats who had endowed their monasteries in the first place. Even Gandersheim, shortly after the death of Hroswitha, lost its independence, as the Emperor, Henry II, handed the monastery, including its members over to the local bishop. The Abbess Sophia of Gandersheim did not accept this state of affairs easily and managed to prevail for a while. Finally, the Emperor Henry III, of supposedly pious disposition, combined the great Abbeys of

Gandersheim and Quedlinberg into one huge estate for his daughters.[16] This was an age of massive institutional reform, and women were involved only peripherally – that is, if and when they got in the way. None of the reform was aimed at the betterment of women's lives.

It must not be forgotten that the Cluniac reform of the tenth century coincided with the disastrous troubles of the papacy, and that Europe was still struggling to survive the long series of depredations by Viking, Saracen and Magyar. When Hroswitha is placed in this context, her whole life – her very existence – becomes even more mysterious. But exist she did, and in the process, managed to become the first ever Christian dramatist, the first Saxon poet, and the first woman historian of Germany.[17] It is no wonder that Hroswitha's work focused on the re-writing of women's conventional literary roles, because all the evidence points to the fact that women, from the ninth century on, are beginning to internalise the often vicious language used to describe them. Neither is it an accident that this period also sees a new impetus given to Marian devotion. In Hroswitha's account of the foundation of Gandersheim, she writes that it was exactly 881 years 'after a virgin, without loss of her maidenly chastity, brought forth the King.'[18]

The Abbey of Gandersheim was founded in the mid-ninth century by the Duke of Saxony, apparently at his wife's request. All of his daughters were attached to it; one, Hathumod, was its first abbess. Eventually, it became a centre of female learning for the whole of Western Europe. It always enjoyed the imperial protection of Otto I and his successors, and was cultivated by them as part of their German renaissance. We know the names of several of its nuns but, doubtless, the most famous was Hroswitha. Her dates are usually given as 932-1002, though there is no real way of verifying them. She is presumed to be from an aristocratic background, as the royal abbey would not have welcomed other than noblewomen. The structure of the abbey community presents something of an anomaly, as it seems to have been composed both of nuns, with the customary three vows, and canonesses, who would have led a somewhat less constricted life, but with both following the Benedictine rule. Besides, as we have seen, it is something of a miracle that there were any canonesses, as all the reforms aimed to eliminate them and their less enclosed and less restricted lifestyle. Canonesses took vows of obedience and chastity, but were allowed to receive guests, come and go somewhat freely, and own books and some other property. Besides, as befitted their aristocratic lineage, the canonesses were allowed to have servants. Gandersheim, thus, presents itself as one more refuge, in that less than woman-friendly time, for many royal and aristocratic women. Gandersheim became famous for its school and the excellence of its teachers, and seems to have had a particularly well-endowed library.[19] It seems to have been a true haven for women in one of the darkest periods of European cultural and ecclesiastical history.

Hroswitha honoured her teachers in her writings, especially the emperor's niece, Gerberga, who later became abbess. It is clear that Hroswitha was an excellent student and she stands out as a literate and privileged woman in a most unpropitious age. Hroswitha compiled her writings into three volumes, of legends, dramas, and histories. As a woman writer, even one as privileged as she was, Hroswitha, nevertheless feels compelled to engage in the act of self-diminishment as she begins to write:

Although prosody may seem a hard and difficult art for a woman to master, I, without any assistance but that given by the merciful grace of heaven (in which I have trusted, rather than in my own strength), have attempted in this book to sing in dactyls. I was eager that the talent given to me by heaven should not grow rusty from neglect ... Yet if my work is examined by those who know how to weigh things fairly, I shall be more easily pardoned on account of my sex and my inferior knowledge, especially as I did not undertake it of my own will but at your [the abbess] command.[20]

It was safe for Hroswitha to write as long as she accepted her place in the scheme of things and did not claim equality with the male. Nevertheless, the theme of her writings shows that this aristocratic woman was well aware of the situation of women. The tradition she received, both from the Latin playwright, Terence, whom she copied, and from most other writings, was one that rarely showed women in a positive light. Women's frailty, deception, and ignorance were constantly emphasised. As Hroswitha borrows these old stories, like feminists of today, she re-writes them to show female heroism, fidelity and heroic devotion to chastity. The scope of her reading seems extraordinary. It included a whole range of Latin authors, from Horace and Vergil to Terence and even Boethius, as well as dozens of Christian authors, from Jerome to Alcuin, as well as the Vulgate, a host of liturgical texts, and a great deal of apocryphal literature.[21] She says that she wants to give her audience some good literary models of exemplary conduct, rooted in the monastic ideal, which she seems to have loved. In her eight legends, six plays, two epics and some short poems, she presents the triumph of good over evil and the inevitable triumph of the Christian faith.

Some of Hroswitha's choice of topics are conventional, but she manages to give them her own particular and creative twist. One of her plays, *Pelagius,* seems to follow the conventional Christian storyline of the wicked ruler challenging the virginity of young believers, and then executing them for their insistence on maintaining their virginity. But Pelagius is a young man, and his challenger is not a Roman provincial governor, but is portrayed as a preying Saracen homosexual. Hroswitha is careful not just to paint her *dramatis personae* in the stark colours of good and evil, but offers contrast and tension. Her martyrs are never simply passive, but are active in their own defence. One can imagine the young nuns, who must have played these parts, deriving the greatest pleasure from their enactment:

Embracing with his left the martyr's sacred neck,
So that thus he may place at last a single kiss.
But the martyr thwarted the King's shrewd playful act
And swung at the King's lips promptly with his fist.

He dealt such a blow to the King's face below
That the blood gushing forth from the inflicted wound
Stained the King's beard and wetted all his garments.[22]

Pelagius was eventually killed by being flung from the ramparts to the river below (the scene is set in Cordoba), and when found to be still alive, was beheaded. Some fishermen found the body and, after the 'sacred funeral rites', gave it a fitting burial. When healings began to occur in great numbers, the outraged king had the body disinterred and burnt. Even then, the head remained intact, 'and the folk rejoiced in the patron granted them by God'.

All six plays of Hroswitha deal with the confrontation between the early Christians and paganism, but each bears her own creative signature. All commentators agree that her dramatic masterpiece is the play, *Abraham*, which recounts the fall and redemption of Abraham's niece, Mary. Abraham is a hermit, and after an exemplary life in a cell next to his, Mary 'jumped from her window' to follow a young monk with whom she had fallen in love. Mary despaired of ever gaining forgiveness and takes on the life of a prostitute, thus heaping sin upon sin. A friend reports to Abraham:

She has chosen as her abode the house of a certain procurer who treats her with tender love. And not without profit, I may say, for every day he receives large sums of money from her lovers.

Abraham decides to disguise himself as one of these lovers and sets off to save his niece. He arrives at the inn where Mary is set up as a prostitute, pays the required fee, telling the procurer, 'That is why I burn and for her love so yearn.' Mary arrives and is greeted by Abraham: 'Come on, Mary, give me a kiss.' Mary replies: 'I will not only give you a taste of sweet kisses, but will caress your ancient neck with close embraces.' 'That is what I am after,' Abraham replies. But Mary suddenly smells the odour of sanctity from Abraham, while he persists in being lustful 'in the manner of lewd young men'. Mary suddenly, to everyone's consternation, begins to lament her sins, but Abraham still gamefully keeps up his pretence: 'I didn't come all this way to join you in lamenting your sins but to be joined to you in making love and being gay.' He persuades her to retire to the bedroom, and there reveals himself to her. Mary disposes of her ill-gotten gains because 'It is neither sanctioned nor acceptable that gifts be given to God which were acquired through sin.' Mary returns, enters on a life of penance and strives 'to appear as brightly radiant as she was once foul'.[23]

It is almost impossible on reading this and the other plays not to hear the laughter of the convent players as they enact these 'edifying' and far from prudish tales. Hroswitha seems to be able to enter with ease into the world of prostitutes as procurer, lover and harlot in order to redeem them all by God's grace. They are definitely tongue-in-cheek productions, challenging the restrictive male world of her time with skill and playfulness. Her aim, however, is clear. Where Terence harped on the frailty and deception of women, Hroswitha, with many variations, emphasises their heroic attachment to chastity.

Hroswitha's work disappeared until the fifteenth century, but since then she has been the subject of continuous study. Peter Dronke, a contemporary literary critic, is very sympathetic to her work and has done much to make it better known. He suggests that 'women write from inner need, ardent yet unfanatical, seeking solutions that are apt and truthful existentially.'[24] One of the most frequently quoted sayings of Terence is the one used by the bishops of Vatican II at the opening of the Pastoral Constitution on the Church, *Gaudium et Spes: nihil humanum alienum mihi*, nothing human is alien to me. This certainly can be said also of Hroswitha's work. She has the ability to portray many levels of human existence, even though, in the end, her main objective is not to portray character, but to emphasise the power of faith and of God's grace. She mirrors her age in making most of her saints to be members of the aristocracy, at the same time both beautiful and gifted with charming manners and polite speech .

Hroswitha is perhaps best remembered for her dramas, and

her place as the first Christian dramatist. It is, then, appropriate to leave her the last word:

Therefore I, the Strong Voice of Gandersheim, have not found it objectionable to imitate him [Terence] in composition, whom others study in reading, so that in that very same form of composition through which the shameless acts of lascivious women were depicted, the laudable chastity of sacred virgins may be praised within the limits of my little talent.[25]

Conclusion

From the women of the biblical stories to the learned and aristocratic Hroswitha at the end of the tenth century, the story of Christian women traverses an astonishing terrain. Women travelled this territory as disciples and apostles, house-church leaders and prophets, martyrs and virgins, princesses and slaves, wives, lovers, concubines and widows, abbesses and canonesses, evangelists and missionaries, founders and members of religious organisations, and, perhaps, even one pope. Their names may sound strange to our ears at first, because for most people, the Christian story has been handed on without a trace of their passing. Hopefully, in time, these names will sound familiar to a new generation.

I name some of them again, because women have been virtually nameless in the Christian tradition, and there is a continuing need to honour the memory of these forgotten foremothers. Readers of this volume will have met, among many others, Mary of Magdala and Mary of Bethany, Martha and Salome, Phoebe and Prisca, Thecla and Maximilla, Perpetua and Felicitas, Blandina and Sabina, Marcella and Paula, Macrina and Melania, Brigid and Bertha, Clothilde and Ethelburga, Radegund and Hilda, Frideswide and Ermengarde, Leoba and Papissa Joanna, Tetta and Dhuoda. These women are Jewish, Greek, Phoenician, Syrian, Roman, Celtic, Frankish, and Saxon. They lived in an astonishing variety of circumstances and all of them were rooted in a particular expression of the Christian story. To these, it is necessary to add the uncountable numbers of nameless women Christians, whose passing left little discoverable trace in the annals of their time. All of them, without exception, have brought Christianity to where it is today, and for the most part, continue to remain unacknowledged by the wider tradition.

For it is an unaccountable fact of the Christian tradition that it found itself able to tell its own story without any inclusion of women. Indeed, as this book reveals, women were intentionally omitted from the central core of Christianity's version of itself. From its beginning as a faith, rooted in a message of inclusion and equality, the Christian story progressively became at once a universal faith and a virtually woman-free zone. Women were, of course, present in every stage of the church's life, but each ecclesiastical reform could envisage Christian continuity only as a virtually all-male community. As this volume shows, this was not done with the consent of women, but against their explicit hopes and desires. More than anything else, I hope to have demonstrated the glorious resilience of women, as they find ways to tread their own spiritual path despite every conceivable obstacle. When women are marginalised in one area, they almost magically pop up somewhere else. The spasmodic and episodic nature of this evidence about women's lives, however, offers a distinctive challenge to the historian. Here, I hope to have avoided some of the pitfalls. It has not been my wish to make women seem either innocent or perfect, but the fact remains that almost all the women known to us in the sources appear there because of the desirability of their witness in a patriarchal world.

One of the increasingly obvious tragedies of women's Christian story is the use of marriage, in particular, for the silencing of women. Virginal women did not fare much better, but they illustrate the fact that the sometimes violent rejection of the patriarchal household was an essential pre-requisite for any kind of independent spiritual life. We are left, therefore, with barely a record of the married woman. The biblical edicts about the silencing of women represent one of the most perfectly worked out aspects of the biblical legacy. The resulting tragedy will mark Christianity forever. No amount of contemporary educational opportunities, even where these are freely offered, will fill the two-millennial void. The Christian message has been articulated intentionally and with continually renewed emphasis without the voice, insight, reflection or genius of women. The contemporary and traditional doctrinal structure of Christianity has been intentionally formulated using the Christian insights of a very small minority of ordained men. The integrity of this theological monolith seems quite tenuous when viewed through a feminist historical lens.

And yet, women did achieve their own authoritative and powerful space within the tradition. When, and if, a more complete story of Christianity is written, it will be discovered that the women, in fact, were the carriers and maintainers of the essential Christian message. Starting with their role as the exemplary faith-filled disciples, through that of foundational biblical witnesses of the crucifixion, burial and resurrection scenes, and continuing with their ongoing role as missionary evangelists through the Mediterranean and later the Celtic and Anglo-Saxon worlds, Christian women can lay claim to a definitive role in spreading the core aspects of the good news. Without too much exaggeration, it can be claimed that, while men cared specifically for the political and institutional dimensions of the faith, women expressed in their lives their allegiance to the good news.

While there is truth in these statements, all historical observations about women remain partial, distorted, eccentric and ultimately profoundly dissatisfying. We are left with fragments and each historian has to cobble together a credible story from such pitiably sparse remains. The doing of history depends on sources, their verification and interpretation, and finally, their presentation in some coherent and integrated format. My intention here has been to try to convey some continuity in women's Christian story, and to illustrate some sense of what might have been a more complete and true form of Christianity, had Jesus' message of inclusion and equality been taken seriously. I have also tried to present some extraordinary women whose presence on the Christian scene has been erased, distorted or simply found irrelevant. Leoba's biographer spoke, however unwittingly, for all his brothers, when he voiced his opinion about the apparent uselessness of her story to the real historical record. I am reminded of my early teaching days, when seminarians pointedly laid down their pens whenever I included women in the history of Christianity, and just as pointedly resumed their note-taking when I returned to the real history of men's doings. It is my profound hope that this book will serve, in some small way to make the telling of the Christian story an impossibility without the complete and ongoing witness of women.

Select Bibliography

Adomnan of Iona, *Life of St Columba*, Penguin Books, 1995.

Allen, Prudence, R.S.M., *The Concept of Woman: The Aristotelian Revolution 750 BC-AD 1250*, Eden Press, 1985.

Armstrong, Karen, *A History of God*, Mandarin, 1994.

Armstrong, Karen, *The End of Silence: Women and the Priesthood*, Fourth Estate, 1993.

Armstrong, Karen, *The Gospel According to Women: Christianity's Creation of the Sex-War in the West*, Elm Tree Books, 1986.

Atkinson, Clarissa, *et al.*, *Immaculate and Powerful: The Female in Sacred Image and Social Reality*, Harvard: Women's Studies in Religion, 1985.

Augustine, Saint, *Confessions*, Penguin Books, 1979.

Baker, Derek, (Ed.), *Medieval Women*, Blackwell, 1978.

Barstow, Anne Llewellyn, *Married Priests and the Reforming Papacy: The Eleventh Century Debates*, Edwin Mellen Press, 1982.

Behr-Siegel, Elisabeth, *The Ministry of Women in the Church*, Oakwood Publications, 1987.

Benstock, Shari , (Ed.), *The Private Self: Theory and Practice of Women's Autobiographical Writings*, University of North Carolina Press, 1988.

Beresford Ellis, Peter, *Celtic Women: Women in Celtic Society and Literature*, Eerdmans, 1996.

Bordo, Susan, *Unbearable Weight: Feminism, Western Culture and the Body*, University of California, 1993.

Borresen, Kari Elisabeth, (Ed.), *The Image of God: Gender Models in Judaeo-Christian Tradition*, Fortress Press, 1995.

Bowman Thurston, Bonnie, *The Widows: A Women's Ministry in the Early Church*, Fortress Press, 1989.

Bridenthal, Renate, *et al.*, *Becoming Visible: Women in European History*, Houghton Mifflin Co., 1977.

Brown, Peter, *The Cult of the Saints*, University of Chicago Press, 1981.

Brown, Peter, *The Body and Society: Men, Women and Sexual Renunciation in Early Christianity*, Columbia University Press, 1988.

Peter Brown, *The World of Late Antiquity*, Thames and Hudson, Reprinted 1989.

Bullough, V. I, *et al.*, *Sexual Practices and the Medieval Church*, Promotheus, 1982.

Burrus, Virginia, *Chastity as Autonomy: Women in the Stories of Apocryphal Acts*, Edwin Mellen Press, 1987.

Bynum, Caroline Walker, *The Resurection of the Body in Western Christianity, 200-1136*, Columbia University Press, 1995.

Bynum, Caroline Walker, *et al.*, *Gender and Religion: On the Complexity of Symbols*, Beacon Press, 1986.

Cameron, A. (Ed.), *History as Text: The Writing of Ancient History*, Duckworth, 1981.

Caputi, Jane, *Gossips, Gorgons and Crones: The Fates of the Earth*, Bear and Co., 1993.

Carlson Brown, Joanne and Bohn, Carole R. (Eds.), *Christianity, Patriarchy and Abuse: A Feminist Critique*, Pilgrim Press, 1989.

Carr, Anne E., and Schüssler Fiorenza, Elisabeth, (Eds.), *The Special Nature of Women*, SCM, 1991.

Carroll, Bernice, *Liberating Women's History: Theoretical and Critical Essays*, University of Illinois, 1976.

Chopp, Rebecca S. and Davaney, Sheila Greeve, *Horizons in Feminist Theology: Identity, Tradition and Norms*, Fortress Press, 1997.

Cioran, E.M., *Tears and Saints*, University of Chicago Press, 1992.

Clark, Elizabeth A., *Jerome, Chrysostom and Friends*, Edwin Mellen Press, 1979.

Clark, Elizabeth, *Women in the Early Church*, Michael Glazier, 1983.

Clark, Elizabeth A., *Ascetic Piety and Women's Faith: Essays in Late Ancient Christianity*, Edwin Mellen Press, 1986.

Clark, Gillian, *Women in Late Antiquity: Pagan and Christian Life-Styles*, Clarendon Press, 1994.

Clarke, W.K.L., *The Lausiac History of Palladius*, SPCK, 1929.

Connolly, R.H., *Didascalia Apostolorum*, Oxford University Press, 1929.

Condren, Mary, *The Serpent and the Goddess: Women, Religion and Power in Celtic Ireland*, Harper and Row, 1989.

Cooey, Paula, Eakin, William and McDaniel, Jay, (Eds.), *After Patriarchy: Feminist Transformations of the World Religions*, Orbis, 1991.

Cooey, Paula M., *Religious Imagination and the Body: A Feminist Analysis*, Oxford University Press, 1994.

Corish, Patrick, *The Irish Catholic Experience: A Historical Survey*, Gill and MacMillan, 1986.

Crossan, John Dominic, *The Birth of Christianity: Discovering What Happened in the Years Immediately After the Execution of Jesus*, Harper, 1998.

Daly, Mary, *The Church and the Second Sex, With the Feminist Postchristian Introduction and New Archaic Afterwords by the Author*, Beacon Press, 1985.

Danielou, Jean, SJ, *The Ministry of Women in the Early Church*, The Faith Press, 1961.

De Paor, Máire and Liam, *Early Christian Ireland*, Thames and Hudson, 1978.

Douglas, Mary, *Purity and Danger: An Analysis of the Concepts of Purity and Taboo*, Ark, 1984.

Dowell, Susan and Williams, Jane, *Bread, Wine and Women: The Ordination Debate in the Church of England*, Virago, 1994.

Dronke, Peter, *Women Writers of the Middle Ages: A Critical Study of Texts from Perpetua (d. 203) to Marguerite Porete (d. 1310)*, Cambridge University Press, 1984.

Duby, George and Perrot, Michelle, (General Editors), *A History of Women*, Belknap Press, 1992– : Vol. 1. *From Ancient Goddesses to Christian Saints*, Pauline Smith Pantel (Ed.), Harvard, 1992; Vol. 2. *Silences of the Middle Ages*, Christiane Klapisch-Zuber, (Ed.), Harvard, 1992.

Early Christian Writings, Penguin Books, 1980.

Eckenstein, Lina, *Women Under Monasticism: Chapters on Saint-Lore and Convent Life Between AD 500 and AD 1500*, Cambridge University Press, 1986.

Erler, Mary, *et al.*, *Women and Power in the Middle Ages*, University of Georgia Press, 1988.

Fletcher, Richard, *The Conversion of Europe: From Paganism to Christianity 371-1386 AD*, Fontana Press, 1997.

Frend, W.H.C., *The Rise of Christianity*, Darton, Longman and Todd, 1984.

Frend, W.H.C., *Martyrdom and Persecution in the Early Church: A Study of a Conflict from the Maccabees to Donatus*, Basil Blackwell, 1965.

Gies, F. and Gies, J., *Women in the Middle Ages*, Harper, 1978.

Gregory of Tours, *History of the Franks*, Ten Volumes, Translated by Lewis Thorpe, Penguin Books, 1974.

Gryson, Roger, *The Ministry of Women in the Early Church*, Liturgical Press, 1986.

Gudorf, Christine E., *Victimization: Examining Christian Complicity*, Trinity Press International, 1992.

Haskins, Susan, *Mary Magdalen: Myth and Metaphor*, Harper Collins, 1993.

Hayter, Mary, *The New Eve in Christ: The Use and Abuse of the Bible in the Debate about Women in the Church*, SPCK, 1987.

Heine, Susanne, *Women and Early Christianity*, Augsburg Publishing House, 1986.

Jay, Nancy, *Throughout Your Generations Forever: Sacrifice, Religion and Paternity*, University of Chicago Press, 1992.

Jedin, Hubert, (Ed.), *History of the Church*, Ten Volumes: Vol. I. *From the Apostolic Community to Constantine*, Karl Baus, Vol. II. *The Imperial Church from Constantine to the Early Middle Ages*, Karl Baus, *et al.*, The Seabury Press, 1980; Vol. III. *The Church in the Age of Feudalism*, Friedrich Kempf, *et al.*, Burns & Oates, 1980.

Johnson, Elizabeth A., *She who is: The Mystery of God in Feminist Theological Discourse*, Crossroad, 1992.

Johnson, Elizabeth A., *Friends of God and Prophets: A Feminist Theological Reading of the Communion of Saints*, Continuum, 1998.

Johnson, Paul, *A History of Christianity*, Penguin Books, 1976.

Kadel, Andrew, *Matrology: A Bibliography of Writings by Christian Women from the First to the Fifteenth Centuries*, Continuum, 1995.

Kelly, Joan, *Women, History and Theory*, (Chicago, 1984).

Kelly, J.N.D., *Jerome: His Life, Writings and Controversies*, Harper and Row, 1975.

Kemp, Sandra and Squires, Judith, *Feminisms*, Oxford University Press, 1997.

Kenney, James F., *The Sources for the Early History of Ireland*, New York, 1929, with additions by Ludwig Bieler, 1966.

Kleinberg, Aviad M., *Prophets in Their Own Country: Living Saints and the Making of Sainthood in the Later Middle Ages*, University of Chicago Press, 1992.

Kleinberg, S. Jay, *Retrieving Women's History: Changing Perceptions of the Role of Women in Politics and Society*, Oxford, 1988.

Küng, Hans, *Christianity: The Religious Situation of Our Time*, SCM Press, 1995.

Kushner, J. and Wemple S., *Women of the Medieval World*, Blackwell, 1985.

Labarge, Margaret Wade, *Women in Medieval Life*, London, 1984.

LeGoff, Jacques, (Ed.), *The Medieval World*, Collins and Brown, 1990.

Lerner, Gerda, *The Creation of Patriarchy*, Oxford University Press, 1986.

Lerner, Gerda, *The Creation of Feminist Consciousness: From the Middle Ages to 1870*, Oxford University Press, 1993.

MacDonald, Margaret, *Early Christian Women and Pagan Opinion: The Power of the Hysterical Woman*, Cambridge University Press, 1976.

MacHaffie, Barbara J., *HerStory: Women in Christian Tradition*, Fortress Press, 1986.

MacHaffie, Barbara J., *Readings in HerStory: Women in Christian Tradition*, Fortress Press, 1992.

Maisch, Ingrid, *Mary Magdalene: The Image of a Woman Through the Centuries*, The Liturgical Press, 1998.

Maitland, Sara, *A Map of a New Country: Women and Christianity*, Routledge, 1979.

Maitland, Sara and Mulford, Wendy, *Virtuous Magic: Women Saints and Their Meanings*, Mowbray, 1998.

Malone, Mary T., *Christian Attitudes to Women in the Fourth Century: Background and New Directions*, Unpublished Ph.D. Dissertation, University of Toronto, 1971.

Malone, Mary T., *Who Is My Mother?: Rediscovering the Mother of Jesus*, William C. Brown, 1984.

Malone, Mary T., *Women Christian: New Vision*, Brown Roa, 1985.

Malone, Mary T., 'Unfinished Agenda: A Critical Look at the History of Celibacy,' in *The Way Supplement*, Vol. 77, 1993, pp. 66-75.

Malone, Mary T., 'Mary, Advocate of Justice,' in *All Generations Shall Call Me Blessed*, Edited by Francis A. Eigo, OSA, Proceedings of the Theology Institute of Villanova University, 1994, pp. 73-105.

Markale, Jean, *Women of the Celts*, Inner Traditions International, 1975.

May, Melanie H., *Women and the Church: The Challenge of Ecumenical Solidarity in an Age of Alienation*, Eerdmans, 1991.

Mayeskie, Mary Anne, *Women: Models of Liberation*, Sheed and Ward, 1988.

McAlister, Linda Lopez, (Ed.), *Hypatia's Daughters: Fifteen Hundred Years of Women Philosophers*, Indiana University Press, 1996.

McGinn, Bernard, (Ed.), *Christian Spirituality: Origins to the Twelfth Century*, Crossroad, 1985.

McNamara, Jo Ann Kay, *Sisters in Arms: Catholic Nuns Through Two Millennia*, Harvard University Press, 1996.

Miles, Margaret, *Carnal Knowing: Female Nakedness and Religious Meaning in the Christian West*, Beacon Press, 1989.

Miles, Rosalind, *The Women's History of the World*, Paladin, 1988.

Morris, Joan, *The Lady Was a Bishop*, MacMillan, 1973.

Morris, Joan, *Pope John VIII – an English Woman; Alias Pope Joan*, Vrai Publishers, 1985.

Musurillo, Herbert, (Ed. and Trans.), *The Acts of the Christian Martyrs*, Clarendon Press, 1972.

Nelson, James B., and Longfellow, Sandra P., (Eds.), *Sexuality and the Sacred: Sources for Theological Reflection*, Westminster/ John Knox Press, 1994.

Nichols, J.A. and Shank, Lillian T., (Eds.), *Medieval Religious Women*, 3 Volumes: Vol. 1. *Distant Echoes*, Vol. 2. *Peace Weavers*, Vol. 3. *Hidden Springs*, Cistercian Publications, 1984-1995.

O'Faolain, Julia, *Women in the Wall*, Penguin Books, 1978.

Osborne, M.L., *Women in Western Thought*, Random House, 1979.

Pagels, Elaine, *The Gnostic Gospels*, Houghton Mifflin Co., 1977.

Pagels, Elaine, *Adam, Eve, and the Serpent*, Vintage Books, 1989.

Perrot, Michelle, (Ed.), *Writing Women's History*, Blackwell, 1984.

Petroff, Elizabeth Avilda, *Medieval Women's Visionary Literature*, Oxford University Press, 1986.

Petroff, Elizabeth Avilda, *Body and Soul: Essays on Medieval Women and Mysticism*, Oxford University Press, 1994.

Philips, John A., *Eve: History of an Idea*, Harper and Row, 1984.

Rader, Rosemary, *Breaking Boundaries: Male/Female Friendship in Early Christian Communities*, Paulist Press, 1983.

Ranke-Heinemann, Uta, *Eunuchs for the Kingdom of Heaven: Women, Sexuality and the Catholic Church*, Doubleday, 1990.

Rankka, Kristine M., *Women and the Value of Suffering: An Aw(e)ful Rowing towards God*, The Liturgical Press, 1998.

Ricci, Carla, *Mary Magdalen and Many Others: Women Who Followed Jesus*, Burns and Oates, 1994.

Robinson, J.M., (Ed.), *Nag Hammadi, Gnosticism and Early Christianity*, New York, 1977.

Robinson, J.M., *The Nag Hammadi Library in English*, Harper and Row, 1977.

Ruether, Rosemary Radford and McLaughlin, Eleanor, *Women of Spirit: Female Leadership in the Jewish and Christian Traditions*, Simon and Schuster, 1979.

Ruether, Rosemary Radford, *Womanguides: Readings toward a Feminist Theology*, Beacon Press, 1985.

Ruether, Rosemary Radford, *Women and Redemption: A Theological History*, Fortress Press, 1998.

Schillebeeckx, Edward and Halkes, Catharina, *Mary: Yesterday, Today, Tomorrow*, Crossroads, 1993.

Schmitt, Miriam and Kulzer, Linda (Eds.), *Medieval Women Monastics: Wisdom's Wellsprings*, Liturgical Press, 1996.

Schneiders, Sandra, *Beyond Patching: Faith and Feminism in the Catholic Church*, Paulist Press, 1991.

Schneiders, Sandra, *The Revelatory Text: Interpreting the New Testament as Sacred Scripture*, Harper, 1991.

Schottroff, Luise, *Lydia's Impatient Sisters: A Feminist Social History of Early Christianity*, Westminster/John Knox Press, 1995.

Schüssler Fiorenza, Elisabeth, *In Memory of Her: A Feminist Theological Reconstruction of Christian Origins*, Crossroad, 1983.

Schüssler Fiorenza, Elisabeth, *But She Said: Feminist Practices of Biblical Interpretation*, Beacon Press, 1992.

Schüssler Fiorenza, Elisabeth, (Ed.), *Searching the Scriptures: Volume One, A Feminist Introduction*, Crossroad, 1993.

Schüssler Fiorenza, Elisabeth, (Ed.), *Searching the Scriptures: Volume Two, A Feminist Commentary*, Crossroad, 1994.

Sells, Michael A., *Mystical Languages of Unsaying*, University of Chicago Press, 1994.

Shahar, Shulamith, *The Fourth Estate: A History of Women in the Middle Ages*, Methuen, 1983.

Sheldrake, Philip, *Spirituality and History: Questions of Interpretation and Method*, Crossroad, 1992.

Smith, Sidonie, *A Poetics of Women's Autobiography: Marginality and the Fictions of Self-Representation*, Indiana University Press, 1987.

Soskice, Janet Martin, *After Eve*, Collins, 1990.

Southern, Richard W., *Western Society and the Church in the Middle Ages*, Pelican History of the Church, Vol. 2, 1970.

Stanford, Peter, *The She-Pope: A Quest for the Truth Behind the Mystery of Pope Joan*, Arrow Books, 1998.

Swidler, Leonard, *Biblical Affirmations of Women*, The Westminster Press, 1979.

Swidler, Leonard and Swidler, Arlene, (Eds.), *Women Priests: A Catholic Commentary on the Vatican Declaration*, Paulist Press, 1977.

Tong, Rosemary, *Feminist Thought: A Comprehensive Introduction*, Routledge, 1994.

Torjeson, Karen Jo, *When Women Were Priests*, Harper, 1993.

Tucker, Ruth A. and Liefeld, Walter, *Daughters of the Church: Women and Ministry from New Testament Times to the Present*, Zondervan, 1987.

Warner, Marina, *Alone of all Her Sex*, Quartet books, 1978.

Warner, Marina, *Monuments and Maidens: The Allegory of the Female Form*, Picador, 1985.

Weaver, Mary Jo, *New Catholic Women: A Contemporary Challenge to Traditional Religious Authority*, Harper and Row, 1985.

Webster, Margaret, *A New Strength, A New Song: The Journey to Women's Priesthood*, Mowbray, 1994.

West, Angela, *Deadly Innocence: Feminism and the Mythology of Sin*, Cassell, 1985.

White, Erin and Tulip, Marie, *Knowing Otherwise: Feminism, Women and Religion*, David Lovell Publishing, 1991.

Wiethaus, Ulrike, (Ed.), *Maps of Flesh and Light: The Religious Experience of Medieval Women Mystics*, Syracuse University Press, 1993.

Williams, Marty and Echols, Anne, *Between Pit and Pendulum: Women in the Middle Ages,* Princeton, 1994.

Wilson, Katharina, *Medieval Women Writers,* University of Georgia Press, 1984.

Wire, Antoinette, *The Corinthian Women Prophets: A Reconstruction Through Paul's Rhetoric,* Fortress, 1990.

Primary Sources

It would be impossible to list all the primary sources on which I depended for this book. Here I simply list some of the more accessible collections in translation.

Women:
The most complete collection is in Andrew Kadel, *Matrology: A Bibliography of Writings by Christian Women From the First to the Fifteenth Centuries,* Continuum, 1995.
Perhaps the most helpful anthology is that of Elizabeth Avilda Petroff, *Medieval Women's Visionary Literature,* Oxford University Press, 1986.
See also Barbara MacHaffie, *Readings in HerStory: Women in Christian Tradition,* Fortress Press, 1992.

Early Christianity:
The two volumes, *Searching the Scriptures: A Feminist Introduction,* and *Searching the Scriptures: A Feminist Commentary,* edited by Elisabeth Schüssler Fiorenza, are invaluable. Crossroad, 1993 and 1994. The patristic writings are voluminous, but the best entry point still is *Patrology,* edited by Johannes Quasten, Christian Classics, Inc., 1983-1992: Vol. 1. *The Beginnings of Christian Literature: From the Apostles Creed to Irenaeus;* Vol. 2. *The Ante-Nicene Literature after Irenaeus;* Vol. 3. *The Golden Age of Greek Patristic Literature;* Vol. 4. *The Golden Age of Latin Patristic Literature: From the Council of Nicea to the Council of Chalcedon.*
A very useful small collection is *Early Christian Writings,* Penguin Books, 1980.
See also Henry S. Bettenson, *Documents of the Christian Church,* Holt, Rhinehart and Winston, 1965.

Celtic Church:
Hart, Richard, *Ecclesiastical Records of England, Ireland and Scotland: From the Fifth Century Till the Reformation,* MacMillan, 2nd Ed., 1846.
Hughes, Kathleen, *Early Christian Ireland: Introduction to the Sources,* Cambridge University Press, 1977.

Beresford Ellis, Peter, *Women in Celtic Society and Literature*, Eerdmans, 1995. This has a good up-to-date bibliography.

Kenney, J. F., *Sources for Early History of Ireland*, Cambridge University Press, 1929, remains an indispensable source as does *Early Christian Ireland*, by Máire and Liam de Paor, Thames and Hudson, 1978. The recent Penguin Edition of *Adomnan's Life of St Columba*, translated by Richard Sharpe (1995) is a wonderful introduction to the Celtic Church in Dal Riada.

Anglo-Saxon Church:
The work of Bede is still the gateway to the Anglo-Saxon Church: *Ecclesiastical History of the English People*, Translated by Leo Sherley-Price, with a revised translation by R. E. Latham, Penguin, 1955, 1960. See also the *Anglo-Saxon Chronicle*, J. M. Dent, and *Councils and Ecclesiastical Documents Relating to Great Britain and Ireland*, Clarendon Press, 1964 reprint, edited and translated by Arthur Haddan and William Stubbs.

Frankish Church:
The huge *Monumenta Germaniae* lists the works of Venantius Fortunatus, Gregory of Tours and a host of others, Paris, 1908. J. M. Wallace-Hadrill, *The Frankish Church*, is one of the best and most accessible contemporary interpretations, Oxford, 1983.

Notes

CHAPTER ONE: READING WOMEN INTO HISTORY

1. See *Origins,* October 6, 1988, Vol. 18: No. 17.

2. See *Origins,* November 15, 1990, Vol. 20: No. 23.

3. The text of the document is published in *Women Priests: A Catholic Commentary on the Vatican Declaration,* Edited by Leonard Swidler and Arlene Swidler, Paulist Press, 1977, pp. 37-49.

4. Anne Llewellyn Barstow, *Married Priests and the Reforming Papacy: The Eleventh Century Debates,* The Edwin Mellen Press, 1982, p. 60

5. *The Woman in the Modern World,* arranged and edited by the Monks of Solesmes, St Paul Editions, 1959.

6. The Decree on Ecumenism, *Unitatis Redintegratio,* was published on November 21, 1964, to be followed in 1965 by the Declaration on the Relation of the Church to Non-Christian Religions, *Nostra Aetate.*

7. The first wave of the feminist movement is associated with the mid-nineteenth century search for women's rights culminating in the demand for suffrage. Protestant Christian women, in their study of the scriptures, found no support for the religious and cultural restrictions on women, and began to challenge many facets of conventional living arrangements, from the use of 'masculine' language to the exclusion of women from political and religious leadership. The normative marital arrangement of male headship and female silence and submission was particularly challenged. With the achievement of the vote and the advent of the two world wars, much of this debate had been forgotten.

8. The Pontifical Biblical Commission was founded by Leo XIII at the beginning of the twentieth century to oversee proper biblical interpretation. One of its most influential documents was the 1964 *Instruction on the Historical Truth of the Gospels.*

9. Adrienne Rich, 'When We Dead Awaken: Writing as Re-Vision' in *Adrienne Rich's Poetry,* selected and edited by Barbara Charlesworth Gelpi and Albert Gelpi, W.W.W. Norton & Co. Inc., 1975.

10. Joan Kelly-Gadol, 'Did Women Have a Renaissance?' in *Becoming Visible: Women in European History,* Edited by Renate Bridenthal and Claudia Koonz, Houghton Mifflin Co., 1977, pp. 137–164.

11. There is an abundance of literature on feminist historiography. The following are helpful: Pauline Schmitt Pantel, 'Women and Ancient History Today,' pp. 464-471 in *A History of Women: From Ancient Goddesses to Christian Saints*, Harvard University Press, 1992. This is Volume 1 of a five volume series on *A History of Women in the West*, with Georges Duby and Michelle Perrot as General Editors. For a very readable account of the 'new historiography', see Philip Sheldrake, *Spirituality and History: Questions of Interpretation and Method*, Crossroad, 1991.

12. One hopeful sign is the publication of *A World History of Christianity*, edited by Adrian Hastings, Cassell, 1999. While attentive to the worldwide diversity of the Christian reality, it does not yet take the case of women seriously, but it is a step in the right direction.

13. The phrase was coined by the biblical scholar, Elisabeth Schüssler Fiorenza, but is now part of the lexicon of every feminist. It draws the attention of women to the fact that no traditional document was written with the welfare of women in mind, not even, as she would assert, the biblical documents. It therefore serves women well to reserve judgement about the intent and purpose of all such documents, however well-meaning. This is especially the case with writing addressing or making statements about the 'whole of mankind,' and even more so about religious documentation of God's will for 'all mankind'.

14. Joan W. Scott, 'Gender: A Useful Category of Historical Analysis', in *American Historical Review*, Vol. 71, 1986, pp. 1053-1075.

15. Sheila Briggs, 'A History of Our Own', in Rebecca S. Chopp and Sheila Greeve Davaney, (eds.), *Horizons in Feminist Theology: Identity, Tradition and Norms*, pp. 165-178, Fortress Press, 1997.

CHAPTER TWO: THE WOMEN DISCIPLES

1. The two most familiar gospel texts on Mary are, of course, the nativity scenes in Matthew and Luke which, even though they differ remarkably in their theological meaning, have been combined into the 'Christmas Story' (Mt 2 and Lk 1, 2). Each of the synoptic gospels contains appearances of Mary during the public ministry of Jesus. Mark (Mk 3:31-35) seems to be the earliest and there are parallels with interesting variations in Mt 12:46-50 and Lk 8:19-21. Mk 6:1-5 portrays the astonishment of Jesus at the unbelieving attitudes of his family and townspeople, and Lk 11:27-28 shows Jesus yet again deflecting attention from his biological family to his family of disciples. Finally, John's gospel has provided Christians with images of Mary's presence in two very familiar biblical scenes – the wedding at Cana (Jn 2:1-12) and the crucifixion (Jn 19:25-27).

2. There was much debate at the Second Vatican Council about the role of Mary in Roman Catholic life. Chapter Eight of the Dogmatic Constitution on the Church, *Lumen Gentium,* had explicitly warned Catholics about 'false exaggerations' in their devotion to Mary. The end result was that a certain falling off in devotion to Mary has always been associated with the Council. At any rate, it was not until about ten years later that Paul VI published his remarkable document on Mary. Despite subsequent papal statements, this remains one of the best summaries of the contemporary official Roman Catholic position on Marian devotion.

3. The Greek word, *akolouthon,* has always been interpreted as the official designation of discipleship.

4. *In Memory of Her: A Feminist Theological Reconstruction of Christian Origins,* Crossroads, 1983.

5. *Mulieris Dignitatem,* dated August 15, 1988. In the sections headed, Guardians of the Gospel Message, and First Witnesses of the Resurrection, the Pope shows his familiarity with recent feminist and other biblical scholarship. (Sections 15 and 16).

6. Lk 8:4-15. As we shall see in Chapter 4, this attribution of the 'hundredfold' came to be particularly associated with all those who had taken and remained faithful to a vow of virginity.

7. See the chapter on this story in Elisabeth Schüssler Fiorenza's *But She Said: Feminist Practices of Biblical Interpretation,* Part 1, Chapter 2, 'Arachne – Weaving the Word: The Practice of Interpretation', pp. 51–76, Beacon Press, 1992.

8. See the long section on the story of the woman of Samaria in Sandra M. Schneiders, *The Revelatory Text: Interpreting the New Testament as Sacred Scripture,* Harper, 1991, p. 180-199.

9. Section 15.

10. For a wonderful examination of the biblical story and its subsequent historical development, see Susan Haskins, *Mary Magdalen: Myth and Metaphor,* Harper Collins, 1993.

11. Mk 16:1-8; Mt 28:1-8; Lk 24:1-12; Jn 20:1-10.

12. Mk 16:9-11 (perhaps a later addition to the gospel); Mt 28:8-10; Lk 24:4-5 (men in dazzling clothes); Jn 20:11-18.

13. Jn 20:18.

14. In addition to the books by Elisabeth Schüssler Fiorenza already mentioned, see the following two volumes edited by her: *Searching the Scriptures: A Feminist Introduction,* Crossroad, 1993, and *Searching the Scriptures: A Feminist Commentary,* Crossroad, 1994. For a selection of views by other feminist scholars, see Letty M. Russell, Editor, *Feminist Interpretation of the Bible,* The Westminster Press, 1985, and Adela Yarbro Collins, Editor, *Feminist Perspectives on Biblical Scholarship,*

Scholars' Press, 1985. For an excellent journalistic overview of feminist biblical activity, see Cullen Murphy, 'Women and the Bible,' in *The Atlantic Monthly*, August, 1993, pp. 39-64.

15. 'Politicizing the Sacred Texts: Elizabeth Cady Stanton and The Women's Bible', Carolyn De Swarte Gifford, in *Searching the Scriptures: A Feminist Introduction*, Part 1, Chapter 3. For full reference, see note 24 above.

16. Sandra M. Schneiders, *The Revelatory Text: Interpreting the New Testament as Sacred Scripture*, tells us that she wrote this book because she was 'increasingly plagued by questions that had no answers' (p. 2, Introduction). Her book is an erudite yet accessible attempt to provide some answers.

CHAPTER THREE: EARLY CHRISTIAN WOMEN

1. Karen Jo Torjesen, 'Reconstruction of Women's Early Christian History,' p. 290 in *Searching the Scriptures: A Feminist Introduction*, Edited by Elisabeth Schüssler Fiorenza, Crossroad, 1993.

2. Elisabeth Schüssler Fiorenza, *In Memory of Her: A Feminist Theological Reconstruction of Christian Origins*, Crossroad, 1984, p. 211.

3. There is something of a consensus among mainline scripture scholars about the dating of New Testament texts. Here, I am following the dating suggested in the two volumes of *Searching the Scriptures* edited by Elisabeth Schüssler Fiorenza. For convenience, these texts will be referred to henceforth as SSFI for Vol. 1, and SSFC for Vol. 2. For full references, see note 14, Chapter Two.

4. See Jo Ann Kay McNamara, *Sisters in Arms: Catholic Nuns Through Two Millennia*, Harvard University Press, 1996, p. 13.

5. 'Early Christian Women and their Cultural Context: Issues of Method in Historical Reconstruction', in *Feminist Perspectives on Biblical Scholarship*, Scholars Press, 1985, pp. 65 -91.

6. For a detailed feminist analysis of the role of women in the Acts of the Apostles, see the appropriate section in SSFC, Chapter 37, by Clarice J. Martin.

7. See Acts 9:1-2 and Acts 22:4-5.

8. For an extended reflection on the role of women in positions of theological leadership, see 'Prisca, Teacher of Wisdom' in *But She Said: Feminist Practices of Biblical Interpretation*, by Elisabeth Schüssler Fiorenza, Beacon Press, 1992, pp. 167-194.

9. For contemporary commentaries on Junia and Phoebe, see Bernadette Brooten, 'Junia ... Outstanding among the Apostles (Romans 16:7),' in *Women Priests: A Catholic Commentary on the Vatican Declaration*, edited by Leonard Swidler and Arlene Swidler, Paulist

Press, 1977, chapter 15. It is Brooten who has done the intensive research on the name Junia. See also the relevant sections of *In Memory of Her*, and especially Elizabeth A. Castelli, 'Romans,' in SSFC, pp. 272-300.

10. op. cit., p. 278.

11. Lone Fatum, '1 Thessalonians', p. 251 in SSFC.

12. For this whole discussion, see Antoinette Clark Wire, *The Corinthian Women Prophets: A Reconstruction through Paul's Rhetoric*, Fortress Press, 1990, and her article on '1 Corinthians' in SSFC, pp. 153-195.

13. See Mary Rose D'Angelo on 'Colossians' in SSFC, pp. 313-324.

14. *Sexism and God-Talk: Toward a Feminist Theology*, Beacon Press, 1983, pp. 18-19. Her more recent work carries this 'critical feminist principle' through the whole of Christian history: *Women and Redemption: A Theological History*, Fortress Press, 1998.

15. See the important discussion of Roman households in 'Ephesians,' SSFC, pp. 325-348, by Sarah J. Tanzer.

16. *Mulieris Dignitatem*, Section VII, 'The Church – The Bride of Christ: The "Great Mystery".'

17. See the discussion on 1 Peter by Kathleen E. Corley in SSFC, pp. 349-360.

18. See the excellent commentary by Linda M. Maloney in SSFC, pp. 361-380.

CHAPTER FOUR: WOMEN IN APOCRYPHAL AND GNOSTIC LITERATURE

1. *Acts of Paul and Thecla*, 34, in Elizabeth Clark, *Women in the Early Church*, Michael Glazier, 1983.

2. *The Gospel of Mary Magdalen*, in SSFC, p. 612, by Karen L. King.

3. Paula M. Cooey, 'Bad Women: The Limits of Theory and Knowledge', in *Horizons in Feminist Theology: Identity, Tradition, and Norms*, Fortress Press, 1997, p. 149, edited by Rebecca S. Chopp and Sheila Greene Davaney.

4. Elisabeth Schüssler Fiorenza, in the 'Introduction: Transgressing Canonical Boundaries,' in SSFC, p. 7.

5. The literature on this topic is huge and complex. For an accessible summary, see Hans Küng, *Christianity: The Religious Situation of Our Time*, SCM Press, 1995, p. 136ff. See also, of course, the many chapters of SSFC which deal with individual texts.

6. The literature about both Gnosticism and the Apocrypha continues to grow. Here I mention only a few of the most general discussions. Of special interest to the present topic are two books by Elaine Pagels, *The Gnostic Gospels*, Random House, 1977 and *Adam, Eve, and the Serpent*, Vintage Books, 1989. A more detailed study can be found in *Nag*

Hammadi, Gnosticism, and Early Christianity, edited by J. M. Robinson, New York, 1977. The texts can be found in *The Nag Hammadi Library in English*, edited also by J. M. Robinson, Harper and Row, 1977. For the Apocrypha, I will be depending heavily on SSFC and the sources annotated there.

7. For an exhaustive discussion of these texts, see John Dominic Crossan, *The Birth of Christianity: Discovering what happened in the years immediately after the Execution of Jesus*, Harper San Francisco, 1998.

8. SSFC, Introduction, p. 7.

9. See the discussion of Thecla in Elaine Pagels, *Adam, Eve, and the Serpent*, p. 18-19. And for a discussion of authorship and a detailed commentary on the text, see Sheila E. McGinn, 'The Acts of Thecla', in SSFC, pp. 800-828. For the texts of most of the Apocrypha, see the revised edition of *New Testament Apocrypha* by Edgar Hennecke, Westminster/John Knox Press, 1992.

10. One of the best commentaries on these issues is *The Body and Society: Men, Women and Sexual Renunciation in Early Christianity*, by Peter Brown, Columbia University Press, 1988.

11 Jane Schaberg gives a thorough critique of this document in 'The Infancy of Mary of Nazareth,' in SSFC, pp. 708-727.

12. See Elizabeth Moltmann Wendell, *The Women around Jesus*, SCM and Crossroad, 1982.

13. Susan Haskins, *Mary Magdalene: Myth and Metaphor*, Harper Collins, 1993.

14. In SSFC, pp. 601-634, by Karen L. King.

15. See the excellent references in 'The Gospel of Mary Magdalene'. My dependence on this article is obvious throughout.

CHAPTER FIVE: WOMEN MARTYRS

1. From *Acta minora*, a later version of Perpetua's life, quoted in *Carnal Knowing: Female Nakedness and Religious Meaning in the Christian West*, by Margaret R. Miles, Beacon Press, 1989, p. 60.

2. 'On the Apparel of Women,' Book, Chapter 2, Ancient Christian Writers.

3. Peter Brown, *The Body and Society: Men, Women, and Sexual Renunciation in Early Christianity*, Columbia University Press, 1988, p. 81.

4. Kristine M. Rankka, *Women and the Value of Suffering: An Aw(e)ful Rowing Toward God*, A Michael Glazier Book, The Liturgical Press, 1998, p. 91.

5. For this whole section, see W. H. C. Frend, *The Rise of Christianity*, Darton, Longman and Todd, 1984, especially, pp. 119ff. Important insights are also provided by Robin Lane Fox, *Pagans and Christians*, Penguin, 1986.

6. The text can be found in *Early Christian Writings*, Penguin Books, 1968.

7. See the account in Peter Brown, op. cit., p. 73f. See also the section on 'Martyrdom' in Rosemary Rader, *Breaking Boundaries: Male/Female Friendship in Early Christian Communities*, pp. 44-61, Paulist Press, 1983. One of the most comprehensive accounts of the martyr period is W. H. C. Frend, *Martyrdom and Persecution in the Early Church: A Study of a Conflict from the Maccabees to Donatus*, Basil Blackwell, 1965.

8. The texts of the martyrs' stories can be found in *The Acts of the Christian Martyrs*, Clarendon, 1972, translated and edited by Herbert Musurillo.

9. Quoted from Irenaeus in Brown, op. cit., p. 73

10. 'The Passion of Perpetua and Felicitas', Translated by H. R. Musurillo, in *Medieval Women's Visionary Literature*, edited by Elizabeth Avilda Petroff, Oxford University Press, 1986, pp. 70-77. For an excellent commentary on the text by Maureen A. Tilley, see SSFC, pp. 829-858.

11. The main work of Irenaeus is usually called *Against the Heresies*. These quotations are from the first book.

12. For a general overview of this situation, see Hans Küng, op. cit., pp. 153ff. For more specific information, see Bonnie Bowman Thurston, *The Widows: A Women's Ministry in the Early Church*, Fortress Press, 1989, and for many relevant primary texts, see Elizabeth A. Clark, *Women in the Early Church*, Michael Glazier, 1983. Peter Brown, op. cit., discusses the theological ramifications of this period in great and illuminating detail.

13. For suffering and martyrdom, see Philip Sheldrake, *Spirituality and History: Questions of Interpretation and Method*, Crossroad, 1992; Johannes-Baptist Metz and Edward Schillebeeckx, *Martyrdom Today*, The Seabury Press, 1983, Vol. 163 of *Concilium*, and Kristine M. Rankka, op. cit..

14. One of the most famous *Christa* images is by Almuth Lutkenhaus; see the reproduction in Rosemary Radford Ruether, *Womanguides: Readings Toward a Feminist Theology*, p. 104, Beacon Press, 1985; see the whole discussion of 'Male and Female Saviours,' ibid. pp. 105-133. See also Erin White and Marie Tulip, *Knowing Otherwise: Feminism, Women, and Religion*, David Lovell Publishing, 1991, pp. 43ff.

CHAPTER SIX: DEACONESSES, WIDOWS, AND VIRGINS

1. *The Apostolic Constitutions*, 8.3. 19-20. Translation from the *Ante-Nicene Fathers*, Vol. VII, p. 492.

2. *Didascalia Apostolorum*, Translated by R.H, Connolly, Oxford, 1929, Chapter 15.

3. Bonnie Bowman Thurston, *The Widows: A Women's Ministry in the Early Church,* p. 104, Fortress Press, 1989.

4. Jo Ann Kay McNamara, *Sisters in Arms: Catholic Nuns Through Two Millennia,* p. 67, Harvard University Press, 1996.

5. W. H. C. Frend, quoting Origen in *The Rise of Christianity,* p. 289. My reliance on Frend's work is obvious throughout this section.

6. Frend, op. cit., p. 320.

7. Eusebius of Caesarea, quoted in Frend, op. cit., p. 452.

8. Docetists taught that Jesus just appeared to have a body. They could not imagine divinity lowering itself to actually inhabit the human body, tainted by sex.

9. Peter Brown, op. cit., p. 136. Brown deals with Clement's teaching in great detail and credits him with some of the sanest Christian teaching on marriage for centuries.

10. For a brief overview of Origen and his relevance to our theme, see Peter Brown, op. cit., p. 160ff. And also Hans Küng, op. cit., p. 169ff.

11. See Frend, op. cit., p. 222ff.

12. ibid., p. 322.

13. Brown, op. cit., p. 163.

14. One of the earliest studies of these ministries is *The Ministry of Women in the Early Church* by Jean Danielou, SJ, The Faith Press, 1961. At this period of the early sixties, several attempts were under way to restore the ministry of the diaconate for women, in the spirit of Vatican Council II. Several doctoral theses were produced at this time. This chapter relies heavily on Mary T. Malone, 'Christian Attitudes Towards Women in the Fourth Century: Background and New Directions', Unpublished doctoral thesis, University of Toronto, 1971.

15. Quoted in Malone, p. 53.

16. Quoted in Monique Alexandre, 'Early Christian Women,' p. 433, in Chapter Nine of *A History of Women: From Ancient Goddesses to Christian Saints,* Edited by Pauline Schmitt Pantel, Harvard University Press, 1992.

17. Quoted in Malone, p. 66-67.

18. Malone, p. 64.

19. Danielou, p. 28.

20. ibid. p. 19.

21. 1 Tim 5:3-16.

22. For this whole section on widows, see Malone, op. cit., pp. 67-78 and notes; also Thurston, op. cit., especially Chapter 6.

23. Quoted in Thurston, op. cit., p. 96.

24. Malone, p. 77.

25. W. K. L. Clarke, *The Lausiac History of Palladius,* SPCK, 1918.

26. This section depends heavily on Malone, op. cit., as well as Brown, op. cit. See also J. N. D. Kelly, *Jerome: His Life, Writings and Controversies,* Harper and Row, 1975. Many of the citations are from my own translations, but see also for a good selection Ross Kraemer, Ed., *Maenads, Martyrs, Matrons, Monastics,* Fortress Press, 1988, and Elizabeth A Clark, *Women in the Early Church,* Michael Glazier, 1983, and her earlier work, *Jerome, Chrysostom and Friends,* The Edwin Mellen Press, 1979.

27. Much of this information comes from the *Letters of Jerome,* one of the most prolific correspondents of the ancient world. His brilliant style makes for excellent reading, but his attraction for the pithy phrase often overcomes his devotion to the truth. All epistolary references are in Malone.

28. Letter 45.

29. Letters 38, 39.

30. Letter 108.

31. Quoted in Malone, pp. 203-204.

32. op. cit., p. 78

33. The Life of St Macrina by Gregory of Nyssa is reprinted, almost in its entirety, in Elizabeth Avilda Petroff, Ed., *Medieval Women's Visionary Literature,* Oxford University Press, 1986, p. 77ff.

34. Linda Lopez McAlister, Ed., *Hypatia's Daughters: Fifteen Hundred Years of Women Philosophers,* Indiana University Press, 1996, p. 1ff.

CHAPTER SEVEN: THE LIFE OF VIRGINITY

1. Gregory of Nyssa, *Life of St Macrina.* Gregory is, of course, talking about his sister.

2. Jerome, in his inflammatory tract against Jovinian, uses the most extreme language to advocate the ascetic life against Jovinian's defence of marriage.

3. Jo Ann Kay McNamara, *Sisters in Arms: Catholic Nuns Through Two Millennia,* Harvard University Press, 1996, p. 55.

4. Margaret R. Miles, *Carnal Knowing: Female Nakedness and Religious Meaning in the Christian West,* Beacon Press, 1989, p. 54.

5. Every male writer of these centuries wrote about women. We have chosen these three as the most influential and the most accessible for readers. All their writings have been published in *Patrologia Latina,* and have been published in English in a variety of ways, but most completely in *The Library of the Nicene and Post-Nicene Fathers* and its various revisions. A most helpful resource is *Patrology, Vol. IV, The Golden Age of Latin Patristic Literature from the Council of Nicea to the Council of Chakcedon,* edited by Angelo Di Berardino, with an introduction by Johannes Quasten, Christian Classics, Inc., 1992.

6. Every church figure known to us, from this period, wrote several tracts about virginity. In the vast majority of cases, this writing deals only with women. These texts carry more or less the same titles, and references to them in the major secondary sources can be very confusing. Here, I shall refer sometimes to the original Latin text in my own translation, sometimes to translations as found in other contemporary authors. The main secondary sources used for this chapter are: Peter Brown, *The Body and Society: Men, Women, and Sexual Renunciation in Early Christianity*, Columbia University Press, 1988; Gillian Cloke, *This Female Man of God: Women and Spiritual Power in the Patristic Age, AD 350-50*, Routledge, 1995; Elizabeth A. Clark, *Women in the Early Church*, Michael Glazier, Inc., 1983; Prudence Allen, *The Concept of Woman: The Aristotelian Revolution, 750 BC-AD 1250*, Eden Press, 1985; Margaret R. Miles, *Carnal Knowing: Female Nakedness and Religious Meaning in the Christian West*, Beacon Press, 1989; and Mary T. Malone, *Christian Attitudes Towards Women in the Fourth Century: Background and New Directions*, unpublished Ph.D. thesis, 1971.

7. Brown, p. 279f.

8. Malone, p. 213.

9. John Chrysostom, *On Virginity*, quoted in Brown, p, 307.

10. Augustine, Letter 262, quoted in Brown, p. 403-404.

11. Brown, p. 6.

12. For a discussion of Clement of Alexandria, see Brown, p. 122f.

13. One of the best discussions of Augustine's life is Peter Brown's *Augustine of Hippo*, (University of California Press, 1967); and see his discussion in Brown, op. cit., p. 387 and following.

14. See Malone, p. 256f., and Brown, p. 341f.

15. Symmachus, *Relatio*, 10.

16. See references in Malone, p. 259.

17. *On Virgins*, 3, 9. Quoted in Malone, p. 260.

18. Brown, p. 352f.

19. Brown, p. 361f.

20. See J. N. D. Kelly, *Jerome: His Life, Writings and Controversies*, Harper and Row, 1975, p. 104f.

21. Malone, p. 267f.

22. Letter 22, To Eustochium. Quoted in Malone, p. 270.

23. See Uta Ranke-Heinemann, *Eunuchs for the Kingdom of Heaven: Women, Sexuality and the Catholic Church*, Doubleday, 1990, p. 82f.

24. See Brown, pp. 387-427, on which this whole section relies heavily.

25. For the controversies with both Helvidius and Jovinian, see Malone, pp. 237ff.

26. All quotations are from Malone, p.244f.

27. Malone, p. 254.

28. Allen, op. cit., p. 218f.

29. Augustine, *The Trinity*, Book 12, Chapter 7. Quoted in Allen, p. 222.

30. See Mary T. Malone, *Who is My mother: Rediscovering the Mother of Jesus*, Wm. C. Brown, 1984, p. 21f.

31. ibid., p. 25f.

32. The development of Marian devotion in Eastern Christianity followed a different trajectory. See Malone, ibid., for a description of the main features of this development.

CHAPTER EIGHT: THE ABBESSES

1. Baudonivia's *Life of Radegund*.

2. Bede on Hilda.

3. 'A Legacy of Miracles: Hagiography and Nunneries in Merovingian Gaul,' p. 41, by Jo Ann McNamara, from Julis Kirshner & Suzanne F. Wemple, *Women of the Medieval World*, Basil Blackwell, 1985.

4. Joan Morris, *The Lady was a Bishop*, The Macmillan Company, 1973, p. 13.

5. Augustine, *The City of God*, Book xix, 17. Quoted in Richard Fletcher, *The Conversion of Europe: From Paganism to Christianity, 371-1386 AD*, Fontana Press, 1998, p. 31.

6. The Christian sources for this period overlap with the foundation stories of the different nations. For the Franks, the primary source is the *History of the Franks* by Gregory of Tours in ten volumes. The most recent translation is by Lewis Thorpe, Penguin, 1974. Bede's *Ecclesiastical History of the English People*, with a recent commentary by J.M. Wallace-Hadrill, Oxford, 1988, is excellent. For Celtic Christianity, there are voluminous writings. I have used *Early Christian Ireland* by Máire & Liam de Paor, Thames and Hudson, 1978, and *The Irish Catholic Experience: A Historical Survey*, Gill and MacMillan, 1986, by Patrick Corish, as well as the voluminous primary sources collected by James F. Kenney in *The Sources for the Early History of Ireland*, New York, 1929 with additions by Ludwig Bieler, 1966.

7. For this whole section, see Fletcher, p. 97ff.

8. Quoted in Fletcher, p. 111.

9. op. cit., p. 115.

10. For an engaging study of evangelisation and catechesis in this period, see Marianne Sawicki, *The Gospel in History*, Fortress Press, 1988.

11. There were several Rules written prior to Benedict's, such as that of Caesarius of Arles, but all the Western monastic rules have the same characteristics. Benedict's is the one we know best, and so it is convenient to qualify all of them as Benedictine.

12. There is an excellent discussion of women's monasticism, in Penelope D. Johnson, *Equal in Monastic Profession: Religious women in Medieval France*, The University of Chicago Press, 1991.

13. There are various accounts of Radegund's life. See the following: Suzanne Foney Wemple, 'Female Spirituality and Mysticism in Frankish Monasticism: Radegund, Balthild and Aldegund, 'in *Peace Weavers: Medieval Religious Women*, Vol. 2, edited by John A. Nichols and Lillian Thomas Shank, pp. 39-54, Cistercian Publications, Inc., 1987; 'A Legacy of Miracles: Hagiography and Nunneries in Merovingian Gaul', by Jo Ann McNamara, in *Women of the Medieval World*, edited by Julius Kirshner & Suzanne F. Wemple, pp. 36-55, Basil Blackwell, 1985; Jo Ann Kay McNamara, *Sisters in Arms: Catholic Nuns Through Two Millennia*, Part II, passim, Harvard University Press, 1996; and Sara Maitland and Wendy Mulford, *Virtuous Magic: Women Saints and Their Meanings*, Mowbray, 1998, pp. 54-61.

14. 'Abbess Hilda of Whitby: All Britain Was Lit by Her Splendor', by Nancy Bauer, O.S.B., in *Medieval Women Monastics: Wisdom's Wellsprings*, The Liturgical Press, 1996, Edited by Miriam Schmitt and Linda Kulzer, pp. 13-32.

15. The *agapetae* were representatives of a group of women and men, who lived together in a kind of spiritual marriage. Evidence for this practice abounds in the early years of Christianity, even though it is constantly condemned.

16. ibid., p. 23

17. Maitland and Mulford, p. 106

CHAPTER NINE: WOMEN AS MONASTIC MISSIONARIES

1. *Life of Leoba* by Rudolf of Fulda, quoted in *Medieval Women's Visionary Literature*, edited by Elizabeth Avilda Petroff, Oxford University Press, 1986, p. 86.

2. Idung of Prufening on the cloistering of women, quoted in *Distant Echoes: Medieval Religious Women*, Vol. 1, edited by John A. Nichols and Lillian Thomas Shank, Cistercian Publications, 1984, p. 63.

3. Jo Ann Kay McNamara, *Sisters in Arms: Catholic Nuns Through Two Millennia*, Harvard University Press, 1996, p. 162.

4. Lina Eckenstein, *Women Under Monasticism: Chapters on Saint-Lore and Convent Life Between AD 500 and AD 1500*, Cambridge University Press, 1986, p. ix. Quoted in *Medieval Women Monastics: Wisdom's Wellsprings*, The Liturgical Press, p. 38-39.

5. *The Lady was a Bishop*, MacMillan, 1973.

6. Richard Fletcher, *The Conversion of Europe: From Paganism to Christianity 371-1386 AD*, Fontana Press, 1997, p. 180.

7. op. cit., note 5 above.

8. Morris, p. 30.

9. See Morris, Chapter 6 for the often hilarious events of the history of the Royal Abbey at Jouarre. The original abbey had been founded at the time of Columbanus, but the history of the site goes back for centuries, when it was known to be a pagan centre for the worship of Jove.

10. Morris, chapter 7, p. 38.

11. Quoted from the *Life of Frideswide* by the medieval English historian, William of Malmesbury in *Medieval Women Monastics: Wisdom's Wellsprings*, p. 34

12. op. cit., p. 33-47.

13. Richard Southern, from a sermon preached in Christ Church Cathedral on Sunday, 19 October, 1980; quoted in *Medieval Women Monastics*, p. 39.

14. op. cit., p. 63ff.

15. See Petroff, op. cit., p. 87, who includes in her anthology the translation of the *Hodoeporicon* by Talbot, pp. 92-106.

16. Petroff, op. cit., p. 104-105.

17. *Peace Weavers: Medieval Religious Women*, Vol. 2, edited by John A. Nichols and Lillian Thomas Shank, Cistercian Publications Inc., 1987, p. 56.

18. Fletcher, op. cit., p. 204ff., and see E. Emerton, *The Letters of Boniface* New York, 1940.

19. Quoted in *Medieval Women Monastics*, p. 85.

20. See *Medieval Women Monastics*, p. 81ff.

21. For the text of Rudolf's biography of Leoba, see Petroff, op. cit., pp. 106-114.

22. See Fletcher, op. cit., p. 204ff.

23. Petroff, p. 113.

24. ibid., p. 114; *Medieval Women Monastics*, p. 92.

25. Fletcher, p. 216ff.

26. See *Sisters in Arms*, p. 150ff. for an excellent account of this process, an account on which this chapter substantially relies.

27. See the very detailed article by Jane Tibbets Schulenberg, 'Strict Active Enclosure and Its Effects on the Female Monastic Experience (ca. 500-1100)', in *Distant Echoes: Medieval Religious Women*, Volume One, pp. 51-86, Cistercian Publications, 1984, edited by John A. Nichols and Lillian Thomas Shank.

28. Marie Anne Mayeskie, *Women: Models of Liberation*, Sheed and Ward, 1988, Chapter 2, 'A Troublesome Puppy': Dhuoda of Septimania,' pp. 31-56.

29. See text in Mayeskie, op. cit.

30. *Sexual Practices and the Medieval Church,* by Vern L. Bullough and James Brundage, Prometheus Books, New York, 1982, passim, but especially Chapter 3, 'Chaste Marriage and Clerical Celibacy,' by Jo Ann McNamara, pp. 22-33, and Chapter 9, 'The Marriage of Mary and Joseph in the Twelfth Century Ideology of Marriage,' by Penny Shine Gold, pp. 102-117.

31. 'Bishops as Marital Advisors,' p. 55, quoting the famous Bishop Hincmar of Rheims, in *Women of the Medieval World,* edited by Julius Kirshner and Suzanne Wemple, Basil Blackwell, 1985.

CHAPTER TEN: THE POINT OF THE STORY: JOAN AND HROSWITHA

1. *The Chronicle of Adam of Usk,* edited by Edward Maunde Thompson (London, 1876). This purports to be an eye-witness account of the election of Innocent VII in 1404 and is quoted in Peter Stanford, *The She-Pope: A Quest for the Truth Behind the Mystery of Pope Joan,* Arrow Books, 1998, p. 33-34.

2. This is Hroswitha's own translation of her name, in Latin *clamor validum.*

3. Stanford, op. cit., p. 182.

4. 'The Saxon Canoness, Hrosvit of Gandersheim,' by Katharina M. Wilson, p. 30, in *Medieval Women Writers,* edited by Katharina M. Wilson, Manchester University Press, 1984.

5. For a good conventional overview of this period, see *The History of the Church,* edited by Hubert Jedin and John Dolan, Vol. III, 'The Church in the Age of Feudalism', by Friedrich Kempf, Hans-Georg Beck, Eugen Ewig and Josef Andreas Jungmann, Burns & Oates, 1980.

6. A rather jaundiced account of the period can be found in Peter de Rosa, *Vicars of Christ: The Dark Side of the Papacy,* Bantam, 1988.

7. Stanford, op. cit., p. 138ff.

8. I rely here primarily on the collection of documents assembled by Joan Morris in *Pope John VIII – an English Woman: Alias Pope Joan,* Vrai Publishers, 1985, and the already mentioned work of Peter Stanford, *The She-Pope.* Both these authors accept the fact of Joan's papacy with some caution, since the trail of evidence continually grows cold. Both are, however, fair to both opponents and proponents.

9. This is from one of the most famous of the sources for Joan's story, Martin of Poland's *Chronicon Pontificum et Imperatum,* quoted from Stanford, p. 19.

10. Stanford and Morris, op. cit.

11. Stanford, p. 110ff.

12. ibid., p. 19.

13. These were, especially, Cardinal Baronius (1538-1607), and the two

Jesuits, Cardinal Robert Bellarmine (1542-1625) and Philippe Labbe (1607-1667), who tried to prove that, in the list of popes, there was no room for Joan between Leo and Benedict. See Morris, p. 106ff.

14. Stanford, p. 151.

15. ibid. p. 155f. Peter Stanford has a remarkable list of contemporary literary references to Joan.

16. Jo Ann Kay McNamara, *Sisters in Arms*, p. 214ff.

17. Katharina M. Wilson, op. cit.

18. *Sisters in Arms*, p. 216.

19. *Medieval Women Monastics*, Chapter 9 on 'Hrotsvit: Medieval Playwright,' pp. 137-147.

20. Quoted in *The Subordinate Sex: A History of Attitudes Towards Women*, Penguin Books, 1974, by Vern L. Bullough, p. 159.

21. Wilson, p. 31.

22. Quoted from the translation of the play in *Medieval Women's Visionary Literature*, edited by Elizabeth Alvilda Petroff, Oxford University Press, 1986, p. 120.

23. ibid. p. 124ff.

24. Peter Dronke, *Women Writers of the Middle Ages:A Critical Study of Texts from Perpetua (203) to Marguerite Porete (1310)*, Cambridge University Press, 1984, p. 852. Quoted in *Medieval Women Monastics*, p. 144.

25. Quoted from Wilson, p. 38.

Index of People and Places